T0073235

Praise for *Intelligence-Driven Incident Response*

In today's world, where cyber crime continues to rise—costing the global economy trillions of dollars, and impacting all aspects of our lives including our access to healthcare, education, food supply, utilities, and financial services—one of the biggest challenges we face is gaining a clear picture of what's actually happening so we can determine the best response. Building and sharing threat intelligence is a critical element of addressing this issue. Brown and Roberts bring incredibly deep experience of the topic from a range of sectors and organizational sizes, and even from the government intelligence point of view, and as such have thoroughly explored the topic and its challenges and opportunities. They offer that expertise to you in this second edition of their book to help drive greater understanding and availability of threat intelligence and reduce cyber risk over time.

—Jen Ellis, cochair, Ransomware Task Force,
and founder, NextJenSecurity

Detecting, investigating, and remediating active cyber security incidents is one of the greatest thrills you can experience as a security analyst. This book teaches you how to squeeze every ounce of value from that work so that we can prevent similar incidents from impacting multiple targets in the future. This is how we begin to shift the balance in favor of defenders.

—Wade Woolwine, security program architect

Intelligence-Driven Incident Response is the definitive resource for CTI analysts, thrunters, and blue teams on updated and practical threat intelligence strategy. A must read for analysts and cybersecurity leaders serious about their defense.

—Mick Baccio, White House Threat Intelligence POTUS 44/45,
and founder, ThruntCon

SECOND EDITION

Intelligence-Driven Incident Response

Outwitting the Adversary

Rebekah Brown and Scott J. Roberts
Foreword by Jeannie L. Johnson and Rob Lee

Beijing · Boston · Farnham · Sebastopol · Tokyo

Intelligence-Driven Incident Response

by Rebekah Brown and Scott J. Roberts

Published by O'Reilly Media, Inc., 1005 Gravenstein Highway North, Sebastopol, CA 95472.

O'Reilly books may be purchased for educational, business, or sales promotional use. Online editions are also available for most titles (*http://oreilly.com*). For more information, contact our corporate/institutional sales department: 800-998-9938 or *corporate@oreilly.com*.

Acquisitions Editor: Jennifer Pollock	**Indexer:** WordCo Indexing Services, Inc.
Development Editor: Angela Rufino	**Interior Designer:** David Futato
Production Editor: Elizabeth Faerm	**Cover Designer:** Karen Montgomery
Copyeditor: Nicole Taché	**Illustrator:** Kate Dullea
Proofreader: Kim Wimpsett	

June 2023: Second Edition

Revision History for the Second Edition
2023-06-12: First Release

See *http://oreilly.com/catalog/errata.csp?isbn=9781098120689* for release details.

978-1-098-12068-9

[LSI]

Table of Contents

Part I.   The Fundamentals

Part II.   Practical Application

Part III. The Way Forward

Foreword to the Second Edition

The cyber threat landscape continues to outpace the numbers of talented cyber experts needed by government and industry. The raw truth is that the competition for cyber professionals is likely to get only sharper over the next five years. Generative AI and other enabling factors mean cyber incursions are becoming possible for a widening range of highly motivated actors. This, combined with our expanding digital life, makes Scott Roberts and Rebekah Brown's second edition of *Intelligence-Driven Incident Response* a particularly critical and timely resource. Institutions competing for the cyber talent necessary to protect internal systems and data from the malicious activity of commercially driven criminals, "glass breaking" hacktivists, or the punitive action of geopolitical actors will need to have a strategy in place that draws top tier recruits to rewarding and meaningful cyber work and cultivates a team dynamic that is proficient at finding, fixing, and finishing cyber intruders. Roberts and Brown explain how this is done. Their book is a goldmine resource for those who are tasked with their organization's mandate for cyber proficiency.

In this second edition, Scott Roberts and Rebekah Brown provide refinements and updates to cyber analytic concepts and processes and deliver these across a conversational, witty, and insightful text that supplies tactical and strategic best practices for enterprises at every level of cyber investment. Readers of the first edition have offered a groundswell of thanks for their refreshingly accessible step-by-step guide to thinking through and implementing highly effective cyber team structures and functions. In response, this updated guide offers an expanded range of examples and professional tips for applying leading-edge models in cyber threat intelligence. The authors engage the reader on every page and supply detailed explanations of both the *why* and *how* behind each recommended intelligence practice.

The cyber education supplied by most university (and other) training institutions tends to focus on technical skills. In *Intelligence-Driven Incident Response*, Roberts and Brown provide the vital *missing* education, the one necessary to transform technically proficient individuals into sophisticated and threat-wise teams of cyber hunters. This transformation process includes onboarding the global perspective and methods of intelligence professionals. Roberts and Brown have achieved this fusion in their own professional lives and now offer the seminal tradecraft text for how it might be achieved by others. The authors draw on their years of combined experience in both the public and private sector to deliver detection and denial strategies, frank advice about security trade-offs, and important warnings about tempting modes of retributive action against the "enemy" that are most likely to backfire and result in unproductive blowback. Their recommendations are sound, pragmatic, accessible even for those new to the cyber arena, and will save state and corporate cyber teams hours, months, and perhaps years of trial and error in order to discover the same things.

Roberts and Brown decrypt the intelligence side of cyber security for C-suite executives, cyber team leads, state and federal officials, and educators seeking to deliver the leading edge of cyber training. They make clear that savvy investments in fused cyber security and intelligence practices are the right resources trade-off for institutions seeking to save time and money. Experienced cyber teams will find great value in the chapters discussing internal communications and dissemination of intelligence. Roberts and Brown offer articulate and compelling data points to teams frustrated with their inability to communicate the importance of the cyber role to institutional leadership. Security ops and intelligence teams that have been operating separately are provided with a blueprint for maximizing the function of both of their shops by fusing their practices into an effective detection, response, assessment, lesson-extraction loop that keeps both teams ahead of consistently evolving threats. As experience across the cyber landscape demonstrates, collaborative, cross-functional practices are the hallmark of the most effective teams. Roberts and Brown show how it is done.

Cyber professionals know they are in high demand. As a rare market resource, they will seek meaningful and rewarding work with institutions that have invested in understanding the critical role of active cyber protections in the enterprise's success. Cyber teams who operate ad hoc will fail to serve their institutions well and will fail to attract the talent they seek. Teams that exude professionalism and operate with a high degree of proficiency will attract the best the market has to offer. *Intelligence-Driven Incident Response* is the guide to creating those teams.

Most public and private institutions now recognize that they represent a security frontier that in previous eras was typically defended by governments. All of us who head organizations, large and small, must construct our own cyber defense structure and practices. Roberts and Brown emphasize that this need not be done alone. Collaborative structures which facilitate intelligence sharing across institutions provide a "play as a team" approach that has the potential to speed up response time and strengthen resistance, recovery, and resurgence (coming back stronger) strategies for all parties. Being faster than the adversary matters.

As professionals in the field of anticipatory intelligence, my leadership team seeks out the best strategic practices across the wide horizon of this century's threatscape. I am convinced that the cyber intelligence approach offered by Roberts and Brown— smart, collaborative, adaptive, and crafted to achieve and keep strategic initiative—is the only way to stay ahead of the swelling ranks of cyber proficient adversaries. I am profoundly grateful to have come across their work and continue to recommend it at every opportunity. You will thank yourself for picking up this book.

— Jeannie L. Johnson
Founding Director,
Center for Anticipatory Intelligence
Utah State University

Foreword to the First Edition

Over 20 years ago, I was involved in my first large scale intrusion by a nation state actor from Russia called Moonlight Maze. My job for the Air Force Office of Special Investigations was to aid in data collection, interception, and analysis of adversary activity that occurred on the network and compromised systems. We learned through analyzing multiple attacks across many targets that this adversary was not going away by only "pulling the plug" from the back of the hacked systems. The enemy was extremely patient. Once they detected our response measures, they would persist in not reaccessing the same target for weeks. The attackers would ensure survival by hitting more than one target across the network and leave back doors on many systems. Across multiple intrusions by the same attackers, the task force started to put together a playbook on who this adversary was, how they operated, and what they were after. This playbook helped inform the defenses of many DoD locations worldwide. What was one of the outcomes of the Moonlight Maze intrusion? The scope and urgency of the attacks led to the formation of the Joint Task Force–Computer Network Defense (JTF-CND) that later became the gestation of U.S. Cyber Command.

We learned a lot from these advanced attacks in the late '90s. First and foremost, we learned that to detect the adversary, we had to learn from the enemy. Early on we discovered tools and practices that would allow us to pinpoint the same adversary on other networks. The information that helped inform our defenses and detect specific attackers became the formation of, likely, the most significant information security development since the intrusion detection system and the firewall: cyber threat intelligence.

Having responded to hundreds of incidents through my career in the DoD, US Government, Mandiant, and my own company, the one thing we always rely on is that incident responders' primary objective is to use the opportunity to learn about the adversaries attacking you. With this information, we can observe another network and assess if the same enemy compromised them. This intelligence lays the bedrock for our approach to proper information security and defensive posturing against these specific threats. Organizations aren't likely to be hit by any hacker, they are likely part of a group, and they have your organization's name on a hit list. Without cyber threat intelligence as the primary consumer of incident-response data, the security defenses could never improve and reduce the dwell time for the adversaries inside the networks they're compromising.

Threat intelligence was vital to intrusions over 20 years ago, starting with the story told in the *Cuckoo's Egg*, written by Cliff Stoll, and has been ever since. But somehow, most organizations are still learning to adopt the same principles. Part of the reason is the failure of proper resources that groups can follow. Another factor is bad advice from security vendors. Lucky for us, this book now exists and steps the reader through proper threat-intelligence concepts, strategy, and capabilities that an organization can adopt to evolve their security practice. After reading this book, your operations can grow to become an intelligence-driven operation that is much more efficient than ever in detecting and reducing the possible impact of breaches that will occur.

As the SANS Institute's Digital Forensics and Incident Response Curriculum Director and Lead, I have been discussing the importance of proper threat assessment and intelligence for many years. Many argued that it was a "nice to have" and "not as important" as stopping the adversary until analysts started to learn there was little they could do to eliminate an adversary without it.

I have advised many executives over the years that money would be better spent on developing proper threat intelligence than on vendor hardware that will likely not detect the next intrusion without being fed indicators learned and extracted as a part of the threat-intelligence analytical process. Part of that advice came from listening to conversations with the authors of this book, Scott and Rebekah.

Scott and I worked together at Mandiant and have remained friends ever since. I regularly follow up with him over the years and am an avid reader of his papers and articles. Scott is currently one of our instructors for the SANS Institute's Cyber Threat Intelligence course (FOR578). Listening to Scott present on this topic for many years is always a breath of wisdom that is equivalent to hearing Warren Buffet give financial advice. I can hear Scott's voice in my head as I read his thoughts pouring off the pages in this book.

Similar to my background, Rebekah is former military and worked across the board in cyber operations. She is formerly the Cyber Unity Operations Chief for the U.S. Marine Corp. She was also a cyber-operation exercise planner in the DoD, a network warfare analyst while at the NSA, and worked to create threat intelligence in Fortune 500 companies and across information security vendors. Rebekah's knowledge is on point and intuitive. She knows and understands this space like no other, having lived it by working inside and outside the DoD (both Intel and cyber communities) and across many companies. Rebekah has provided cyber threat intelligence briefs at the White House, based on her theories of coordinated defensive and offensive cyber operations. Getting to know Rebekah has been amazing and enlightening, especially as I continue to learn how traditional intelligence methods are applied to cyber-operations analysis. I am also proud to highlight that Rebekah is also a course author and instructor for the SANS Institute's Course in Cyber Threat Intelligence (FOR578).

Together, Scott and Rebekah have put together their thoughts on paper in one of the most informed cyber-operations strategy guides you could ever pick up. You should consider making this book mandatory reading for all cyber analysts in your organization. This book is at the top of my recommended reading list for any cyber security analysts old and new. The ideas expressed in this book don't solve technical challenges, hacking tactics, or configuring security defenses, but instead, focuses on concepts, strategy, and approaches that indeed work at improving the posture, detection, and response inside the security operations of your organization.

One of the most important chapters of the book for cybersecurity management to read is how to build an intelligence program. Watching Scott and Rebekah go through this with many organizations has been impressive. Organizations that have benefited from their knowledge understand that "threat intelligence" is not a buzz-word, and their approaches and requirements to step through is worth the read several times over.

For those who are security analysts, the book's main content steps an analyst through the intricacies of proper incident-response approaches, utilizing a threat intelligence mindset. Once exposed to the information contained in this book, it will permanently change the way you approach cyber security in your organization. It will transition you from being an average analyst into one with advanced operational skills that will continue to pay off throughout your career.

I wish I had this book 20 years ago in my first intrusion cases while investigating Russian hackers during Moonlight Maze. Luckily, we have this book today, and I can now point to it as required reading for my students who want to move beyond tactical response and apply a framework and strategy to it all that works.

— *Rob Lee*
Founder, Harbingers Security/DFIR Lead,
SANS Institute

Preface

Welcome to the exciting world of intelligence-driven incident response! Intelligence—specifically, cyber threat intelligence—has a huge potential to help network defenders better understand and respond to attackers' actions against their networks.

With the first edition of *Intelligence-Driven Incident Response*, our goal was to demonstrate how intelligence fits into the incident-response process and make the case for taking what seemed to be at the time, a novel approach to understanding adversaries and reducing the time it takes to detect, respond to, and remediate intrusions. In the years that have passed since the first edition was released, we have seen tremendous growth in the field, both in numbers and capabilities. Our goal in this second edition is to continue to grow along with the community, adding in additional techniques, methods, lessons learned, and case studies to help more seamlessly integrate these concepts into the critical work that is being done every day to secure the technology that we rely on every day.

Wherever you are in your journey, whether you are just starting in cybersecurity, are transitioning from another security domain into cyber threat intelligence, or are a seasoned professional, we hope you find this book a valuable tool to help you in your mission of making the world a more secure place.

Why We Wrote This Book

In recent years, we have seen a transition from approaching incident response as a standalone activity to viewing it as an integral part of an overall network security program. At the same time, cyber threat intelligence is rapidly becoming more and more popular, and more companies and incident responders are trying to understand how to best incorporate threat intelligence into their operations. The struggle is real—both of us have been through these growing pains as we learned how to apply traditional intelligence principles into incident-response practices, and vice versa—but we know that it is worth the effort. We wrote this book to pull together the two worlds, threat intelligence and incident response, to show how they are stronger and more effective together, and to shorten the time it takes practitioners to incorporate them into operations.

Who This Book Is For

This book is written for people involved in incident response, whether their role is an incident manager, malware analyst or reverse engineer, digital forensics specialist or intelligence analyst. It is also for those interested in learning more about incident response. Many people who are drawn to cyber threat intelligence want to know about attackers—what motivates them and how they operate—and the best way to learn that is through incident response. But it is only when incident response is approached with an intelligence mindset that we start to truly understand the value of the information we have available to us. You don't need to be an expert in incident response, or in intelligence, to get a lot out of this book. We step through the basics of both disciplines in order to show how they work together, and give practical advice and scenarios to illustrate the process.

How This Book Is Organized

This book is organized as follows:

- Part I, "The Fundamentals" includes Chapters 1, 2, and 3, and provides an introduction to the concept of intelligence-driven incident response (IDIR) and an overview of the intelligence and incident-response disciplines. We introduce the concept of F3EAD, the primary model for IDIR that will be used in the rest of the book.

- Part II, "Practical Application" includes Chapters 4, 5, and 6, which step through the incident-response-focused portion of F3EAD: Find, Fix, and Finish, as well as Chapters 7, 8, and 9, which cover the intelligence-focused steps in the F3EAD process: Exploit, Analyze, and Disseminate.

- Part III, "The Way Forward" includes Chapter 10, an overview of strategic-level intelligence and how it applies to incident response and network security programs, and Chapter 11, which discusses formalized intelligence programs and how to set up an intelligence-driven incident response program for success.

- An index helps you find key topics or concepts throughout the book.

Typically, people who are interested in integrating threat intelligence into incident response have a stronger background in one of those disciplines over the other, so it may be appealing to skim through the sections you are more familiar with and focus only on the parts that are new to you. While that is perfectly fine, you may find that we have discussed a new model or approaches to better integrate the two disciplines, so don't skip through too much, even if you think you know it already!

Conventions Used in This Book

The following typographical conventions are used in this book:

Italic
> Indicates new terms, URLs, email addresses, filenames, and file extensions.

`Constant width`
> Used for program listings, as well as within paragraphs to refer to program elements such as variable or function names, databases, data types, environment variables, statements, and keywords.

`Constant width bold`
> Shows commands or other text that should be typed literally by the user.

`Constant width italic`
> Shows text that should be replaced with user-supplied values or by values determined by context.

 This element signifies a general note.

 This element indicates a warning or caution.

O'Reilly Online Learning

 For more than 40 years, *O'Reilly Media* has provided technology and business training, knowledge, and insight to help companies succeed.

Our unique network of experts and innovators share their knowledge and expertise through books, articles, and our online learning platform. O'Reilly's online learning platform gives you on-demand access to live training courses, in-depth learning paths, interactive coding environments, and a vast collection of text and video from O'Reilly and 200+ other publishers. For more information, visit *https://oreilly.com*.

How to Contact Us

Please address comments and questions concerning this book to the publisher:

O'Reilly Media, Inc.
1005 Gravenstein Highway North
Sebastopol, CA 95472
800-889-8969 (in the United States or Canada)
707-829-7019 (international or local)
707-829-0104 (fax)
support@oreilly.com
https://www.oreilly.com/about/contact.html

We have a web page for this book, where we list errata, examples, and any additional information. You can access this page at *https://oreil.ly/intelligence-driven-incident-response-2e*.

For news and information about our books and courses, visit *https://oreilly.com*.

Find us on LinkedIn: *https://linkedin.com/company/oreilly-media*.

Follow us on Twitter: *https://twitter.com/oreillymedia*.

Watch us on YouTube: *https://youtube.com/oreillymedia*.

Acknowledgments

Rebekah would like to thank the following people:

First and foremost, thank you to my brilliant and steadfast partner, Gordon, for always supporting me, even when I had to give up coffee for six months, which was rough on everyone. Your love and encouragement allow me to turn the dreams in my head into reality.

Thanks to my amazing kiddos, who continue to grow into amazing humans and inspire me every day to make the world (digital and IRL) a better place.

My parents and the rest of the Ramey clan, thank you for making—literally—my entire life one big adventure. And thank you for the "Big Fam" group chat that kept us all connected when we couldn't leave our houses.

All of the amazing people I have worked with throughout the years—you all know that I am the biggest believer in the power of teams, and I feel humbled and honored to have worked with so many brilliant minds who have helped make me a better person and analyst.

To my ShameCon crew—our origin story versions may be inconsistent, but I love you all the same.

To Scott—what can I say to my BFFFA? Thank you for being the ultimate creative coauthor, for always being up for brainstorming on complex topics, and for bringing your better half and mini-me into my world.

We wrote the bulk of this update during COVID-19 lockdowns, so I would also like to thank the first responders and essential workers who put themselves at risk in their never-ending quest to help others. We owe you a debt that can never be repaid. A special thank-you to the staff and leadership of Bellden Café for all of the decaf lattes and avocado toasts delivered curbside that fueled the writing of this book—this little bit of normalcy and consistency meant more than I can express.

Scott would like to thank the following people:

Kessa: my spouse, partner, inspiration, challenger, supporter, everything. We're a long way from Hershey, and I would never have expected all the places we've been, the things we've done, and the challenges we've taken on, but I wouldn't change any of it for the world. You never pushed me, but you've made me want to do more than expected; seeing how much you've done drives me daily! I love you more every day. JTMC.

SJR4: Hey, Little! You're not reading this now and won't for a while, but you were a part of it. Hopefully, you'll see what a person can do when they put their mind to it and follow their passion. I can't wait to see what you'll do! Until then, thanks for all the smiles.

My family: I'm a long way from basecamp (though closer to mountains) but will forever appreciate the foundation to build on. The hardware support was excellent, from our Family's first Apple II to Palm Pilots to my first laptop. Still, the emotional and intellectual support meant even more, which will never be obsolete.

Mentors: to the many friends, coworkers, mentors, and managers I've had who have challenged me, pushed me, and helped me explore the many facets of this crazy industry. You have helped make me the analyst, engineer, responder, and author I am now.

USU: I thought I'd be a die-hard Nittany Lion for the rest of my life, but now, I'm fully an Aggie. I couldn't have lucked into better programs, from the Center for Anticipatory Intelligence to Huntsman School DAIS program to the SOC. After 20 years of professional life, I didn't imagine something would blow my worldview up so much.

Rebekah, I think now you're technically the BFFFA at this point, but no matter where I couldn't ask for a better coauthor, work partner, hypothetical foil, or friend.

## PART I

The Fundamentals

When you begin implementing intelligence-driven incident response, it is important to have a solid understanding of both intelligence and incident-response processes. Part I provides an introduction to cyber threat intelligence, the intelligence process, the incident-response process, and how they all work together.

## CHAPTER 1

Introduction

But I think the real tension lies in the relationship between what you might call the pursuer and his quarry, whether it's the writer or the spy.

—John le Carré

Once relegated to the secretive realms of national security and military operations, intelligence has become something that is fundamental to the daily functioning of many organizations around the world. At its core, intelligence seeks to give decision makers the information that they need to make the right choice in any given situation.

Previously, decision makers experienced significant uncertainty because they did not have enough information to make the right decisions. Today they are likely to feel there is *too much* information, but just as much ambiguity and uncertainty as in the past. This is especially the case with network security, where there are fewer traditional indications that a significant action is actually about to take place. To make decisions about how to prepare for and respond to a network security incident, decision makers need analysts who understand intelligence fundamentals, the nuance of network intrusions, and how to combine the two into an accurate assessment of a situation and what it means for their entire organization. In short, they need analysts who can conduct intelligence-driven incident response.

Before diving into the application of intelligence-driven incident response, it is important to understand the evolution of cybersecurity incidents and their responses, and why it is so relevant in this field. This chapter covers the basics of cyber threat intelligence, including its history, recent activity, and the way forward, and sets the stage for the concepts discussed in the rest of this book.

Intelligence as Part of Incident Response

As long as there has been conflict, there have been those who watched, analyzed, and reported observations about the enemy. Wars have been won and lost based on an ability to understand the way the enemy thinks and operates, to comprehend their motivations and identify their tactics, and to make decisions—large and small—based on this understanding. Regardless of the type of conflict, whether a war between nations or a stealthy intrusion against a sensitive network, intelligence guides both sides. The side that masters the art and science of intelligence—analyzing information about the intent, capability, and opportunities of adversaries—and is able to act on that information will almost always be the side that wins.

History of Cyber Threat Intelligence

One of the best ways to understand the role of intelligence in incident response is by studying the history of the field. Each of the events discussed in the following paragraphs could (and often do!) fill entire books. From the iconic book *The Cuckoo's Egg* by Cliff Stoll (Pocket Books) to recent revelations about decades-old intrusions, such as Moonlight Maze, the history of cyber threat intelligence is intriguing and engaging and offers many lessons for those working in the field today.

The first intrusion

In 1986, Cliff Stoll was a PhD student managing the computer lab at Lawrence Berkeley National Laboratory in California when he noticed a billing discrepancy in the amount of 75 cents, indicating that someone was using the laboratory's computer systems without paying for it. Our modern-day network security–focused brains see this and scream, "Unauthorized access!" but in 1986 few administrators would have jumped to that conclusion. Network intrusions were not something that made the daily news, with claims of millions or even billions of dollars stolen; most computers connected to the internet belonged to government and research institutes, not casual users, and it was easy to assume everyone using the system was friendly. The network defense staple tcpdump was a year from being started. Common network discovery tools such as Nmap would not be created for another decade, and exploitation frameworks such as Metasploit would not appear for another 15 years. The discrepancy Stoll noticed was more easily expected to be a software bug or bookkeeping error, as it seemed that someone had simply not paid for their time.

Except that it wasn't. As Stoll would discover, he was not dealing with a computer glitch or a cheap mooch of a user. He was stalking a "wily hacker" who was using the Berkeley lab's network as a jumping-off point to gain access to sensitive government computers, such as those used by the White Sands Missile Range and the National Security Agency (NSA). Stoll monitored incoming network traffic, printing reams of paper to keep a record, and began to profile the intruder responsible for the first documented case of cyberespionage. He learned the typical hours the attacker was active, monitored the commands he ran to move through the interconnected networks, and observed other patterns of activity. He discovered how the attacker was able to gain access to the Berkeley lab's network in the first place by exploiting a vulnerability in the movemail function in GNU Emacs, a tactic that Stoll likened to a cuckoo bird leaving its egg in another bird's nest to hatch and inspiring the name of his book on the intrusion, *The Cuckoo's Egg*.

Understanding the attacker meant that it was possible to protect the network from further exploitation, identify where he may target next, and allow a response—both on the micro level (identifying the individual carrying out the attacks) and on the macro level (realizing that nations were employing new tactics in their traditional intelligence-gathering arsenal and changing policies to respond to this change). Sharing this understanding was key to protecting Lawrence Berkeley National Lab and many other government organizations as well.

Destructive attacks

In 1988, Cornell University student Robert T. Morris (*https://oreil.ly/LtI5x*) hacked into a computer lab at the Massachusetts Institute of Technology (MIT) and released a computer program that was designed to replicate itself to as many computers as possible without being detected. It did this by exploiting a backdoor in the internet's email delivery system as well as a flaw in the "finger" program that identified network users. It may have just been a harmless experiment—or a prank, as some have described it—that few people ever knew about, but it did not work exactly as Morris intended and became part of cybersecurity history (which is just like regular history, but cooler). Morris's cyber "worm" ended up crashing 6,000 computers, which was about 10% of the internet of the time, with systems at Harvard, Princeton, Stanford, Johns Hopkins, NASA, and the Lawrence Livermore National Laboratory among the many victims. Investigators from the FBI were struggling to inspect the activity, unsure if it was an outage or an attack, when Morris called two friends and admitted that he was the one behind the worm. One of the friends called the *New York Times*, which led to the eventual identification and conviction of Morris for violations of the new Computer Fraud and Abuse Act of 1986 (CFAA).

Although there was no nefarious intent behind this worm—it was really just another example of how programs don't always behave exactly the way that their creator intended them to—there were far-reaching implications that can still be seen today. As the internet became more and more critical to operations, it became even more important to be able to quickly identify and remediate other intrusions or destructive attacks. The Computer Emergency Response Team (CERT) was established in 1998 at Carnegie Mellon University as a professional, trained response team responsible for providing assessments and solutions for cyberattacks. Morris's worm also highlights why it is important to be able to quickly attribute an attack. In 1988 there had been significant "warming" of the Cold War, with Reagan and Gorbachev meeting in Moscow and Soviet troops beginning to withdraw from Afghanistan. If this worm had inaccurately been blamed on Soviet activity—which was actually the case for the activity from *The Cuckoo's Egg*—it could have significantly changed the course of history.

Moonlight Maze

In the decade following *The Cuckoo's Egg* and Morris's worm, the field of incident response improved, not just with the creation of CERT, but because of the professionalization of the field itself across the government, military, and private sectors. In addition, the emergence of proper network monitoring tools meant that defenders weren't reliant on printers scattered around a basement to identify malicious network activity. This increase in capabilities was fortuitous, as intrusions not only continued but grew in scope and sophistication. In 1998, the US government identified what is believed to still be the largest and longest-running intrusion into government networks—codenamed Moonlight Maze (*https://oreil.ly/DT6G8*).

In March 1998, the US government noticed anomalous activity within several sensitive and restricted networks, including the Pentagon, NASA (yes, NASA has apparently always been a target for intrusions), and the Department of Energy (DOE). Further analysis identified the same malicious activity at several universities and revealed that the activity had been ongoing for at least two years. The sustained nature of this activity was unlike any of the previous intrusions (as far as was known at the time), which had seemed more targeted and short-lived. Unlike those instances, the adversaries had left strategic backdoors in different parts of the network so that they could return at will. Information was being gathered from numerous locations that often seemed unrelated.

We have been fortunate enough to work closely with people who directly investigated and responded to Moonlight Maze, both in the 1990s and today, as there are still many unknowns and many insights to be gained from this intrusion. Talking with these individuals and reading through the numerous reports on the intrusion hammers home the point that intelligence work is critical to incident response and that cyber threat intelligence bridges the gap between what is happening on the strategic level with national interests and foreign adversaries and how those adversarial goals and actions show up on a computer network. By 1998, the US had a full-scope intelligence community actively looking and listening for signs of foreign interference, but the largest network attack went unnoticed until it was detected "by accident" because intelligence work had not yet been fully modified to account for actions taken against a network.

Moonlight Maze kicked cyber threat intelligence capabilities into the modern era. Computer networks were not something that might be impacted from time to time; these networks were now being targeted directly for the information and access they held. Computer networks were part of intelligence collection, and intelligence needed to play a role in their defense.

Modern Cyber Threat Intelligence

Over the decades, cyber threats have grown and morphed. Adversaries are not just foreign governments or curious students. Organized criminals, identity thieves, scammers, ideologically motivated activists, and others have realized the impact that their activities could have when directed at digital targets instead of physical ones. These adversaries use an ever-expanding set of tools and tactics to attack their victims and actively attempt to evade detection. At the same time, our reliance on our networks has increased, making incidents even more impactful. Understanding the attacker has gotten much more complicated and much more important.

Understanding how to identify attacker activity and how to use that information to protect networks are the fundamental concepts behind a more recent addition to the incident responder's toolkit: cyber threat intelligence. *Threat intelligence* is the analysis of adversaries—their capabilities, motivations, and goals. *Cyber threat intelligence* (sometimes abbreviated as CTI) is the analysis of how adversaries use the cyber domain to accomplish their goals. See how these levels of intelligence play into one another in Figure 1-1.

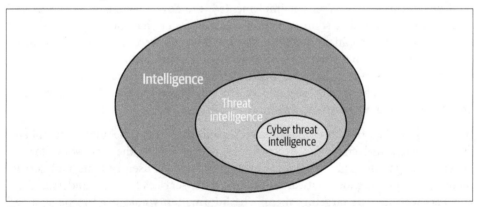

Figure 1-1. From intelligence to cyber threat intelligence

Initially, intelligence analysts came into the picture after an intrusion like Moonlight Maze to understand what the overall intrusion told us about the adversary. What were their goals, their motivations, their capabilities? What was their organizational structure? These were all things that were important for a strategic understanding and long-term planning, but not things that would immediately provide value to those trying to defend their networks from the attacks of today, tomorrow, or sometimes even last week. Cyber threat intelligence began to focus more on tactical and technical details that were more immediately actionable, learning along the way what types of information were most valuable in different situations. Cyber threat intelligence analysts didn't just bring data; they also brought insights.

In information security, we traditionally focus on observable concepts; we like things that are testable and reproducible. Cyber threat intelligence, meanwhile, lives in the area between observations and interpretation. We may not know *for sure* that an adversary will attempt to access employee financial records, but we can conduct analysis on data about past intrusions and successful attackers outside of our network and make recommendations for the systems and types of data that may need additional protection. Not only do we need to be able to interpret information, but we also need to be able to convey it in a way that is meaningful to the intended audience to help them make decisions. Looking back on his historic analysis of the intrusions in *The Cuckoo's Egg*, Stoll identified "the need for a story" as one of his key takeaways from the entire experience. "I thought I could just show people the data and they would understand," he said. "But I was wrong. You need to tell a story" (SANS CTI Summit 2017).

The Way Forward

New technologies give us more information about the actions that attackers take as well as additional ways to act on that information. However, we have found that with each new technology or concept implemented, the adversary adapted; worms and viruses with an alphabet soup of names changed faster than our appliances could identify them, and sophisticated, well-funded attackers were often more organized and motivated than many network defenders. Ad hoc and intuitive intelligence work would no longer suffice to keep defenders ahead of the threat. Analysis would need to evolve as well and become formal and structured. The scope would have to expand, and the goals would have to become more ambitious.

In addition to detecting threats against an organization's often nebulous and ephemeral perimeter, analysts would need to look deeper within their networks for the attacks that got through the lines, down to individual user systems and servers themselves, as well as look outward into third-party services to better understand the attackers who may be targeting them. The information would need to be analyzed and its implications understood, and then action would have to be taken to better prevent, detect, and eradicate threats. The actions taken to better understand adversaries would need to become part of a formal process and a critical part of information security operations: threat intelligence.

Incident Response as a Part of Intelligence

Intelligence is often defined as data that has been refined and analyzed to enable stakeholders to make better decisions. Intelligence, therefore, requires data. In intelligence-driven incident response, there are multiple ways to gather intelligence that can be analyzed and used to support incident response. However, it is important to note that incident response will also generate cyber threat intelligence. The traditional intelligence cycle—which we cover in depth in Chapter 2—involves direction, collection, processing, analysis, dissemination, and feedback. Intelligence-driven incident response involves all of these components and helps inform direction, collection, and analysis in other applications of threat intelligence as well, such as network defense, secure software development, and user awareness training. Intelligence-driven incident response doesn't end when the intrusion is understood and remediated; it generates information that will continue to feed the intelligence cycle.

Analysis of an intrusion, no matter if it was successful or failed, can provide a variety of information that can be used to better understand the overall threat to an environment. The root cause of the intrusion and the initial access vector can be analyzed to inform an organization of weaknesses in network defenses or of policies that attackers may be abusing. The malware that is identified on a system can help expose the tactics that attackers are using to evade traditional security measures such as antivirus or host-based intrusion-detection tools and the capabilities they have available to them. The way an attacker moves laterally through a network can be analyzed, and that intelligence can be used to create new ways to monitor for attacker activity in the network. The final actions that an attacker performed (such as stealing information or changing how systems function), whether they were successful or not, can help analysts understand the enemy's motivations and goals, which can be used to guide overall security efforts. There is essentially no part of an incident-response engagement that cannot be used to better understand the threats facing an organization and improve future defense and response.

For this reason, the various processes and cycles outlined in this book are aimed at ensuring that intelligence-driven incident response supports overall intelligence operations. Although they provide specific guidance for utilizing cyber threat intelligence in incident response, keep in mind that wider applications can be used as intelligence capabilities expand.

What Is Intelligence-Driven Incident Response?

Cyber threat intelligence isn't a new concept, simply a new name for an old approach: applying a structured analytical process to understand an attack and the adversary behind it. The application of threat intelligence to network security is more recent, but the basics haven't changed. Cyber threat intelligence involves applying intelligence processes and concepts—some of the oldest concepts that exist—and making them a part of the overall information security process. Threat intelligence has many applications, but one of the fundamental ways it can be utilized is as an integral part of the intrusion-detection and incident-response process. We call this *intelligence-driven incident response* and think it is something every security team can do, with or without a major capital investment. It's less about tools, although they certainly help sometimes, and more about a shift in the way we approach the incident-response process. Intelligence-driven incident response will help not only to identify, understand, and eradicate threats within a network, but also to strengthen the entire information security process to improve those responses in the future.

Why Intelligence-Driven Incident Response?

Over the past few decades, our world has become increasingly interconnected, both literally and figuratively, allowing attackers to carry out complex campaigns and intrusions against multiple organizations with the same effort that it used to take to target a single entity. We are long past the point where we can automatically assume that an intrusion is an isolated incident—in fact, while we used to be stunned to find overlaps and connections between intrusions, now we are suspicious when we *don't* see overlap. When we better understand the adversary, we can more easily pick up on the patterns that show commonalities between intrusions. Intelligence-driven incident response ensures that we are gathering, analyzing, and sharing intelligence in a way that will help us identify and respond to these patterns more quickly.

Operation SMN

A good example of intelligence-driven incident response is the analysis of the Axiom Group, which was identified and released as a part of a Coordinated Malware Eradication (CME) campaign in 2014 called Operation SMN.

What's in a Name?

The *SMN* in Operation SMN stands for *some marketing name*, a not-so-subtle but amusing jab indicating how widespread the belief is that marketing often takes over intelligence products. For better or worse, threat intelligence has been eagerly embraced by marketing forces all touting the best threat-intelligence products, feeds, and tools. The first time many people are exposed to threat intelligence

---

is through marketing material, making it difficult for many to fully understand threat intelligence.

It is important that intelligence work is done with the end goal of better understanding and defending against adversaries. Sometimes marketing gets in the way of that, but ideally marketing can help with messaging and ensuring that the "story" behind threat intelligence reaches the right audience in the right way.

For more than six years, a group of attackers known as the Axiom Group stealthily targeted, infiltrated, and stole information from Fortune 500 companies, journalists, nongovernmental organizations, and a variety of other organizations. The group used sophisticated tools, and the attackers went to great lengths to maintain and expand access within the victims' networks. As malware was detected and the incident-response process began within various victim organizations, coordinated research on one of the malware families used by this group revealed that the issue was far more complex than originally thought. As more industry partners became involved and exchanged information, patterns began to emerge that showed not just malware behavior, but the behaviors of a threat actor group working with clear guidance. Strategic intelligence was identified, including regions and industries targeted.

This was an excellent example of the intelligence cycle at work in an incident-response scenario. Not only was information collected, processed, and analyzed, but it was disseminated in such a way as to generate new requirements and feedback, starting the process over again until the analysts had reached a solid conclusion and could act with decisiveness, eradicating 43,000 malware installations at the time that the report was published. The published report, also part of the dissemination phase, allowed incident responders to better understand the tactics and motivations of this actor group.

SolarWinds

In December 2020, news broke of a massive intrusion at the Texas-based company SolarWinds, which makes software for monitoring and managing IT networks and is a very popular tool in many large networks, including cybersecurity companies, governments, and Fortune 500 companies. The activity was detected after the cybersecurity firm FireEye, a SolarWinds customer, identified that their networks had been compromised and a set of tools they developed for identifying intrusions had been accessed by an unknown entity. Their own investigation (*https://oreil.ly/U214f*) into the intrusion on their network led them to identify SolarWinds as the source of the intrusion.

Their analysis indicated that the SolarWinds networks had been compromised in late 2019 and their software tampered with, in that a software update that was pushed to all its clients contained a backdoor that would allow the adversaries access to those networks as well. This was not the first software-based supply chain attack; however, it was notable for its size and scale—estimates suggested that more than 18,000 SolarWinds customers were impacted. It was also notable for its response, which, 20 years after Moonlight Maze, showed how far cyber threat intelligence has come as a discipline. Once identified, FireEye published a blog post with details about the incident and ways for others to detect activity on their network. Additional teams jumped in to analyze activity on their networks and continued to share indicators and findings, both publicly and through established threat-sharing groups, allowing a picture of the overall attack to quickly develop. The Department of Homeland Security published guidance on supply chain attacks, taking the response from a mentality of just reacting to one isolated incident to thinking about how this new information shapes the way the industry should think about preparing for intrusions in the future. While certainly not a perfect process, the SolarWinds compromise illustrates the role that cyber threat intelligence can play in incident response and how it not only can help the organizations directly impacted but also can help to surface important lessons for others.

Both the Axiom Group attacks and the SolarWinds software supply chain intrusion were information-seeking, espionage-related attacks, but nation-state-sponsored attackers aren't the only thing that incident responders have to worry about. Financially motivated criminal activity is also evolving, and those actors are also working hard to stay ahead of defenders and incident responders. One of the most significant tactical changes for financially motivated criminals in recent years is the move to ransomware. Ransomware attacks use tools to encrypt data on a network and then charge a ransom for the key to decrypt the data. The concept of ransomware has been around for decades; however, its usage has increased drastically since 2012, along with its impact. Although ransomware attacks do not always involve strategic and coordinated attacks against multiple organizations, the groups executing ransomware attacks often target different victims using the same tactics, the same toolsets, and often the same targeting information. Defenders working against these financially motivated attacks can also leverage intelligence-driven incident response to identify early indications that their networks have been breached by these actors before the actual encryption process has begun.

Conclusion

Despite the many advances in the computer security field, attackers continue to adapt—but they do not have to outpace defenders. Intelligence-driven incident response allows us to learn from attackers; to identify their motivations, processes, and behaviors; and to identify their activities even as they seek to outwit our defenses and detection methods. The more we know about attackers, the better we can prevent, detect, and respond to their actions.

We have reached the point where a structured and repeatable process for implementing intelligence in the incident-response process is necessary, and this book aims to provide insight into that process. Throughout this book, we provide various models and methods that can be viewed as the building blocks of intelligence-driven incident response. We discuss why these models are beneficial and how they integrate with incident response. There is no one-size-fits-all approach. In many cases, the incident or the organization will dictate which specific combination of models and approaches fits best. Understanding the foundational principles of intelligence and incident response, as well as the specific methods for integrating them, will allow you to develop and build a process for intelligence-driven incident response that will work for you and the needs of your organization.

## CHAPTER 2

Basics of Intelligence

It consists of gathering facts. ... It consists of forming hypotheses on the basis of these facts, of testing these hypotheses for traces of one's own ignorance or bias, of cleansing them if possible. The goal is to build better hypotheses than already exist and to establish them as relatively more true: it is to reveal a sharper picture of what happened and to make a closer approach to actuality than anyone has yet contrived.

—Sherman Kent

Intelligence analysis is one of the oldest and most consistent concepts in human history. Every morning people turn on the news or scroll through feeds on their phones, looking for information that will help them plan their day. What is the weather report? What implications does that have for their activities for that day? How is the traffic? Do they need to plan for extra time to get to where they need to go? External information is compared to an internal set of experiences and priorities, and an assessment is made of the impact on the target subject—the individual in question.

This is the basic premise of intelligence analysis: taking in external information from a variety of sources and analyzing it against existing data to provide an assessment that will affect decision making. This occurs at the individual level as well as at higher levels; this same process is implemented at the group, organization, and government level every single day. There is one big catch though—unlike many forms of day-to-day analysis, intelligence analysis involves trying to understand something about an adversary who very much wants to stay hidden from you. The weather report—although occasionally inaccurate—was not intentionally tricking you into leaving your umbrella at home so that you would get soaked in a downpour. Because of this, intelligence analysis almost always involves some aspect of secrecy. Even when it is not part of a classified government program, it involves an entity that does not want you to have the whole picture. Likewise, you don't want that entity to know what *you* know about it, otherwise it might change tactics and cause you to start over at the beginning. In fact, a significant debate in intelligence work is around the concept of intelligence-gain-loss where analysts need to determine how much intelligence value will be lost by taking an action that would warn the adversary that their presence, tactics, or tools have been identified.

Although there are a growing number of intelligence training programs inside and outside of traditional government and military fields, many individuals currently conduct some form of intelligence analysis on their own without formal training, and many security teams work through similar processes as they conduct investigations without realizing that they are, in fact, engaged in intelligence analysis. While intuitive analysis can be beneficial to a security program, it is even more useful when basic structures, such as processes and models, are utilized to streamline intelligence work, account for biases, and make the analytic judgments defensible and repeatable.

When businesses and governments conduct intelligence operations, it is based on a formalized process and doctrine that has been captured over the years. In addition, there are formalized processes that have been specialized for intelligence operations in information security and incident response. This chapter walks through key concepts of intelligence and security. We'll start with abstract concepts that are primarily pulled from intelligence doctrine and move toward the more concrete concepts that can be applied directly to your incident-response investigations.

Intelligence and Research

Intelligence as a discipline follows the same basic principles of other types of applied research, but there are several significant differences, including secrecy, timeliness, and lack of reproducibility. The first, as we mentioned, is the understanding that intelligence often deals with matters that the subject or the target is actively trying to keep hidden. Intelligence analysts cannot go to an archive or search online repositories and find *all* of the information that they need. They may be able to find a great deal of relevant information, but there will always be an unspoken understanding that key pieces of information are intentionally not included in public information.

The second difference is that timeliness is far more significant with intelligence analysis than in other forms of research. If the information is not analyzed and presented to decision makers ahead of when it is needed, then it is likely no longer relevant. The third difference is that with intelligence analysis, reproducibility, or being able to replicate findings, is often not done because of the first two principles. Most analysts will not have access to the exact same information to provide external validation of an analytic judgment, and the timeliness required of intelligence products means that the peer-review process is a rarity in the field and often conducted only in the aftermath of an intelligence failure.

Data Versus Intelligence

Before tackling anything else, it's important to clear up one of the most important distinctions of this discussion: the difference between data and intelligence. These are significant terms in the security community and unfortunately are often used interchangeably, to the point that many practitioners have a difficult time articulating the difference between them.

Joint Publication 2-0 (JP 2-0) (*https://oreil.ly/_dwGY*), the US military's primary joint intelligence doctrine, is one of the foundational intelligence documents used today. In its introduction, it states, "*Information* on its own may be of utility to the commander, but when related to other information about the operational environment and considered in the light of past experience, it gives rise to a new understanding of the information, which may be termed *intelligence*."

Data, in contrast, is a piece of information, a fact, or a statistic. Data is something that describes something that *is*. In terms of a weather report, the temperature is a piece of data. It is a fact, something that has been measured using a proven and repeatable process. Knowing the temperature is important, but to be useful for decision making, it must be analyzed in the context of what else is going on that day. In information security, an IP address or a domain is a piece of data. Without any additional analysis to provide context, they are simply facts. When various data points are gathered and analyzed to provide insight around a particular requirement, they become intelligence.

Intelligence is derived from a process of collecting, processing, and analyzing data. Once it has been analyzed, it must be disseminated to be useful. Not only does intelligence need to be disseminated, but it needs to reach its intended audience in a timely manner. Intelligence that does not get to the right audience is wasted intelligence. Wilhelm Agrell, a Swedish writer and historian who studied peace and conflict, famously said, "Intelligence analysis combines the dynamics of journalism with the problem solving of science."

The difference between data and true intelligence is *analysis*. Intelligence requires analysis that is based on a series of requirements and is aimed at answering questions relevant to decision makers. Without analysis, most of the data generated by the security industry remains simply data. That same data, however, once it has been properly analyzed in response to requirements, becomes intelligence, as it now contains the appropriate context needed to answer questions and support decision making.

Indicators of Compromise

There was a time when many people considered indicators of compromise, or IOCs, to be synonymous with threat intelligence. IOCs, which we will reference a *lot* and cover in depth later in the book, are things to look for in a system or in network logs that may indicate that a compromise has taken place. This includes IP addresses and domains associated with command-and-control servers or malware downloads, hashes of malicious files, and other network- or host-based artifacts that may indicate an intrusion. As we will discuss throughout this book, however, there is far more to threat intelligence than IOCs, although IOCs remain one of the most common types of technical intelligence around intrusions.

IOCs have gotten a bad reputation over the years, and while analysts once loved collecting as many as they could, IOCs may now be rejected out of hand as the pendulum swung too far in the other direction. Just because data is not intelligence does not mean that the data has no value—in fact without data there can be no intelligence! So rather than dismissing IOCs as useless artifacts of simpler times, value them for what they are—pieces that can help both detect threats on the network and be used in post-incident analysis and strategic research. We will discuss how to use IOCs for both of these use cases in later chapters.

Sources and Methods

Now that we have cleared up the distinction between data and intelligence, the natural next question is, "Where should I get this data from so that I can analyze it and generate intelligence?"

Traditional intelligence sources are most often centered around the following *INTs*, which describe where the data is collected from:

HUMINT

Human-source intelligence is derived from humans, either through covert or clandestine methods or from overt collection such as from diplomats. Human-source intelligence is the oldest form of intelligence collection. There is serious debate about whether cyber threat intelligence can be derived from HUMINT. However, there is a growing body of evidence to suggest that HUMINT can be a crucial part of the story. One example is interviews or conversations with individuals who are involved with or have firsthand knowledge of intrusions, such as when researchers from Kaspersky Labs were able to connect with a systems administrator from a network that had been compromised as part of Moonlight Maze. Not only did the sysadmin give inside information and perspective that only a person who experienced an intrusion can, he also provided access to a server from the intrusion that had been sitting under his desk—HUMINT can often lead to additional data collection. Another example that many describe as HUMINT is information gained from interactions with individuals via restricted or members-only online forums. This type of intelligence gathering could also be considered SIGINT, as it is derived from electronic communications.

SIGINT

Signals intelligence includes intelligence derived from the interception of signals, including communications intelligence (COMINT), electronic intelligence (ELINT), and foreign instrumentation signals intelligence (FISINT). Most technical intelligence collection falls under SIGINT. After all, computers function using electronic signals, so anything derived from a computer or other networking device could be considered SIGINT.

OSINT

Open source intelligence is gathered from publicly available sources, including news, social media, and commercial databases as well as a variety of other unclassified sources. We discussed previously that intelligence analysis, including cyber threat intelligence, involves some aspect of secrecy. This does not mean, however, that *all* intelligence sources must be secret. Published reports on cybersecurity threats are one type of OSINT that can be incredibly useful in intelligence analysis. When dealing with government-backed actors, publications that detail the organizational structure of that government's offensive cyber forces can provide a wealth of knowledge. OSINT can also help reveal technical details about things like IP addresses or domain names that are publicly accessible, for example, a WHOIS query detailing who registered a malicious domain.

IMINT

Imagery intelligence is collected from visual representations, including photography and radar. IMINT is not typically a source of cyber threat intelligence, but there are always cases where visual representations can provide critical information, such as the ability to watch troop movements during large-scale, government-backed denial-of-service attacks, as were previously seen with the Russia and Georgia conflict.[1]

MASINT

Measurement and signature intelligence is gathered from technical means, excluding signal and imagery. MASINT often includes signatures from nuclear, optical, radio frequency, acoustics, and seismic activity. As MASINT specifically excludes signals intelligence, it is also not a typical source of cyber threat intelligence.

---

1 Sarah Pruitt, "How a Five-Day War with Georgia Allowed Russia to Reassert Its Military Might" (*https://oreil.ly/nSW7h*), HISTORY, updated September 4, 2018.

GEOINT

    Geospatial intelligence is collected from geospatial data, including satellite and reconnaissance imagery, maps, GPS data, and other sources of data related to locations. Some organizations consider IMINT to be a part of GEOINT, and some believe it is a separate discipline. Similar to IMINT, GEOINT is not a typical source of cyber threat intelligence, but it can provide contextual information on threats to help you understand how attackers may use the cyber domain to achieve their goals.

There are various other INTs that have popped up over the years, including cyber intelligence (CYBINT), technical intelligence (TECHINT), financial intelligence (FININT), and the most recent one we found—CyberHumint. However, most of these new terms are already covered by other intelligence-collection methods. For example, cyber intelligence is primarily derived from ELINT and SIGINT. What's important is to understand the *source* of the data. At the end of the day, if it helps to refer to a specific collection type as its own INT, then go ahead; just be prepared to deal with the eventual terminology conflicts that tend to pop up in this field.

In addition to these traditional intelligence-collection disciplines, some collection methods are often used specifically in cyber threat intelligence. Specific threat data may come from the following:

Incidents and investigations

    This data is collected from the investigation of data breaches and incident-response activities. This is often one of the richest data sets used in cyber threat intelligence because investigators are able to identify multiple aspects of the threat, including the tools and techniques that are used, and can often identify the intent and motivation behind the intrusion.

Honeypots and honeynets

    These devices are set up to emulate machines or entire networks and gather information about interactions with these devices. There are many types of honeypots: low interaction, high interaction, internal honeypots, and honeypots on the public internet. Honeypot information can be useful if you know which types of honeypots it came from, what they were monitoring for, and the nature of the interactions. Traffic gathered from a honeypot that captures exploit attempts or attempts to install malware on a system are far more useful in analysis than scanning or web-scrapping traffic.

    A honeynet is a network specifically set up with one or more honeypots to both look more realistic to an attacker and to capture additional information about how an attacker may move between devices in a network. As with individual honeypots, it is important to understand how the network was configured in order to understand the attacker data it captures.

Forums and chatrooms

A variety of companies claim to have deep web or dark web collections. In many cases, these companies are referring to data from forums and chatrooms with restricted access. In these forums and chatrooms, individuals often exchange information that is valuable after it's analyzed. There are so many of these types of forums and chatroom sites that it is nearly impossible for any one company to have complete coverage of the dark web, so be aware that the collection is often limited in scope and will differ from that of other companies that claim to have similar data.

Even these techniques are new iterations of common techniques of the past. What's old is new as technology evolves, and intelligence is no different. The philosopher George Santayana's missive about forgetting the past is as true as ever.

Military Jargon

One common point of contention in information security is the use of military terminology. Although intelligence has existed for centuries, it was codified in doctrine by military entities in documents such as the US Joint Publication 2-0: Joint Intelligence (*https://oreil.ly/2bo9V*) and the UK Joint Doctrine Publication 2-00: Understanding and Intelligence Support to Joint Operations (*https://oreil.ly/BHjV-*). The majority of nonmilitary intelligence applications still pull heavily from the general principles captured in these documents, which results in a high volume of military terms in modern intelligence analysis. This means that related fields, such as cyber threat intelligence, often pull heavily from military doctrine. However, just as with marketing, military jargon is useful in some situations and not useful in others. If the use of military terminology gets in the way of conveying your message, it may be a good time to use different terms.

Models

Models are a critical tool in the analyst's toolkit. Without models, many analysts would not be able to keep up with the quantity of data that exists in the world or the requirements for providing meaning around the data. They would struggle to not only synthesize the information that they collected from all the various sources but also to make meaning and insights that are relevant to decision makers.

One of the best working definitions of "models" for intelligence purposes comes from the book *Quantitative Intelligence Analysis* by Edward Waltz.[2] In the book, Waltz writes: "Models refer to the cognitive, conceptual, mathematical, physical, or otherwise logical representation of systems, entities, phenomena, or processes." The two most common types of models used in cyber threat intelligence are mental models and conceptual models. Mental models are cognitive models that hold an analyst's perception of reality. Even when analysts have gone through similar courses of formalized training, their mental models may be very different because of the many diverse ways that individuals perceive and process information.

Conceptual models, on the other hand, are representations of explicit knowledge and are commonly the result of intelligence synthesis based on mental models that have been codified. Some of the most useful models have been derived from an analyst capturing and codifying a way that they intuitively approached or thought about problems. One example of this is the Diamond Model of Intrusion Analysis (*https:// oreil.ly/x6R3P*), which we cover in depth in Chapter 3. Sergio Caltagirone, one of the creators of the model, described the generation of a new model as:

> a long progression of understanding the work we were repeatedly doing, until we understood it well enough to abstract it. Once abstracted, it became infinitely more useful because we could then ask new questions [of the model].

Caltagirone also described models as formulas—you have to understand its parts and their relationships before you can fully utilize them.

The goal of codifying a conceptual model is to be able to structure information so that it can be analyzed and acted on. Many models that are frequently used in intelligence analysis, including the Diamond Model, are covered further in Chapters 3 and 7.

Using Models for Collaboration

One of the key benefits of using explicit, conceptual models (rather than exclusively using mental models) is that it enables collaboration. Intelligence collaboration has been likened to "thinking in public," because it requires analysts to verbalize or otherwise articulate mental processes of analysis and synthesis that can be difficult to describe. Models are critical to analytic collaboration and will result in higher quality intelligence. Therefore, it is worth the time investment to make sure that team members understand the different conceptual models that are commonly used and also understand the process for codifying the mental models that they commonly use in analysis.

---

2 Edward Waltz, *Quantitative Intelligence Analysis: Applied Analytic Models, Simulations, and Games* (Lanham: Rowman & Littlefield Publishers, 2014).

Process Models

Conceptual models can be divided into two broad categories: models that represent our thinking, and models that represent the subject of analysis. The first type of model can be thought of as being used to give structure to processes—such as how we think or the process of generating intelligence.

This section covers two process models that are used to effectively generate and act on intelligence. The first model is the OODA loop, which can be used in making quick, time-sensitive decisions. The second model is the intelligence cycle, or intelligence process, which can be used to generate more formal intelligence products that will be used in a variety of ways, from informing policy to setting future intelligence requirements.

Using Models Effectively

British statistician George E.P. Box said, "All models are wrong; some models are useful." Every model is an abstraction that's useful for understanding a problem. On the other hand, by its very nature, every model is reductionist and throws out important details. It's not important to fit all data into a particular model, but it's always valuable to use models to understand and improve your thought processes.

OODA

One of the most referenced military concepts in security is *OODA*, an acronym for observe, orient, decide, act. The OODA loop, shown in Figure 2-1, was developed by fighter pilot, military researcher, and strategist John Boyd in the 1960s. He believed that a fighter pilot who was at a disadvantage against an adversary with more advanced equipment or capabilities could be victorious by using OODA to respond more quickly to stimuli and effectively attack the opponent's mind through decisive actions.

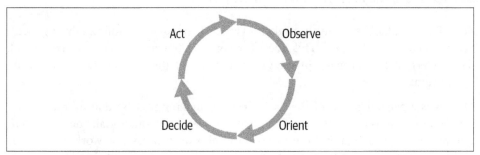

Figure 2-1. The OODA loop

Let's discuss each of the four phases.

Observe. The Observe phase centers around the collection of information. In this phase, an individual collects information from the outside world—anything and everything that could be useful. If the individual is planning to catch a baseball, this phase is about observing the baseball to determine its velocity and trajectory. If the individual is trying to catch a network attacker, the observation includes gathering logs, monitoring systems, and collecting any outside information that could help identify the attacker.

Orient. The Orient phase puts the information collected during the Observe phase into context with already known information. Past experience, preconceived notions, expectations, and existing models are taken into account. For the baseball example, orientation uses what the observer knows about how a ball moves, taking into account its velocity and trajectory, to predict where it will go and how much force the impact will generate when it is caught. In terms of a network attacker, orientation takes the telemetry pulled from the logs and combines it with knowledge about the network, relevant attack groups, and previously identified artifacts such as specific IP addresses or process names. The orientation phase is heavily reliant on the mental models we previously discussed. Without a way to quickly and accurately "sort" the data you have observed, orientation becomes a very difficult task.

Decide. At this point, information has been collected (observed) and contextualized (oriented), and now it is time to determine a course of action. The Decide phase is not about executing an action. It is about debating various courses of action until the final course of action is determined.

In the baseball example, this phase includes determining where to run and how fast, how the fielder should move and position their hand, and anything else needed to attempt to catch the ball. In the case of dealing with a network attacker, it means deciding whether to wait and continue to observe the attacker's actions, whether to start an incident-response action, or whether to ignore the activity. In either case, the defender *decides* on the next steps to achieve their goal.

Act. The Act phase is relatively straightforward: The individual follows through with the chosen course of action. This doesn't mean it's 100% guaranteed to be successful. That determination is made in the Observe phase of the next OODA loop, as the cycle begins again.

OODA is a generalization of the basic decision-making process that everyone goes through thousands of times a day. This explains how individuals make decisions, but also how teams and organizations do so. It explains the process a network defender or incident responder goes through when gathering information and figuring out how to use it.

The OODA loop is used by not only one side. While we, as defenders, go through the process of observing, orienting, deciding, and acting, in many cases the attacker does as well. The attacker is observing the network and the defender's actions in that network and deciding how to respond to changes in the environment and attempts to kick them out. As with many things, the side that can observe and adapt faster tends to win. Figure 2-2 shows the OODA loop for both an attacker and a defender.

One thing to note about the OODA loop is that it can often trip analysts up as they try to think through adversarial responses to their actions—*"First I will do X, then they will do Y, and then I will..."*—when in reality it can be difficult to know how the adversary will respond. There will always be some level of uncertainty when dealing with adversaries who are human and may act unpredictably, which can make the risk-averse wary of making any moves. When in doubt, reach back to your requirements or even further back to the goals and mission of your team or program. Are you tasked with defending the network? With safeguarding user data or public safety? Make sure those requirements and missions are included in the Orient phase, which can help to avoid paralysis when it comes time to decide the best course of action.

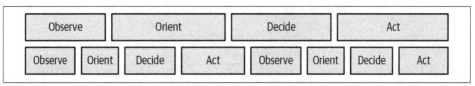

Figure 2-2. Competing OODA loop of the defender and the attacker

Multiple Defender OODA Loops

Beyond attacker-defender OODA loops, it's useful to think about defender-defender OODA loops—that is, how the decisions we make as defenders can impact other defenders. Many decisions that defensive teams can make may essentially set up race conditions for other defenders. For example, if a defender executes an incident response and then publicly shares information about the attack, then the first defender has started the clock on all other defenders to ingest that intelligence and use it. If an attacker can move through the OODA loop faster, find the public information about their activities, and change their tactics before the second defender can use the information, then they've turned inside (outmaneuvered and achieved a more ideal position) the second defender and can avoid serious consequences.

For this reason, it's important to consider how your actions and sharing impact other organizations, both adversaries and allies. In all cases, network defense is about slowing down the OODA loops of the adversary and speeding up the OODA loops of defenders.

This generalized model, which we'll discuss throughout the book, provides a template for understanding the decision-making processes of both defenders and attackers.

Intelligence cycle

The intelligence cycle, pictured in Figure 2-3, is the process model for generating and evaluating intelligence. The cycle begins where the last intelligence process ended and continues to build off itself. The intelligence cycle doesn't need to be followed to the letter. In fact, processes explored later in this book will build upon it. You do have to be careful not to omit critical steps, however. If you start skipping entire steps, you run the risk of ending up with more data and questions instead of intelligence.

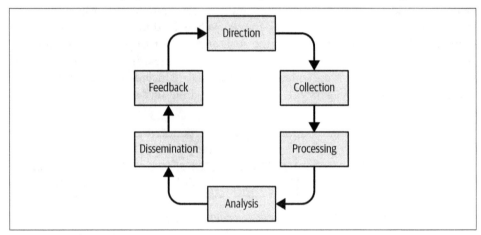

Figure 2-3. The intelligence cycle

To properly use the intelligence cycle, you need to know what is involved in each of its steps: direction, collection, processing, analysis, dissemination, and feedback. Let's dive in and walk through each step.

Direction. The first step in the intelligence cycle is direction—also known as require-ments. *Direction* is the process of establishing the question that the intelligence is meant to answer. This question can be delivered from an outside source, developed by the intelligence team itself, or developed by stakeholders and the intelligence team. (This is sometimes called the *RFI process*, which we'll discuss in Chapter 4.) The ideal outcome of this process is a clear, concise question and an answer the stakeholders will find usable.

Much intelligence work is based around requirements. In the intelligence community, any work done or reports circulated need to be tied directly to an intelligence requirement, whether they be standing (long term) or priority (urgent and time sensitive) requirements.

Collection. The next step in the intelligence cycle is *collection* of the data necessary to answer the question. This is a wide-ranging exercise that should focus on gathering as much data as possible from many sources. Redundant information adds value here because corroboration is often important.

This leads to a key idea of developing an effective intelligence program: *building a collection capability*. It's difficult to know exactly what data might eventually prove useful, so building a broad capability to collect a wide variety of information is important. This includes tactical information such as infrastructure, malware, and exploits, as well as operational strategic information such as attacker goals, social media monitoring, news monitoring, and high-level document exploitation (identifying reports, such as those that vendors release about groups, and gathering information from them). Be sure to document the sources and take care to assess each source: news stories often republish or reference the same original material, making it difficult to know what's corroboration and what's just a rehash of the same material. If it is impossible to determine the source of a particular data set, you may want to avoid using it as a collection source.

Collection is a process, not a one-time action. Using information from the first round of collection (such as gathering IP addresses) leads to a second round (such as using reverse DNS to find domains related to those IP addresses), which leads to a third round (using WHOIS to gather information about those domains). This exploitation becomes exponential as it builds upon itself. The focus at this point is not understanding how the data relates but simply collecting as much information as possible. Combining it comes later. Also, don't forget to consider data from internal sources, such as an incident-management system. It's common for organizations to discover actors or attacks they're already intimately familiar with.

Name Deconfliction

Naming presents a significant challenge in intelligence collection. While in the old days this focused on aliases and cover terms, today the field struggles with the fractured nature of intelligence collection and naming conventions. Every company, every intelligence sharing group, and every intelligence agency has its own names for various threat groups. The intrusion group APT1 is a great example. Commonly referred to as Comment Crew, this group was also known as ShadyRat, WebC2, and GIF89a by industry groups. Mandiant called them APT1. CrowdStrike called them Comment Panda. Ongoing intelligence determined their actual identity as Peoples Liberation Army Military Unit 61398. All of these names matter when collecting data, as overlooking reporting that uses a particular name could lead to missing critical data.

Processing. Data is not always immediately usable in its raw format or in the format in which it was collected. In addition, data from different sources may come in different formats, and it is necessary to get it into the same format so it can be analyzed together. The *processing* necessary to make data usable is often an overlooked task, but without it, generating intelligence would be nearly impossible. In the traditional intelligence cycle, processing is part of collection. However, when dealing with the types of data and organizations involved in incident response, it may be useful to consider processing separately. Here are some of the most common ways to process data related to cyber threats:

Normalization
Processing includes normalizing collected data into uniform formats for analysis. The collection process will generate nearly every conceivable kind of data result. Intelligence data comes in a variety of formats, from JSON to XML to CSV to plain text from email. Vendors share information on websites in blog posts or tables, but also in PDF-based reports or even YouTube videos. At the same time, organizations tend to store data in different formats. Some organizations use a purpose-built threat-intelligence platform, while other organizations build customized solutions from wikis or internal applications.

Indexing
Large volumes of data need to be made searchable. Whether dealing with observables such as network addresses and mutexes or operational data such as forum posts and social media, analysts need to be able to search quickly and efficiently.

Translation
In some cases, regional analysts may provide human translation of source documents, but this is generally not feasible for most organizations dealing with information from all over the world. Machine translation, while imperfect, usually provides sufficient value so that analysts can find items of interest. If necessary, they can then be escalated to specialists for a more accurate translation.

Enrichment
Providing additional metadata for a piece of information is important. For example, domain addresses need to be resolved to IP addresses, and WHOIS registration data fetched. Google Analytics tracking codes should be cross-referenced to find other sites using the same code. This enrichment process should be done automatically so that the relevant data is immediately available to analysts.

Filtering
Not all data provides equal value, and analysts can be overwhelmed when presented with endless streams of irrelevant data. Algorithms can filter out information known to be useless (though it may still be searchable) and bubble up the most useful and relevant data.

The data that has been collected may need to be ranked so that analysts can allocate resources to the most important items. Analyst time is valuable and should be focused correctly for maximum benefit to the intelligence product.

Visualization

Data visualization has advanced significantly. While many analysts fear vendor dashboards because of the clutter they typically contain, designing a visualization based on what analysts need (rather than what marketing and executives think looks good) can assist in reducing cognitive load.

Taking the time to process data effectively enables and improves future intelligence efforts.

Analysis. *Analysis* is as much an art as it is a science. In intelligence analysis, data that has been collected is characterized and compared against other available data, and an assessment is made as to its meanings and implications. Predictions of future implications are often made. There are various methods for conducting analysis, but the most common is to use analytic models to evaluate and structure the information, identify connections, and make assessments and predictions about their implications. In addition to using pre-existing models, which we cover later in this chapter, it is also common for analysts to develop their own models that work with their particular data sets or way of interpreting information.

The goal of the Analysis phase is to answer the questions identified in the Direction phase of the intelligence cycle. The type of answer will be determined by the nature of the question. In some cases, the analysis may generate a new intelligence product in the form of a report or could be as simple as a *yes* or *no* answer, most often backed up with a confidence value. It is important to understand what the output will be before beginning the analysis.

Analysis is not a perfect science and must often be conducted with incomplete information and uncertainty. It is important that analysts identify and clearly state any information gaps in their analysis so that decision makers can be aware of potential blind spots. Information gaps can also drive the collection process to identify new sources in order to reduce those gaps. If the gaps are significant enough that an analyst does not think it is possible to complete the analysis with the current information, then it may be necessary to go back to the Collection phase and gather additional data. It is much better to delay the final analysis than to provide an assessment that the analyst knows is flawed.

It is important to note that *all intelligence analysis is generated by a human*. If it is automated, it is instead considered to be *processing*, which is a critical step in the intelligence cycle but is not by itself analysis.

Dissemination. At this point, the process has generated real intelligence: a contextualized answer to the question posed in the Direction phase. A report with an answer is useless until it's shared with the relevant stakeholders—those who can use this intelligence. In plenty of documented intelligence failures, analysis was spot-on, but dissemination failed. *Intelligence must be shared with relevant stakeholders in the form they find the most useful.* This makes dissemination dependent on the audience. If the product is aimed at executives, it's important to consider length and phrasing. If it's aimed at implementation in technical systems (such as IDS or firewalls), it could require vendor-specific programmatic formats. In any case, the dissemination of intelligence must be usable by the relevant stakeholders.

Feedback. Often forgotten, the Feedback phase is key to continuing intelligence efforts. *The Feedback phase asks whether the intelligence that was generated answers the direction successfully.* This results in one of two outcomes:

Success

If the intelligence process answered the question, the cycle may be over. In many cases, though, a successful intelligence process leads to a request for more intelligence based on either new questions or the actions taken based on the answer given.

Failure

In some cases, the intelligence process fails. In this case, the Feedback phase should focus heavily on identifying the aspect of the original direction that was not properly answered. The following Direction phase should take special care to address the reasons for that failure. This usually comes down to a poorly structured Direction phase that didn't narrow the goal enough, an incomplete Collection phase that was unable to gather enough data to answer the question, or improper analysis that did not extract correct (or at least useful) answers from the data available.

Using the Intelligence Cycle

Let's consider how the intelligence cycle can be used to start learning about a new adversary.

One of the most common questions a chief information security officer, or CISO, should be asking is, "What do we know about this threat group I heard about?" A CISO will want a basic understanding of a group's capabilities and intention, as well as an assessment of relevance to a given organization. So, what does the intelligence cycle look like in this situation? Here is an example of what is involved in each step of the intelligence cycle to meet the CISO's needs:

Direction

Direction comes from a key stakeholder—in our case, the CISO. "What do we know about *X* threat group?" The real answer sought is a target package, which we'll explore in detail later.

Collection

Start with the original source, most likely a news article or report. That document will usually provide at least some context to begin the Collection phase. If the source material includes information about a specific intrusion or attack, it can be helpful to understand more about the entity that had been targeted and identify any potential motivations or goals of the intrusion. If indicators (e.g., IPs, URLs) exist, explore those as deeply as possible by pivoting and enriching. The source may itself point to additional reporting with IOCs; tactics, techniques, and procedures (TTPs); or other analyses.

Processing

The Processing phase is dependent on workflow and organization. Getting all the collected information into a place where it can be used most effectively may be as simple as putting it all into a single text document, or it may require importing it all into an analysis framework. Additional enrichment can be done with technical details related to the group. In addition, translation of reports or other documents may be necessary.

Analysis

Using the collected and processed information, the analyst will start by attempting to answer key questions:

- What are these attackers interested in?

- What tactics and tools do they typically use?

- How can defenders detect those tools or tactics?

- Who are these attackers? (Although this is always a question, it is not always one worth taking the time to answer.)

Dissemination

For a product like this, which aims to answer a specific question from the CISO, a simple email may suffice. While limiting a response makes sense in some cases, a real product for proactive distribution will almost always create greater value.

Feedback

Here, we answer the key question: Is the CISO pleased with the results? Does it lead to other questions? These pieces of feedback help close the loop and may begin a new series of collections.

The intelligence cycle is a generalized model that can be used to answer questions large and small. However, it is important to note that following the steps in this cycle will not automatically result in good intelligence.

Qualities of Good Intelligence

The quality of intelligence relies primarily on two things: collection sources and analysis. In cyber threat intelligence, we often work with data that we did not collect ourselves, and therefore it is critical that we understand as much as possible about the information. When generating intelligence ourselves, we also need to ensure that we understand collection sources and are addressing biases in our analysis. To ensure that quality intelligence is produced, consider the following.

Collection Method

It is important to understand whether the information is collected primarily from incidents or investigations or whether it is being collected from an automated collection system such as a honeypot or a network sensor. Although knowing the exact details of the collection is not imperative—some providers prefer to keep their sources confidential—it is possible to have a basic understanding of where the data comes from without compromising collection resources. The more details you have about the way information was collected, the better your analysis of this information will be. For example, it is good to know that data comes from a honeypot; it is *better* to know that it comes from a honeypot configured to identify brute-force attempts against remote web administration tools.

Date of Collection

The majority of cyber threat data that is collected is perishable. The life span of that data varies from minutes to potentially months or even years, but there is always a period of time when this information is relevant. Understanding when data was collected can help defenders understand how it can be acted upon. It is difficult to properly analyze or utilize any data when you do not know when it was collected.

Context

The collection method and date can both provide some level of context around the data, but the more context that is available, the easier it will be to analyze. Context can include additional details, such as specific activities related to the information and relationships between pieces of information.

Addressing Biases in Analysis

All analysts have biases. Identifying and countering those biases so that they do not influence analysis is a key component of quality intelligence. Some biases that analysts should seek to avoid include *confirmation* bias, which seeks to identify information that will support a previously formulated conclusion, and *anchoring bias*, which leads analysts to focus too heavily on a single piece of information while disregarding other, potentially more valuable, information. We cover biases in depth in Chapter 7.

Levels of Intelligence

The intelligence models we have examined thus far focus on a logical flow of information through pipeline of sorts. But, just as with incident analysis, this approach is not the only way to model the information. We can think about intelligence at different levels of abstraction, ranging from the highly specific (tactical) to the logistical (operational) to the very general (strategic). As we examine these levels of intelligence, keep in mind that they are not discrete buckets. This range of intelligence represents a continuous spectrum with gray areas in between.

Tactical Intelligence

Tactical intelligence is low-level, highly perishable information that supports security operations and incident response. The customers for tactical intelligence include security operations center (SOC) analysts and computer incident response team (CIRT) investigators. In the military, this level of intelligence supports small-unit actions. In cyber threat intelligence, this usually includes IOCs and observables as well as highly granular TTPs describing precisely how an adversary deploys a particular capability. Tactical intelligence enables defenders to respond directly to threats using methods such as hunting in the network for signs of adversary activity, prioritizing critical patching based on reports of active exploitation, or issuing information to employees of active phishing campaigns targeting their organization.

An example of tactical intelligence is IOCs related to an exploitation of a newly discovered vulnerability. These tactical-level IOCs include IP addresses conducting scans for the vulnerability, domains hosting malware that will be downloaded to the host if exploitation is successful, and various host-based artifacts that are generated during exploitation and installation of malware. This tactical intelligence would enable security operations teams to effectively hunt for malicious activity in the network while taking concrete steps to mitigate any future exploitation.

Operational Intelligence

In the military, *operational intelligence* is a step up from tactical. This information supports logistics and analyzes effects of terrain and weather on larger operations—in other words, it involves far more context than just the tactical mission at hand. In cyber threat intelligence, this usually includes information on campaigns and higher-order TTPs, as well as anticipated responses from adversaries and how those actions may impact other operations. It may also include information on specific actor attribution as well as capabilities and intent. Customers for operational intelligence include senior-level digit forensics and incident response (DFIR) analysts and other cyber threat intelligence teams.

This is one of the harder levels of intelligence for many analysts to work with, because it sometimes feels too general to be tactical but too specific to be strategic. Operational intelligence needs to be acted on somewhat urgently; however, there are potentially far-reaching implications of any action taken, so both the "observe" and "orient" phases of the OODA loop have far more components and complexities. In addition, analysts and executive-level decision makers often have differing views on the need to make a decision and act on it. Executive-level decision makers, for example, may want to spend a considerable amount of time weighing the best course of action.

Following the preceding example about tactical-level indicators of active exploitation of a vulnerability, operational-level intelligence would include information on how widespread the exploitation is, whether it is targeted or opportunistic, who else is being targeted, the purpose of the malware that is being installed, and any details on the actors who are carrying out the attacks. Understanding these details can support the generation of follow-up intelligence, including what other actions may be seen and the severity of the threat, to help plan a response.

Strategic Intelligence

In the military or government, *strategic intelligence* deals with national and policy information and is often the accumulation of years of analytic work aimed at providing a holistic picture of a situation. In cyber threat intelligence, we think of this as supporting C-level executives and boards of directors in making serious decisions about risk assessments, resource allocation, and organizational strategy. This information includes threat trends and actor motivations, along with additional information relevant to the organization. In the preceding example, strategic intelligence would include information on the motivations of the attackers, especially if the activity indicates a new or previously unidentified threat, and any information that indicates new tactics or attacker targeting that may require higher-level responses, such as new policies or an architecture change.

Confidence Levels

As mentioned previously, intelligence typically has different confidence levels associated with it. These confidence levels reflect the analysts' trust that the information is correct and accurate. For some types of data, this confidence may be placed on a numeric scale (for example, 0 to 100) and calculated using traditional statistical methods, while in other cases the confidence assessment is provided on a qualitative, subjective basis by analysts directly. It is important to identify confidence in two important areas: confidence in the source of the information, and confidence in an analyst's conclusions.

One common way of describing source reliability is the Admiralty Code or NATO System found in FM 2-22.3 (*https://oreil.ly/nrZ0-*). This consists of two scales. The first evaluates the reliability of a source based on previous information, ranging from A (Reliable) to E (Unreliable). The second scale evaluates the degree of confidence in the information content itself, ranging from 1 (Confirmed) to 5 (Improbable). These two scores are combined for a particular piece of information, based on the source and specific content. So, information known to be true from a source with a history of valid information might be evaluated as B1, but information that is improbable from a source with a history of invalid information would be evaluated as E5.

Sherman Kent, often referred to as the father of intelligence analysis, wrote an essay in 1964 called "Words of Estimative Probability," which describes various qualitative ways to describe confidence in an analyst's judgment. In that essay, Kent shares one of the charts that he and his team use to assign and describe confidence (shown in Figure 2-4). He also writes that other terms may be used in their place as long as the meaning is understood and the terms are used consistently.

100% Certainty
The general area of possibility
93% Give or take about 6% Almost certain
75% Give or take about 12% Probably
50% Give or take about 10% Chances about even
30% Give or take about 10% Probably not
7% Give or take about 5% Almost certainly not
0% Impossibility

Figure 2-4. Sherman Kent's chart on estimative probability

Conclusion

Intelligence has a long and fascinating history and is a field that has adapted time and time again to changes in technology and to the growing complexities of the world. At its foundation are principles that are part of human nature—curiosity, assessing situations for danger, making connections. These foundations have been built upon with structured processes and models so that what is often instinctive becomes more academically rigorous and defensible. Biases, which humans cannot completely escape, can influence analysis and need to be identified and countered to avoid inaccurate assessments.

Intelligence is also a critical component of incident response, and many processes can be used to integrate intelligence principles into incident response investigations. It is important to understand the sources of intelligence that you will be relying on; there is a big difference in the way that you treat intelligence that came from a previous incident-response investigation in your network and the way you treat information that comes from a honeypot. Both types of information are valuable; they just have different applications. The next chapter dives into the specifics of incident response and the models that help analysts implement intelligence-driven incident response.

## CHAPTER 3

Basics of Incident Response

It is a fairly open secret that almost all systems can be hacked, somehow. It is a less spoken secret that such hacking has actually gone quite mainstream.

—Dan Kaminsky

Intelligence is only one half of the intelligence-driven incident-response puzzle. While computer incident response isn't nearly as old as the art of espionage, in the last 40 years it has rapidly evolved into a major industry. *Incident response* is the process of responding to a detected intrusion, whether against a single system or an entire network. It includes identifying the information necessary to fully understand the incident, developing and executing the plans to remove the intruders, and recording information for follow-up actions (such as legal actions, regulatory reporting, or intelligence operations).

Intrusion detection and incident response share many characteristics. Both are abstract. Both are complicated topics. As a result, people have sought to simplify them by abstracting them into cycles or models. These models make understanding the complex interplay between defender and adversary possible and form the basis for planning a response to these incidents. Just like the process models described in Chapter 2—the OODA loop and the intelligence cycle—they are rarely perfect and can't always be followed explicitly. However, they provide a framework for understanding the adversaries' intrusion and the defenders' response processes while also allowing multiple responders to work together to understand an intrusion using the same terminology and methodology. The combination of shared vocabulary and thought processes helps make these complex events less fraught and far more likely to succeed.

Just like our exploration of intelligence, this chapter starts with overarching theory and then moves to more specific applications and models. We'll dig into common defense techniques and introduce the integrated intelligence and operations models we'll use for the rest of the book.

Incident-Response Cycle

In the same way that we need a standard language for discussing intelligence concepts, we need a language to discuss detecting and responding to incidents. This process can be viewed from both the defender's perspective and the adversary's perspective. Let's start with the defenders.

The *incident-response cycle* is made up of the major steps taken in intrusion detection and incident response. The goal of this model is to be agnostic to the type of attack (e.g., phishing, strategic web compromise, service compromise) and generalize the steps that are common to all of those attacks (and many others). Figure 3-1 illustrates this cycle.

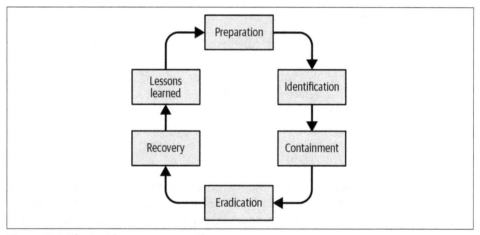

Figure 3-1. The incident-response cycle

There's some argument about where the concept of the incident-response cycle began. The first references seem to come from the National Institute of Standards and Technology's seminal document on incident response, "NIST 800-61 Computer Security Incident Handling Guide" (*https://oreil.ly/tnTt4*). Now in its second revision, this document is the basis for how US government agencies handle incidents. Although this guide introduced a huge number of key concepts, one of the most important is the description of the incident-response cycle, which provides a defender-centric view of the incident-response process. This process includes the following steps, which we will cover in detail: Preparation, Identification, Containment, Eradication, Recovery, and Lessons Learned.

Preparation

From the defender's perspective, the first stage of an incident comes before the attack begins: the *Preparation* phase. Preparation is the defender's chance to get ahead of the adversary by hardening assets, deploying detection capabilities, creating and updating signatures, and understanding baseline system and network activity. This is a combination of network security architecture and security operations. Many of these steps go beyond the security team, impacting and being impacted by general network operations, network architecture, system management, and even help desk and support.

Preparation should focus on five key elements, three technical and two nontechnical:

Attack surface mapping
> It's extremely difficult to defend systems that are unknown. In today's world of shadow IT, cloud providers, and rapid prototyping, it's nearly impossible to have a complete understanding, let alone inventory, of every system in a network. Yet without this understanding, or as close as possible, defense remains a guessing game.

Telemetry and visibility
> You can't find what you can't see. Specialized systems are required for incident responders to identify and investigate intrusions. These systems range from network to host and should provide the ability to investigate a wide variety of activities at multiple levels.

Hardening
> The only thing better than identifying an intrusion quickly is it never happening in the first place. Preparation is the stage for ensuring that patches are deployed, configurations are locked down, unused services are disabled, and tools that limit attacks such as virtual private networks (VPNs) and firewalls are in place.

Process and documentation
> On the nontechnical side, process is the first line of defense that can be prepared ahead of time. Few things are worse during an incident than trying to figure out what you're doing as you're doing it. Along with processes (such as an incident-response plan, notification plan, and communications plan), having documentation for common questions such as network configurations, system configurations, and system owners will also speed up responses.

Practice
> The last thing preparation allows is the chance to practice your plans. This will speed up future incidents and identify issues that can be corrected (something we'll touch on more in "Lessons Learned"). The best incident-response teams are those that have been through incidents together, and the best way to do that

is practice. Practice can include things such as tabletop exercise or red team exercises, with individuals taking on the role of both red and blue team (offense and defense) in a simulated intrusion.

When discussing computer network defense, many (mostly pessimistic) people are quick to point out all the advantages an adversary has. Most of these advantages boil down to surprise: In computer network exploitation, the adversary gets to pick the location and time of the attack. What many don't take into account is the key advantage of the defender: namely, the ability to prepare for an attack by controlling the environment. The adversary can do reconnaissance, but in many cases is attacking a black box, without full understanding of the target until the attack is underway. Defenders can leverage this by preparing adequately and maximizing their "home field" advantage.

Identification

The *Identification* phase is the moment where the defender identifies the presence of an adversary impacting their environment. This can occur through a variety of methods:

- Identifying the adversary entering the network, such as a server attack or an incoming phishing email
- Noticing command-and-control traffic from a compromised host
- Seeing the massive traffic spike when the adversary begins exfiltrating data
- Getting a visit from a special agent at your local FBI field office
- All network devices suddenly displaying a screen announcing you've been hit with ransomware

Regardless of what actions the adversary takes, the Identification phase begins when you first gain awareness of adversary activity against your resources. In the incident-response cycle, the Identification phase is the entire intrusion-detection step, glossing over many details in a complicated topic (we'll dig into other models about this phase specifically later). This is obviously an oversimplification, but it is reasonable given that this cycle focuses on the overarching, end-to-end process of incident response rather than digging into the details of each phase. The Identification phase typically leads to an investigation, discovering even more information about the incident and the adversary, before beginning to respond directly. One of the key goals of threat intelligence is to augment the Identification phase, increasing the accuracy and quantity of methods to identify adversaries earlier.

Identification, at least in the incident-response sense, is not simply hearing about an attack that took place or learning about a new adversary. Identification starts when there is direct impact to your users, systems, or resources. For it to be an incident, there has to be impact.

On the other hand, if an adversary has capability, intent, and opportunity, that adversary does represent a threat. This isn't the start of the incident-response cycle, but the intelligence cycle. Only after the adversary is identified in your environment should an incident begin.

Containment

The first two phases of the cycle can be considered primarily passive and are focused on information gathering. The first phase of actual response, meaning that specific actions are being taken in response to a specific attack, is containment. *Containment* is the initial attempt to mitigate the actions of an adversary, stopping the bleeding in the short term while preparing a longer-term response. These shorter-term responses may not make the attack impossible, but they dramatically reduce the ability of the adversary to continue to achieve their objectives. These actions should be taken in a rapid but controlled manner to limit the adversary's opportunity to respond.

Common containment options are as follows:

- Disabling the network switch port to which a particular system is connected
- Blocking access to malicious network infrastructure such as IPs (at the firewall) and domains or specific URLs (via a network proxy)
- Temporarily locking a user account that is under the control of an intruder
- Disabling system services or software an adversary is exploiting

In many incident responses, defenders may choose to skip over the Containment phase entirely. Containment risks tipping off the adversary by changing the environment while that adversary still may have control. Skipping directly to the Eradication phase may also give comfort to executives who see containment alone as a Band-Aid.

Skipping Containment

Containment tends to be most effective against less-sophisticated adversaries that make limited changes to their approach, such as commodity malware threats. So, what about sophisticated adversaries? In many cases, the Containment phase can tip them off.

They may set up new tools, establish secondary backdoors, or even just start being destructive. For this reason, most of these incident responses may move straight into the Eradication phase. We discuss this more in Chapter 6.

Eradication

Eradication consists of the longer-term mitigation actions meant to remove an adversary from an environment and keep them out for good, unlike the temporary measures in the Containment phase. These actions should be carefully planned out and may take a considerable amount of time and resources to deploy. Eradication actions are focused on completely removing the adversary's ability to regain access to the network once they are kicked out. It includes focusing not just on the specific tactics that allowed them to gain access in the first place, but also additional hardening of the network based on the knowledge of the adversary's objectives and tactics, techniques, and procedures (TTP).

Common eradication actions are as follows:

- Removing all malware and tools installed by the adversary (see the sidebar "Wiping and Reloading Versus Removal" on page 43)
- Resetting and remediating all impacted user and service accounts
- Re-creating secrets that could have been accessed by the adversary, such as shared passwords, certificates, and tokens
- User education and awareness about the incident to reduce future social engineering
- Patching software vulnerabilities and changing vulnerable configurations

Often responders will go for a *scorched-earth* approach to eradication. In these cases, responders will take remediations on resources with no indications of compromise; for example, regenerating all VPN certificates after an adversary accessed one VPN server. Scorched-earth approaches are effective at mitigating the *unknown unknown* situations, where it's impossible to know 100% what the adversary did, but they come with the compromise that it may require a significant effort to make these changes.

The effort necessary for implementing a scorched-earth approach varies based on the sort of service or information involved. Forcing full password resets in an active directory–managed Windows environment is relatively easy. Regenerating and redeploying extended validations (EV) TLS certificates with domain pinning in major browsers is hard. The incident-response team needs to collaborate with the corporate risk management and system/service owner teams to determine how far to go in these situations.

Wiping and Reloading Versus Removal

One of the most common debates between IT and incident-response teams is how to handle malware-infected systems. Antivirus systems claim they can remove malware, but most experienced incident responders have been burned by this in the past and prefer to insist on a full wipe of the system and a reload of its operating system. This process has become both easier and more complicated with the emergence of deterministically built cloud systems using tools like Ansible, Puppet, and Kubernetes that make rebuilding systems easier but require detailed examination to be sure compromised dependencies or builds won't simply be redeployed. An evidence-based approach is key, so each organization needs to fight this battle for themselves.

For example, in the spring of 2015, Pennsylvania State University (*https://oreil.ly/ DnQsH*) took its entire College of Engineering network offline for three days in response to a compromise. Afterward, it had to bring the network back online and return it to normal service. A recovery like this requires removing malware from systems, resetting credentials such as passwords and certificates, patching software, and making many other changes meant to completely remove the adversary from the network and limiting that adversary's ability to return. In this case, the mitigation action, taking the entire network offline (likely to limit the adversary's ability to make changes during the Eradication phase), preceded the remediation actions. This is a common pattern when dealing with persistent adversaries. On one hand it decreases the adversary's ability to react to the mitigation and remediation—except by pre-planned or automated means—but on the other hand it gives a clear signal to the adversary that a response is underway and does cause a significant negative impact to anyone using the network.

Recovery

Containment and eradication often require drastic action. *Recovery* is the process of going back to a non-incident state. In some regards, recovery is less from the attack itself, but more from the actions taken by the incident responders.

For example, if a compromised system is taken from a user for forensic analysis, the Recovery phase includes returning or replacing the user's system so that the user can resume their business functions. If an entire network is compromised, the Recovery phase involves undoing any actions taken by the adversary across the entire network. This can be a lengthy and involved process, sometimes including rebuilding the entire network. Cloud services add a variety of pros and cons; on one hand it can be difficult to track down shadow IT, and on the other these networks can be deterministic (built using configuration management tools) and make resetting and rebuilding easier.

The events of this phase depend on the actions taken during the prior two phases, the adversary's methods, and the resources that were compromised. It generally requires coordination with other teams, such as desktop administrators and network engineering.

Incident response is always a team sport, requiring actions by a wide variety of security and nonsecurity teams, but in no part of the incident is this quite as obvious as during recovery. Security may set certain requirements for the way systems are recovered (most of these will take place during eradication), but recovery, after the incident-response team's all clear, is handled largely by IT and system owners. Figuring out how to work together and collaborate effectively is key and often requires both practice and experience (though good documentation also helps). Few things can compromise a response faster than IT beginning recovery before the incident-response team has fully eradicated the threat.

Lessons Learned

The last phase of the incident-response cycle, akin to many other security and intelligence cycles, includes taking time to assess past decisions and learn how to improve in the future.

This phase can be called many things—an After Action Report, Hot Wash, or Retrospective (Retro). The Lessons Learned phase, no matter what it's called, evaluates the team's performance through each step of the incident. Basically, this takes the incident report and answers some basic questions:

- What happened?
- What did we do well?
- What could we have done better?
- What will we do differently next time?

As an exercise, this can often be daunting. Many teams resist reviewing lessons learned or conducting after-action reviews. This occurs for a wide variety of reasons, from being concerned about mistakes being highlighted (and thus blamed on the incident-response team) to simply not having enough time due to new or ongoing incidents. Whatever the reason, nothing will keep an incident-response team from advancing like skipping lessons learned. The goal of the Lessons Learned phase is to discover how to make the next incident response go faster, smoother, or ideally never happen at all. Without this crucial step, incident-response teams (and the teams they collaborate with) will make the same mistakes, suffer from the same blockers, and fail to identify improvements.

Although it's important, conducting a Lessons Learned phase doesn't have to be daunting; in fact, it should be the opposite. A good after-action doesn't need to take hours or require everyone involved in the incident response. Here are a few detailed starter questions you will want to ask when evaluating each phase during the Lessons Learned process:

Preparation

- How could we have avoided the incident altogether? This includes changes to your network architecture, system configuration, user training, or even policy.
- What policies or tools could have improved the entire process?

Identification

- What telemetry sources (e.g., IDS, net flow, DNS) could have made it easier or faster to identify this attack?
- What signatures or threat intelligence could have helped?

Containment

- Which containment measures were effective?
- Which were not?
- Could other containment measures have been useful if they'd been more easily deployable?

Eradication

- Which eradication steps went well?
- What could have gone better?

Recovery

- What slowed the recovery? (*Hint*: Focus on communication, as that's one of the toughest parts of recovery to do well.)
- What did the response to recovery tell us about the adversary?

Lessons Learned

- Not to be too meta, but even evaluating how the Lessons Learned process could be done more effectively is useful. For example, would it help if responders took notes throughout the process? Did you wait too long to start this phase, and things were lost or forgotten?

Lessons Learned can also be practiced (the same as any other phase of the incident-response cycle). Don't just do Lessons Learned for actual incidents, but take the time to build and follow your Lessons Learned process for red team and tabletop exercises as well (we'll discuss red teaming in more detail in Chapters 8 and 10). In fact, building lessons learned into tabletop exercises is essential.

Ultimately, the key to Lessons Learned is having the understanding that although early lessons learned will be painful, they will improve—and that's the point. Early Lessons Learned exercises will call out flaws, missing technology, missing team members, bad processes, and bad assumptions. Growing pains with this process are common but do take the time and gut through them. Few things will improve an incident-response team and their capability as quickly as some tough Lessons Learned sessions. In addition, capture these lessons and share them with your leadership and related teams. Although it seems like calling out a team's flaws, in many cases these reports provide concrete justification for making changes that will improve your incident-response capability.

The incident-response cycle is one of the first models that incident responders learn for good reason: It succinctly describes the lifecycle of an investigation. Where it becomes key is by taking the time to evaluate your team's ability to execute at each stage, from Preparation through Lessons Learned. As with intelligence work, there are several related models and frameworks that can help in the incident-response cycle.

The Kill Chain

Another military concept that has made its way into cyber threat intelligence vernacular is the *kill chain*. In fact, it has become so popular that finding information on the original kill chains is difficult because of the extent of information security use cases and marketing. While this concept was on the fringes for years, a paper by Lockheed Martin researchers Eric M. Hutchins et al. titled "Intelligence-Driven Computer Network Defense Informed by Analysis of Adversary Campaigns and Intrusion Kill Chains" (*https://oreil.ly/m_ZJ8*) brought the concept into the information security mainstream with a formalized mapping of the most common intrusion pattern: a kill chain.[1]

Since their report, the kill chain has become a go-to model for cyber threat intelligence, referenced by nearly every vendor, and a staple guiding process of defensive teams. The kill chain provides an important abstraction for the phases an adversary moves through when exploiting a target, particularly scenarios that involve phishing-based attacks.

---

1 Eric M. Hutchins et al., "Intelligence-Driven Computer Network Defense Informed by Analysis of Adversary Campaigns and Intrusion Kill Chains" (*https://oreil.ly/m_ZJ8*).

But what is a kill chain? In its simplest form, a *kill chain* is a series of steps an adversary must conduct to achieve an objective (see Figure 3-2). In our case, we're discussing a computer network adversary, but it works for many adversarial activities. This means abstracting the incident process, but whereas the incident cycle is focused on the *defender's* actions, the kill chain focuses on the *adversary's* actions.

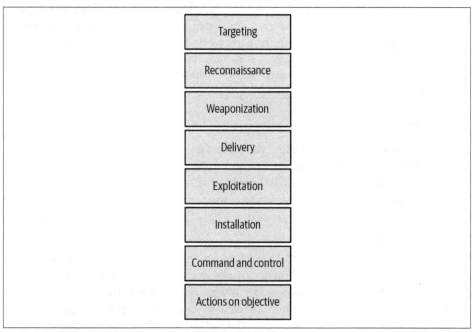

Figure 3-2. Cyber kill chain

The kill chain is a good way to abstract an adversary's TTPs. It provides a structure to understand the abstract actions of an attack.

Though the earlier phases of the kill chain, especially Targeting and Reconnaissance, are sometimes opaque to the defender, usually difficult and circumstantial to detect, they're worth understanding. Defenders tend to think that adversaries succeed every time with zero effort. This is far from the truth. In fact, our ability to disrupt these pre-intrusion phases later might be one of the strongest advantages defenders have.

Kill Chains in General

Kill chains walk through a group of interrelated steps that are necessary to achieve a military objective, originally of lethal nature (going back to Vietnam era airstrikes). That's where the term *kill* comes from. The current US military version of the kill chain is described in "Joint Publication 3-60: Joint Targeting" (*https://oreil.ly/oNHKU*). The kill chain paper by Lockheed Martin is a cyber kill chain model for describing computer network operations; the term *kill* in this case refers to an adversary achieving their objective. There is no "perfect" kill chain. Depending on the attack, certain aspects may be omitted or combined as necessary. Like all models, it's simply a method of thinking about intrusions, and if it is useful for conceptualizing and collaborating on an intrusion, then it is serving its purpose.

For this book, we will make several of our own changes, including adding stages (targeting and breaking out persistence, for instance), as we describe the kill chain. This isn't meant to take away from the great work done by the Hutchins et al. but is meant to enhance it as you build your own model for understanding intrusions and inspire others to modify models based on their own situations.

Targeting

Before the kill chain proper begins, the adversary must decide what to attack (for example, who or what is the potential target). In many cases, this occurs in consultation with some form of sponsor or stakeholder, often as part of their own intelligence or operational requirements. As defenders, we commonly think of the target as the victim organization, but in many cases that is less important than the information or capabilities being targeted.

Targeting is an interesting aspect of the kill chain because it speaks to the motivation and thus the general category (though not necessarily specific identification or attribution) of an adversary. For example, an adversary who wants to steal money needs to go where the money is. Understanding what's being targeted gives insight into what the adversary is after (the adversary's ultimate goals) and may lead to better defensive techniques (discussed later in "Active Defense").

Reconnaissance

After deciding *what* and *who* to target, the adversary begins conducting reconnaissance. In the *Reconnaissance* phase (or simply *recon*), the adversary collects as much information as possible about the planned victim. Reconnaissance can fall into multiple categories based on the type of data sought (hard data versus soft data) and collection methods (passive versus active).

Hard data versus soft data

The intelligence world has multiple ways of dividing intelligence based on subject (e.g., SIGINT, TECHINT), as we discussed in Chapter 2, but for computer network operations, we can think of things a bit more simply.

Hard data includes information about technical aspects of a network and the systems attached to it. For an adversary (and defenders while investigating adversaries), this usually includes open source intelligence:

- Footprinting or enumerating the target network
- DNS information such as reverse DNS
- Operating systems and application versions
- Information about system configurations
- Information about security systems

Soft data includes information about the organization behind the network and its systems:

- Organizational charts, public relationships, and other hierarchy documents
- Business plans and goals
- Hiring information, which can often leak information such as technologies in use
- Information on employees, both professional and personal, for use in social engineering attacks

Active versus passive collection methods

Adversaries may use different methods of collecting information. We can categorize these methods as active or passive.

Active collection methods require interacting directly with the target. An active collection of hard intelligence could be port scanning a system directly. An active collection of soft intelligence could be a social engineering attack to gather information about internal hierarchy and contact information.

Passive collection methods are based on collecting information without interacting directly with the target, often by gathering information from a third-party information service such as DNS or WHOIS. A passive collection of hard intelligence might exploit domain information from a public service. A passive collection of soft intelligence gathers information about an organization from a site such as LinkedIn, where people often share considerable information (even information they shouldn't).

A defender's ability to detect this recon activity varies tremendously. Active methods are much easier to detect than passive methods, for example, and most network defenders have more control over hard information than soft information. Detecting active hard collection in the form of a port scan is easier than detecting soft passive collection in the form of reading job postings for positions that describe specific technologies in use at an organization. In some cases, adversaries can proxy or bounce their reconnaissance activity through public services, some of which execute active methods such as network scans or DNS interrogation at the request of a user. This level of anonymity or hiding in noise benefits defenders and adversaries alike, as many such tools are used by both sides.

Chasing Ghosts

While reconnaissance gathering is useful to add to your kill chains, it's a dubious place to start most kill chains. Gauging the level of intent an actor has simply based on a port scan is virtually impossible. Anything on the internet is likely to be scanned aggressively and not necessarily by bad guys, such as Project Sonar (*https://oreil.ly/fy0yH*), Censys (*https://censys.io*), Shodan (*https://www.shodan.io*), and GreyNoise (*https://www.greynoise.io*), so consider reconnaissance low signal/high noise. On the other hand, taking indicators identified later in the kill chain correlated with reconnaissance activity may give surprising insight into targeting, methods, and even other compromised infrastructures. For example, during the Log4J exploitation in late 2021, GreyNoise was incredibly useful for identifying systems rapidly scanning and attempting to exploit the vulnerability. Early on, this real-time view was highly useful for blocking malicious IPs and identifying adversary strings. Later, as more adversaries and even defenders started scanning for CVE-2021-44228, this data became less useful as the noise became overwhelming.

Weaponization

If all security controls, or all software in general, worked as intended (that is, as their designers imagined, not as they were built), then adversaries would almost always fail. Thus, the goal for adversaries is to find places where the intention and implementation don't match—a vulnerability. This vulnerability must then be exploited reliably and packed into a form that's ready to be delivered to a target (for example, a malicious document or exploit kit). The process of finding this vulnerability, crafting an exploit, and combining it with a payload is *Weaponization*.

Vulnerability hunting

The vulnerability subphase of weaponization is particularly interesting given its effect on what targets can be attacked. This forces the adversary to make a decision. Some widely deployed pieces of software are likely to be found in any environment, such as Adobe Acrobat and Reader or Microsoft Windows and Office. This means that any exploit targeting them is widely usable. However, these pieces of software have been attacked for years, and their respective companies have made considerable efforts to identify and mitigate vulnerabilities. The alternative is attacking a more esoteric piece of software that may be less defended but also less widely deployed. This limits where an adversary can use it. This process can be tied in with the cyber kill chain's Reconnaissance phase. The effort that adversaries are willing to put in may also be influenced by their own direction and intelligence requirements.

As an example of this trade-off, consider the Stuxnet incident, in which unconfirmed adversaries disabled centrifuges within the Iranian nuclear facility at Natanz. Part of this included deploying exploits against programmable logic controllers (PLCs) in Siemens equipment. While this equipment is not widely deployed in most organizations, it existed in the target environment. Vulnerabilities in those PLCs thus provided a vector for the adversaries to carry out their mission.

We, as defenders, disrupt this process constantly by using development-centric security approaches. Good development practices, such as Microsoft Security Development Lifecycle (SDL) (*https://oreil.ly/I5cgG*), reduce the introduction of the mismatches that become vulnerabilities. Application security teams and related reviews constantly hunt for these vulnerabilities in source code. Strong patch management can help eliminate old vulnerabilities within an environment.

Every vulnerability that is patched constrains adversaries a little bit and forces them to find new vulnerabilities to exploit. This is a time-consuming and expensive process. The longer a vulnerability is in the wild, the more value it has to an adversary because of its longer effective life span. In turn, then, disrupting the return on investment (ROI) of a vulnerability brings defensive value.

Imagine that an adversary has a privilege escalation in Windows 95. The adversary uses it for years, and it finally gets fixed in Windows 7. This means the adversary could use that exploit for multiple years across multiple versions. The longer it lasts, the more ROI the adversary receives from the vulnerability hunting and exploit-creation effort.

That same adversary later finds an Internet Explorer 11 code execution vulnerability and uses it in a series of attacks. However, after three months, defenders find and patch the vulnerability. The adversary had less time to get ROI out of that vulnerability, requiring them to go back to the drawing board and find a new one. This requires additional resource allocation for a smaller window of effectiveness.

Exploitability

A vulnerability is just a crack in the armor. It takes an actual exploit to take advantage of that crack. The exploitability process is all about finding a method to trigger the vulnerability and turn that into actual control of program execution. Much like vulnerability hunting, this phase may have its own specialists or occur in conjunction with other exploit phases. This is a topic unto itself, addressed well in the book *Hacking: The Art of Exploitation* by Jon Erickson.[2]

After an exploit is crafted, the adversary must make it reliable. This can be complicated because exploits don't always work, given things like language packs

---

2 Jon Erickson, *Hacking: The Art of Exploitation*, Second Edition (San Francisco: No Starch Press, 2008).

and specific defenses such as Microsoft's Enhanced Mitigation Experience Toolkit (EMET) or Address Space Layout Randomization (ASLR) for Linux. Further, exploits that crash target code or systems will draw attention.

An exploit, though, simply opens the door and gives the adversary a method to access the target (or at least an intermediate target). For the next step, the adversary will need an implant.

Implant development

Generally, the goal of an exploit includes delivering some sort of payload for the adversary to then use to further their goals (such as data exfiltration). The implant will allow the adversary to maintain access to the exploited system without having to continually exploit the device, which can be noisy, and if the system is patched, it would remove the possibility of exploitation at all. As a result, implant development follows many of the same processes as traditional software development, with an emphasis on stealth (to avoid detection) and capabilities (to allow adversaries to achieve their objectives). Thus, if an adversary wants to be able to listen to conversations within range of a compromised system, the implant needs the ability to activate the microphone, record what it hears, and transmit the resulting audio files, all without triggering suspicion from the user or any security software that's running.

There are two primary types of implants. The first is a beaconing implant that calls out to a command-and-control server and will receive commands to be carried out on the target system. The second is an implant that does not beacon but that waits to receive a command and then begins to communicate with a command-and-control server. Implant development is often determined by the network topology and device type. Sometimes a previously developed implant can be used, but in other situations an adversary will need to develop something specifically for the network that is being targeted.

 Although many computer network operations still lean heavily on the need for an adversary to keep persistence and install capabilities with implants, a growing number of actors seek to achieve their objectives without installing any implants. The compromise of Hillary Clinton campaign chairman John Podesta's email was conducted without ever deploying an implant at all, just by stealing his password. In many ways, this style of attack is more difficult for investigators because without an implant, there's one fewer artifact to analyze. Implant-less attacks are another case where understanding the adversary's goals will help contextualize their techniques.

Testing

Both exploits and implants then go through extensive testing as part of the Weaponization phase. Much like software development, testing could be little more than a spot check, or it could mean extensive testing conducted by separate quality assurance teams. For malicious code, the Testing phase focuses on two aspects: *function* and *detectability*.

The functionality aspect is much like any other software development project; the testing team needs to ensure that the software does what it's designed to do. If it's meant to steal files, the implant must be able to read from the filesystem on the target host; find the correct group of files; usually bundle, encrypt, and compress them; and then exfiltrate them to a system the adversary controls. This may seem easy, but there are a wide variety of variables that the development team may not always be able to control and thus need to be tested for.

The detectability aspect is unlike anything seen in normal software development. Testing teams will attempt to verify that their software is undetectable by security tools they might see in their target environment, such as antivirus or other endpoint software. This ties directly into the functionality aspect as many heuristics-based security systems look for certain behaviors that the malicious code may need to achieve its objective, such as setting registry keys to maintain persistence. These detectability requirements may be based on assumptions or, for especially hard targets, based on information gathered during reconnaissance.

Infrastructure development

While not strictly part of the Weaponization phase, infrastructure development is another key preparation task an adversary needs to complete before the attack. Most attacks rely on pieces of infrastructure to support the malicious code deployed onto a victim's machine. Command-and-control servers are needed to direct attack actions. Exfiltration points are needed to upload and then retrieve stolen data. Hot points are needed for adversaries to pivot through to obfuscate their real location if their other infrastructure gets compromised. Adversaries need a wide variety of infrastructure, outlined next, to execute the various phases of their operation:

Certificates. First, it's important to differentiate the two most common types of certificates used in intrusions:

Code signing certificates
> Provided by operating system builders like Apple and Microsoft, are necessary to run new applications without bypassing security controls. Without code signing certificates, users often have to go through multiple steps to execute an unsigned program. These certificates can be difficult to get, especially fraudulently (companies work hard to make this the case).

Transport Layer Security (TLS) certificates

> Encrypt communication with websites, keeping web traffic private. Without these certificates most browsers will throw an error, warning the user their communication is insecure. Even worse is a mismatch between the certificate and the domain, which will throw a more severe error. These certificates used to be very difficult to get, but thanks to services like LetsEncrypt they've become far easier recently.

Adversaries want both code signing and TLS certificates for modern attacks to avoid browser- and operating system–level protections. Some adversaries instead try to encourage users to bypass security controls, but this can be risky both because users are more likely to not bother and because there's a higher chance the user might realize something seems off (and ideally report it to their intrepid security team).

Servers. Like most internet-based activities, most adversaries rely on servers at one or many stages of their attacks. This includes delivery, either to host a downloaded file (for a link in a phishing email) or to host a browser exploit. In later stages, servers can enable communication for the Command and Control phase or as a target to upload stolen files or credentials during the Actions on Objective phase. These may be adversary-owned and run (bare metal), but, like so many organizations, many adversaries have moved to using cloud servers or even directly using public web services. Both of these have the advantage of blending in.

Domains. Few network connections go directly to IP addresses, so most adversaries use domain names. Some domains are chosen as specific lures or confuse analysts, meant to mimic or seem similar to other recognizable domains (e.g., using homograph attacks such as using a lowercase *L* in place of a capital *I*).

Email addresses. Phishing is the first and most obvious usage of email by adversaries. These email addresses are usually built to be throwaway or limited use and, like domains, may emulate related domains or even specific people. Email addresses are also required to set up other infrastructure, to put in certificates, and even to associate with payment sending and receiving methods like cryptocurrency.

Nontechnical Infrastructure Needs

Not all infrastructure needs are technical. Adversaries often need two other things to set up malicious infrastructure: identities and currency. Both are often necessary to buy the resources needed to set up infrastructure. These are both challenging for adversaries because in most cases they tie back directly to real people, something an adversary would most likely want to avoid.

Over the years, adversaries have taken a wide variety of approaches to avoiding these pitfalls. Pseudonyms and fake identities are common, but even these can be

---

tracked as an adversary often uses the same false name, false address, or registration email on domain name and certificate purchases. As for purchasing, some adversaries avoid purchases entirely by compromising other, less well-secured systems, and using those instead of purchasing their own. Others have taken to using semi-anonymous payment systems such as cryptocurrency, which may be used as a laundering mechanism or simply stolen and used for purchases (*https://oreil.ly/WMbI8*). Finally, other adversaries have taken to using online services with free accounts such as GitHub, Twitter, Dropbox, and others for free infrastructure, as was demonstrated in the HammerToss report (*https://oreil.ly/D2QNg*).[3]

Delivery

Once the adversary has gathered enough information to craft an attack, the next kill chain stage is Delivery. Common delivery scenarios include, but are not limited to, the following:

Spear phishing
> The adversary sends a weaponized exploit, either as an attachment or as a link, via direct communications (often email) to a specific target. The communication is usually crafted to appear legitimate and reduce suspicion in the mind of the targeted user. In recent years adversaries have also leveraged instant messaging platforms and SMS to send communications with a malicious link to users.

Service exploitation
> A common group of vectors in the early 2000s—direct exploitation of web-facing services—has reared its head again. In these cases, adversaries find a vulnerability in a web-facing service, such as a web application or VPN, and attack that directly. In many cases these are commodity systems, such as Chinese-nexus adversaries compromising Pulse VPN (*https://oreil.ly/3hKEp*).[4] While some of these attacks are highly targeted, vulnerabilities like Shellshock and Log4J have been widely exploited.

Strategic web compromise (watering hole)
> In a two-stage attack, often based on a previous service exploitation scenario, the adversary first compromises a secondary resource, usually a website the intended target is likely to visit, and places a browser or media exploit on it. The assumption is that the target, usually an entire group rather than a specific individual, will visit the site and become compromised.

---

3 FireEye Threat Intelligence, "HammerToss: Stealthy Tactics Define a Russian Cyber Threat Group" (*https://oreil.ly/D2QNg*) (Special Report, July 2015).

4 Dan Perez et al., "Check Your Pulse: Suspected APT Actors Leverage Authentication Bypass Techniques and Pulse Secure Zero-Day" (*https://oreil.ly/3hKEp*), Mandiant, updated October 27, 2021.

The key to delivery is how simple it is: It's just getting the payload to the victim. This simplicity belies the importance of this stage. Delivery is the first necessarily active stage on the part of the adversary to the victim. While the previous stages can be active (in the case of Targeting and Reconnaissance), Delivery is the first case where an adversary *must* be active, which often results in something the victim (either the intended target or the security team) could detect. This means delivery is the first case where a victim is guaranteed to have indicators of compromise and adversary TTP to build from. In the case of spear phishing, this may be email artifacts such as headers and an email address, while for SQL injection it may be an IP address that initiated the web server/database connections.

Exploitation

Understanding the difference between delivery and exploitation can be challenging. Up through the start of delivery, the adversary has not had direct interaction with the target and does not have any control of the targeted system. Even in the case of a spear phishing email, it is possible that security measures will prevent successful delivery, so even though there was delivery, there was no actual exploitation. Exploitation is the point where the adversary gains control of code execution and begins executing their own code.

In a watering hole attack, this takes place the second a victim hits an infected page. For the spear phishing attack, this is when the victim clicks a malicious attachment or link. From this point forward, the adversary has control of at least one process on the target's system. This foothold is the start of the adversary's move into the network.

Exploitation is a massive topic unto itself, complete with its own specialists (and indeed its own companies, marketplaces, and even economy). For a deeper understanding, take a look at:

- *The Shellcoder's Handbook*, Second Edition by Jack Koziol et al. (Wiley, 2004)
- *The IDA Pro Book* by Chris Eagle (No Starch Press, 2008)
- *Real-World Bug Hunting* by Peter Yaworski (No Starch Press, 2019)
- *A Guide to Kernel Exploitation* by Enrico Perla et al. (Syngress, 2010)

Installation

Initial execution is often difficult and not something an adversary wants to do multiple times. Once adversaries have code execution, their first move is typically to solidify their access by creating a permanent foothold. The Lockheed Martin kill chain paper describes this in the following way: "Installation of a remote-access Trojan or backdoor on the victim system allows the adversary to maintain persistence inside the environment."[5] While this is what the adversary usually does at this stage, we find it useful to look at these actions as establishing system or network persistence (in many cases, the adversary will do both, but it still helps to consider them separately).

System persistence

At this point, the adversary has code execution on a single system, and likely just a single process at that. This is a useful start, but it doesn't persist past a reboot. A shutdown of the compromised application may even remove their access.

Most adversaries begin by solidifying their hold on a small number of hosts by deploying a rootkit or remote-access Trojan (RAT) style of implant. A rootkit establishes kernel-level access to a system and, once installed, permits an adversary to evade many detection methods of the underlying OS. A RAT is a piece of remote-control software meant to persist past reboots without relying on a certain exploit. This allows the adversary to persist on an individual host.

Network persistence

The vast majority of adversaries aren't content to establish a single-system foothold. Instead, they want to establish deeper persistence. To do so, they'll typically establish a wider footprint, using one (or both) of two techniques:

Establish system persistence on multiple systems
> This means using captured credentials and installing RATs or similar access methods on other systems. An adversary has a variety of options for this, from custom software to native tools such as PsExec in Windows or SSH in Nix environments.

Gathering credentials that allow access to broadly utilized network resources without accessing a system on the network
> This often means VPNs, cloud services, or other internet-exposed systems such as web mail. This lowers the risk of detection in many cases and doesn't require a form of malware, instead using native tools.

These techniques can be used individually or together. This combination is often a signature set of techniques for most adversaries.

---

5 Eric M. Hutchins et al., "Intelligence-Driven Computer Network Defense Informed by Analysis of Adversary Campaigns and Intrusion Kill Chains" (*https://oreil.ly/m_ZJ8*).

Command and Control

Once an adversary has established persistence, especially if they've chosen the RAT route, they need a method to deliver commands (either via push or pull). In the past, many pieces of malware, especially distributed denial-of-service (DDoS) tools, communicated by joining IRC channels or HTTP calls to a server under the adversary's control. The Comment Crew (*https://oreil.ly/DBqmG*) got its moniker from doing command and control with HTML comments on otherwise innocuous-looking web pages.[6] Some adversaries use multiple methods, including DNS lookups, social media, or popular cloud applications.

Self-Guided Malware

A relatively small number of malware families operate without any communication at all. These *drones*, or self-guided malware families, are rare and particularly suited to attacking air-gapped networks. The famous example is the Stuxnet malware family, aimed at a group of Iranian nuclear research facilities, where network communication was impossible. Given the success of this family and others like it, it's possible more may be coming. Responding to self-guided malware requires a different approach because defenders can't focus on identifying network traffic used for command and control or exfiltration. Instead, defenders need to identify malware in use on the system and eradicate it before it spreads.

Adversaries focus on making sure that their communication channels avoid notice and provide enough bandwidth to meet the needs of the adversary. In some cases, malware may communicate using only a few lines of text a day, while others include full virtual desktop capability.

Actions on Objective

In most cases, all of the phases we've just described do not represent the ultimate goal, but rather the setup. Adversaries go through the process of setting up access in order to give themselves the capability to affect the target in a way they didn't have before. We call this new capability the actions on objective (AoO).

While many of the earliest AoO were as simple as exploration, since the mid 1990s the most common AoO has been collecting and exfiltrating information on target systems. In a very simple way, it makes a lot of sense: Computers are ultimately meant to process information. Supposedly infamous bank robber Willie Sutton was once asked why he robbed banks. Sutton responded, "Because that's where the money

---

6 "APT1: Q&A on Attacks by the Comment Crew" (*https://oreil.ly/DBqmG*), Endpoint Protection, Broadcom, updated February 19, 2013.

is." In the modern age—where data is money (as ones and zeros in a ledge or blockchain), where plans for the next military technology are in computer-aided design and development files on corporate servers, and where political intelligence is stored as PDFs or Excel spreadsheets—is it any wonder data theft became the dominant AoO?

Next to data exfiltration, the most common AoO, which goes along with the network persistence piece of installation, is pivoting. In many cases, an adversary's true target isn't available to attack directly. People shouldn't be opening phishing emails from the FTP server that holds their most valuable plans (they often do, unfortunately), and they shouldn't be browsing shady websites from the system with all their customer data (they do that, too). But in the cases where these practices are followed, the adversary will often attack related systems that may facilitate further access to get to the ultimate target.

In many cases the adversary wouldn't even know what system they ultimately targeted but would attack anything available, establish persistence, and pivot, essentially starting the entire intrusion process over again (kill chains within kill chains). A common intrusion pattern has been for the initial system to be quite innocuous and unrelated to anything (such as the adversary targeting a recruiter or accountant, who's likely to have Microsoft Office macros enabled), get admin credentials by cracking the Security Account Manager (SAM) file, pivot to the Domain Controller, and steal the SAM file once again. Now the adversary has network-wide administrator credentials and can go after their ultimate target directly.

Aside from data exfiltration and pivoting, the most common AoO by attackers, not just on computers, were categorized by the US Air Force as follows:

Destroy
> The adversary destroys a physical or virtual item. This could mean destroying data, overwriting or deleting files, or otherwise making a system unavailable until it is completely rebuilt. This could also mean destroying a physical object, though this is a rare occurrence in computer attacks. The Stuxnet destruction of Iranian centrifuges is one such example.

Deny
> The adversary denies usage of a resource (such as a piece of infrastructure or a given capability) by the target, such as in the case of denial-of-service attacks that do not permit access to a site. Another example that has gained attention in recent years is *ransomware*, which encrypts a user's data and requires payment before the adversary will (in theory) decrypt the data for use again.

Degrade

The adversary degrades the utility of the target's infrastructure or its capabilities. This most often refers to the target's ability to control and command infrastructure, such as disabling networked services. A slightly less nuanced version of this, with a simple kill chain, is distributed denial of service.

Disrupt

By interrupting the flow of information, an adversary can disrupt the target's ability to carry out normal operations.

Deceive

The adversary seeks to cause the target to believe something that is not true. In this context, the adversary may be inserting false information into a workflow to redirect assets or information or to cause the target to take action that may benefit the adversary.

Most of these are straightforward and basic on the surface. However, the manner in which an adversary puts these together is key and often speaks directly to the adversary's identity and goals. An adversary can often hide malware, obfuscate command and control, and so forth; but ultimately the actions on the objective cannot be obfuscated, encoded, or protected. To steal information, an adversary must steal the files. To execute a DoS, an adversary must use compromised hosts to send massive amounts of network traffic. In short, the AoO phase can't be faked. We'll talk more about what defenders can do to respond to AoO by adversaries later.

It's important to understand that an adversary may combine multiple actions and vectors, including physical/non-cyber actions. This could include anything from recruiting an insider to leak strategic information to a kinetic action (for example, bombing a geographic site).

As you can see in Figure 3-3, the adversary's kill chain stays tightly defined while the incident-response cycle has to react to it, starting with the Identification phase. Identification can occur anywhere between the Targeting and the Actions on Objective phases of the kill chain and causes dramatically different incident responses to occur. An incident identified during the Delivery phase is ideal. The defenders can block the attack at an email or web proxy and keep the attack from ever executing. An attack detected during a later phase, such as Command and Control or Actions on Objective, is likely going to be painful, involving many compromised resources and an expensive and lengthy incident-response investigation.

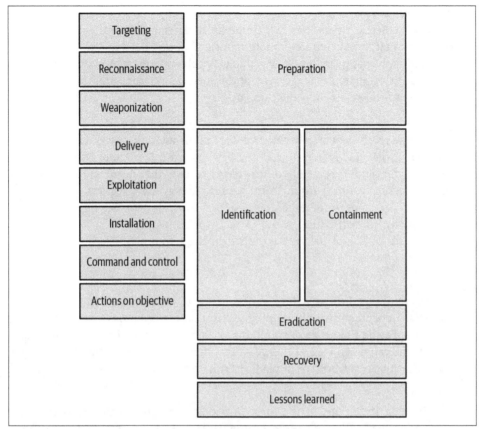

Figure 3-3. The kill chain and the incident-response cycle

Example Kill Chain

To illustrate the kill chain, imagine a series of attacks by a fictitious attack group codenamed Grey Spike. This group conducts political intelligence collection against multiple countries. Most recent reports indicated that they have been targeting election campaigns in the US and UK. They seek to gain information about candidates' stances on economic, foreign policy, and military issues. Here's what their strategy would entail:

Targeting

Grey Spike does not choose its own targets but receives *tasking* (intelligence jargon for which data and organizations they're instructed to target) from national policy makers. This tasking describes specific target countries and candidates as well as key words of interest.

Reconnaissance

Grey Spike begins operations by gaining an understanding of the network foot-print of its targets, including domain names, mail servers, key technologies, and web and mobile applications. The group also gathers information on key person-nel, such as campaign management, social media managers, and the technology consulting firms retained by the campaigns.

Weaponization

Grey Spike receives quarterly resource allocations including zero-day vulnerabil-ities but in general prefers to use these when no other vector is available. In this case, the actor has a suite of download macros that it implants as payloads in documents custom-written in the target languages by regional and cultural specialists on loan from other departments within their intelligence agency. Additionally, infrastructure in the form of private servers used for command and control (C2) and delivery is rented in the name of shell companies from providers around the globe.

Delivery

The operators send the weaponized documents to key managers in the campaign staff. Each document is written to appeal to that manager specifically, including offers to provide financial contributions and endorsements. Because of the rapid pace of the campaign trail, the targets open these documents with a high success rate, allowing the adversary's implants to run on their laptops.

Exploitation

The implant code runs in the form of a document macro that runs an older exploit for the PDF reader used by the campaign. Although a patch has been available for the vulnerability for some time, campaign staff have frozen all updates because of the belief by senior staff that this may cause outages at inopportune times.

Delivery

The exploit code is a downloader that then contacts a malware delivery server in a shared hosting environment at a popular ISP to install a remote-access Trojan (RAT) on the target system. The RAT then contacts a C2 server at a bulletproof ISP in a third country.

Command and control

Grey Spike issues commands to the RAT via the C2 channel, in this case through encoded DNS lookups. Using their covert channel, they conduct searches for the target's email and relevant documents. In addition to some of the informa-tion they've been tasked with acquiring, they find emails documenting shared accounts, including passwords that they can then use to extend their access throughout the network.

Actions on objective

In this scenario, Grey Spike is tasked specifically with information retrieval only. The policy makers do not wish to interfere directly with the campaign, largely because of concern about political consequences, despite having the technical ability to destroy most of the data and online infrastructure of the candidates.

Kill chains help to organize incident-response data in a way that allows you to visualize what the attack looked like as it took place and can help identify patterns in activity. Another method to accomplish this is the Diamond Model, which we will discuss next.

The Diamond Model

The Diamond Model of intrusion analysis differs in many ways from the kill chain (though later in this section we'll discuss how they complement each other). Originally discussed in a seminal paper (*https://oreil.ly/Fi2Lq*) by Christopher Betz, Sergio Caltagirone, and Andrew Pendergast, the model can be summarized as follows:

> An *adversary* deploys a *capability* over some *infrastructure* against a *victim*. These activities are called *events*...events are phase-ordered by an adversary-victim pair into *activity threads* representing the flow of an adversary's operations.

Ultimately, the Diamond Model (Figure 3-4) is a paradigm for understanding the interaction between the various actors (the adversary and the victim) and the adversary's tools (infrastructure and capabilities).

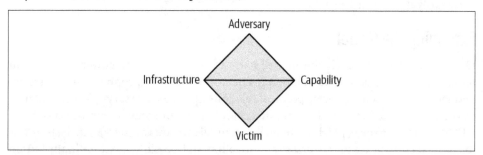

Figure 3-4. The Diamond Model

Basic Model

An *adversary* is an intelligent party (actor) with intent to gather information or do harm to an information system. We can further break this down into the *operator* carrying out the actions and the *customer* who will benefit from the actions. The same person might fulfill both roles (in a small mercenary or financially motivated adversary group), but not always (as in the case of a nation-state SIGINT agency where the customer and operator could come from different agencies or teams).

Adversaries will have an intent, which could be as general as "make money through credit card fraud" or as specific as "acquire the communications of a specified person regarding a particular topic of interest."

An adversary has a set of exploits and techniques, called a *capability*, they can deploy to accomplish their goals. This includes the weaponized software and implants discussed in the kill chain, but it can also include the ability to carry out a social engineering attack or, in some cases, deploy some sort of physical ability, whether for gathering information or disrupting systems.

An adversary uses a set of communication systems and protocols, called *infrastructure*, to deliver or control a capability or to cause some result on a victim. This includes systems owned directly by the adversary (e.g., desktops and network equipment in their physical possession) and systems compromised and re-purposed (e.g., end-user systems in a botnet).

Adversaries target a *victim* against which they deploy their capabilities in the attempt to accomplish a certain intent. The victim includes people and assets and may be targeted together or separately. As noted, a victim's system may then be used as infrastructure against another victim.

Each occurrence in which all four elements are present (an *adversary* using a *capability* across *infrastructure* against a *victim*) represents a single event. Events that feed into each other are then analyzed as *activity threads*, and we can further collect those threads into *activity groups* (related threads that may run in parallel or otherwise not necessarily flow linearly).

Extending the Model

One of the ways in which the model starts to demonstrate its power comes from looking at the axes across the diamond. The north-south axis connecting adversaries and victims represents a social-political relationship. The adversary has some interest in the victim, whether as a class (credit card numbers) or something more specific (a CEO targeted for spear phishing to enable fraudulent wire transfers). Analysis of this axis can shed light on an adversary's motivation and possibly assist with attribution or operational and strategic planning for intrusion detection and incident response.

As mentioned at the beginning of this section, the Diamond Model complements the kill chain, and in fact the two integrate well. Each event in the Diamond Model can be categorized according to its phase in the kill chain. This allows the analyst to have a greater understanding of the relationship between events and consider investigating and documenting phases that have previously been neglected in investigations. (That said, not every phase of the kill chain will be present in every incident.)

This model has also been extended to act as a clustering mechanism, where analysts attempt to compare multiple kill chains together to find similarities and group them into campaigns and actors (something we'll discuss later).

ATT&CK and D3FEND

The MITRE Corporation (usually referred to as MITRE) is a US-based, federally funded research and development center, basically a government think tank, that has released a variety of useful cyber frameworks. This is a pretty logical focus considering that MITRE was one of the companies Cliff Stoll tracked his wily hackers back to in *The Cuckoo's Egg*.

ATT&CK

The kill chain and the Diamond Model for intrusion analysis are two examples of frameworks that you are likely to use frequently, whether explicitly or as mental models. Another more recent addition to the analyst's toolkit is the MITRE ATT&CK framework, which enhances and extends the traditional kill chain. ATT&CK stands for "Adversary Tactics, Techniques, and Common Knowledge" (and yes, if you're thinking it, no one likes the ampersand in the middle, but these are the things you do for good acronyms). MITRE describes ATT&CK as "a globally accessible knowledge base of adversary tactics and techniques based on real-world observations [which is] used as a foundation for the development of specific threat models and methodologies."

Table 3-1 shows how ATT&CK can be broken down into a few key groups of major concepts.

Table 3-1. Key concepts in the ATT&CK framework[a]

Concept	MITRE definition
Tactics	Tactics represent the "why" of an ATT&CK technique or subtechnique. It is the adversary's tactical goal—the reason for performing an action. For example, an adversary may want to achieve credential access.
Techniques	Techniques represent "how" an adversary achieves a tactical goal by performing an action. For example, an adversary may dump credentials to achieve credential access.
Groups	Groups are sets of related intrusion activity that are tracked by a common name in the security community. Analysts track clusters of activities using various methods and terms such as threat groups, activity groups, threat actors, intrusion sets, and campaigns.
Software	Software is a generic term for custom or commercial code, operating system utilities, open source software, or other tools used to conduct behavior modeled in ATT&CK.

[a] Source: *attack.mitre.org*

There are a few other secondary concepts as well, including matrices, data sources, mitigations, and resources. Matrices are important, as they tie other data into various environments. The vast majority of the time, people are referring to the ATT&CK Enterprise matrices, but Mobile and ICS (as in Industrial Control System) could also be important depending on your organization. Data sources is a concept focused on mapping data back to the collection source (i.e., the sensor or type of log). Mitigations, which are split up by matrix, represent ways to respond to various attacks.

The tactics and techniques captured in ATT&CK are not theoretical—they have been observed by cybersecurity practitioners while tracking adversaries who are conducting network operations. These tactics and techniques are captured as individual components that are displayed in a matrix form. ATT&CK is a multifunctional model. It can be used as a library of tactics and techniques to help an incident responder and intelligence team build their understanding of existing and emerging adversary trends.

At this point, ATT&CK has moved beyond the US government, or even being a mental model for cyber threat intelligence analysts and incident responders, and is now in use by vendors who base their detections around ATT&CK, offensive security, technology evaluators, and even ambitious authors. We're going to discuss ATT&CK more throughout this chapter and this book.

Red, Blue, Purple, and Black

While there are a lot of different ways to refer to the different parts of a company's security teams, the easiest shorthand is by color. These are:

Blue team
> The pure defensive team. Typically, this refers to intrusion detection, incident response, cyber threat intelligence (SHOUT OUT!), and even reverse engineers and systems administrators.

Red team
> The red team is typically the way we refer to the faux offensive teams (*faux* because ultimately their goal is to help improve defense, not attack for the sake of it) that probe and test applications and defenses. This usually refers to penetration testers, application security teams, vulnerability analysts, and even vulnerability management.

Purple team
> A somewhat advanced concept, purple team is really more of a process than a set of people (though, some companies have this as a team). While many organizations keep their blue and red teams separate (and sometimes these teams are even, mistakenly, antagonistic) in purple team/teaming, blue and red teams work together directly and try to improve each other by quickly sharing findings, mutually identifying problems, and generally shortening feedback loops.

> *Black team*
>
> This one is a bit of a one-off and less commonly used, but you might hear about it. Black team is what red team is pretending to be: actual attackers trying to do damage. Usually, we'll refer to them as adversaries, but black team is sometimes used as well.

D3FEND

MITRE also released the other side of ATT&CK: D3FEND (and another on the nose, yet delightful, acronym). Created with funding from the NSA, D3FEND enumerates the countermeasures and responses defenders can take to block or respond to an adversary. Similar to the ATT&CK framework, D3FEND splits these into tactics (the overarching goals) and techniques (the technical controls actually being implemented). The goal of D3FEND is to tie specific defensive techniques to specific offensive techniques. Between these two models, it *should* be possible to go from a specific actor (say G0032—Lazarus Group) all the way to the specific system-hardening steps you should take to block them and the type of detections you need to find them.

Will this work? It might be too soon to tell. ATT&CK was slow to get started for the first few years, so it's possible D3FEND will gain speed. These frameworks are a great lead into our next topic.

Active Defense

One of the most talked about and least understood concepts in intelligence-driven incident-response cycles is the idea of active defense.

Active defense is frequently equated with the idea of *hack back*, or attempting to attack a malicious actor directly. Although this qualifies as one aspect of active defense, five other useful pieces of active defense are far more common. This mix-up is based on a fundamental misunderstanding of the purpose of active defense.

Most people who attempt or request some form of hack back are displaying a childish, schoolyard-style form of revenge. It's natural. You get hit, you want to hit someone back. There are reasons we've outgrown these juvenile tactics. First of all, in network intrusions, we often find it difficult to know the adversary's identity, leading to misattribution and thus a misdirected attack. It can be hard to know if a given technology asset is the property of an adversary, something they're purchasing from a vendor (yep, adversaries love the cloud as much as your DevOps team does), a free service that the adversary is leveraging, or even a stolen asset (meaning an attack might not just be against an adversary, but the innocent legitimate owner). Second, proportionate response is difficult for defensively oriented organizations. Third, hacking back usually serves a limited purpose, aside from achieving a sense of revenge and retribution. Fourth, hacking back could, depending on the adversary, cause them to retaliate to the hack back. Lastly, and perhaps most importantly, it is illegal in most countries to attempt to compromise a computer system without permission or appropriate legal authority such as that granted to law enforcement and military organizations, which in theory submit to strict oversight. In short, don't hack back.

Offensive Cyber Operations

You might be saying, "But what about the people who do have the authority and information to hack back?" Well, it turns out that's starting to happen. In December 2021, General Paul Miki Nakasone, head of US Cyber Command and director of the NSA, was quoted in a *New York Times* article acknowledging that "we have taken actions and we have imposed costs" against ransomware operators. How effective this will be long term is yet to be seen.

Apart from hacking back, active defense includes several other valid and useful elements. Wendi Rafferty at the SANS DFIR Summit in 2015 described the goal of active defense as attempting to disrupt the tempo of an adversary. Andrew Thompson of Mandiant uses the same phrasing as General Nakasone, describing active defense as "imposing cost." Like a detective, the goal of incident responders is to catch an adversary in a mistake, providing a chance to expose them. Active defense gives defenders a means to accelerate that by forcing the adversary into an error, generally while responding to a roadblock put into place by the incident-response team.

Defenders, like adversaries, have the option to deny, disrupt, degrade, deceive, and destroy. Thus, we refer to active defense as the D5 model of defense. Originally developed as a series of desired capabilities for computer network attack (CNA), it turns out the same D5 model provides a great list of capabilities for active defense.

Deny

The idea of denying an adversary is so straightforward and common that most organizations wouldn't even imagine it's a type of active defense; most are actively doing deny-style actions. If we go by our traditional definition of disrupting the adversary's tempo, though, this is a perfect example. Denying can be simple, such as implementing a new firewall rule to block an adversary's command and control, applying a system patch for a vulnerability, or shutting down access for a compromised email account. The key to denial is *preemptively excluding a capability or infrastructure from the malicious actor*.

Denial forces adversaries to deviate from their plan and find a different way to achieve their objectives. If the adversaries don't change every single indicator of compromise before continuing, you can force them into revealing TTPs and pivot your investigation to their new activities. Additionally, many deny actions could be interpreted as mere coincidence, such as a user resetting a password because of a required window, not at the direction of the incident-response team.

Disrupt

If the deny action preemptively excludes a capability or infrastructure from the malicious actor, then disrupt *actively excludes a resource from the malicious actor*. In most cases, disruption requires active observation of an adversary in order to know when they're active so that they can be disrupted in real time. This could mean cutting off a command-and-control channel while it's being used or interrupting the exfiltration of a large archive file.

Degrade

Closely related to disrupting and denying an adversary, degrade focuses on *marginal reduction of an adversary's resources while they're actively being used*. An easily understandable example is throttling an adversary's bandwidth during exfiltration, causing a large file to upload over an extremely slow time frame. This degradation of access attempts to frustrate adversaries, ideally driving them to attempt to access the data in a different way and expose additional infrastructure, tools, or TTPs.

Disruption and degradation present interesting but dangerous opportunities for a network defense team. While denial actions may be explained away as coincidence or normal passive defensive operations, disruption and degradation are clearly active. They begin to open a dialogue with an adversary, giving the adversary an indication that the defender is deliberately responding. Adversaries in situations like this can take a variety of actions. They may spool up attack tempo and severity by bringing advanced capabilities to bear, or they may go all the way in the other direction and cease operations entirely while they wait for the heat to go down. This is the risk of these types of active defense actions, and they need to be taken with a measure of caution and preparation.

Deceive

Easily the most advanced of available techniques, the deceive active defense action is based on the counter-intelligence concept of *deliberately feeding adversaries false information* with the hopes they'll treat it as truth and make decisions based on it. This ranges from planting false documents with incorrect values to hosting honeypot systems or even networks.

Deception operations require a deep understanding of the adversary's goals, methods, and even psychology, as well as your own resources. Making deception material that an adversary is willing to accept as truth is incredibly difficult, as skilled adversaries will attempt to corroborate any material they find with other sources. That said, deception has gotten the attention of vendors selling tools ranging from simple honeypots or tokens (a passive deception approach), all the way up to advanced deception suites that mimic entire networks and monitor adversaries as they pivot around (active deception).

Destroy

Destroy actions do actual harm, whether kinetic or virtual, to an adversary's tools, infrastructure, or operators. In most cases, this is the purview of law enforcement, intelligence, or military operators that have the legal authority to commit such acts (in the US, these are Title 10 and Title 50 organizations). For a commercial or private organization to do so is not only generally accepted to be illegal but also dangerous. It is unlikely that they have the tools, methodology, and operators to conduct a successful computer network attack, and there could be significant unintended consequences. Those resources are better allocated to improving defensive operations.

Is active defense for you? Active defense is a trendy topic, but should organizations make it part of their security program? As with almost any simple question about complex topics, the answer is: "It depends." Active defense doesn't have to be implemented in its entirety. Denying an adversary is in the realm of any organization, and in fact most are probably already doing it whether they know it or not. Disruption and degradation require maturity. Deception is an advanced tactic that carries high reward but also high risk and should be reserved for all but the most advanced security teams. As we just discussed, the destroy active defense action requires special legal status that's not available to nongovernment organizations.

F3EAD

The last major framework to cover combines the intelligence-generation aspects of the intelligence cycle with the operations-centric aspect of the incident-response and kill chain cycles. Built as a targeting methodology for special operations teams working with intelligence analysis cells in the field, F3EAD addresses two key issues with the intelligence and operations cycles we've discussed:

- Intelligence cycles shouldn't just lead to more intelligence; they should lead to meaningful operations. In our case, this means that threat intelligence shouldn't just lead us to more threat intelligence but instead to aggressive incident-response actions.

- Operations cycles shouldn't end after the objective is completed. The information gained during any operation should start feeding a new intelligence cycle. In our case, when an incident response is concluded, the information developed during it should be fed into the intelligence apparatus to start developing new intelligence, to learn from previous incidents, and to be better prepared for future intrusion attempts.

Thus, these two cycles, operations and intelligence, *feed into each other* instead of just themselves (Figure 3-5). Each incident-response operation leads to intelligence operations, and each intelligence operation leads to an incident-response operation, continuing the cycle.

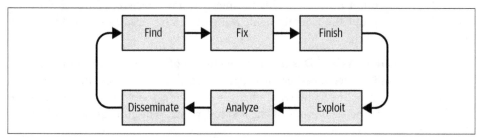

Figure 3-5. The F3EAD operations/intelligence cycle

To facilitate this process, F3EAD (*https://oreil.ly/bZPqP*) uses a modified version of a combined intelligence and operations cycle: Find, Fix, Finish, Exploit, Analyze, Disseminate. As you'll see, this means going through the incident-response cycle and feeding the results into the intelligence cycle, and then connecting those results back into a new incident-response cycle.

Find

The Find phase includes the Targeting phase of the operation, which is where you determine the threats that you will address. This can come from many sources, such as intelligence from a vendor or open source. Ideally, your own previous intelligence cycles should feed this process as well. Depending on the operation or investment, this phase may be determined by the incident-response team itself, in conjunction with the intelligence team, or even working with groups outside these teams, such as the SOC or management. This parallels the Preparation phase of the incident-response cycle.

Fix

Based on the information from the Find phase, the Fix phase establishes telemetry and determines where an adversary is on the network as well any external presence we can detect. Just to be clear, *fix* in this context does not mean "to repair" (we were confused, too!); it refers to the identification of the operational presence of the adversary within the network. This involves taking available information and figuring out which systems, services, or resources an adversary may have compromised, what their channels of communications are, and how they're moving around your network. We can think of this as the Identification phase of the incident-response cycle.

Finish

The Finish phase includes the actual incident-response action (as opposed to the more kinetic and lethal actions intended for the original military version of this process—please do not do these). This is when you take decisive action against the adversary, carrying out the Containment, Mitigation, and Eradication phases of the incident-response cycle.

The major transition in F3EAD is that the conclusion of the incident-response operation doesn't end the cycle. Whether the organization shifts resources and responsibilities between teams or the same team changes its own activity focus, the end of the Finish phase starts the beginning of the Exploit phase. The intelligence half of the F3EAD process then begins.

Exploit

The Exploitation phase roughly maps to the Collection phase of the intelligence cycle, with one primary difference being that this phase is laser-focused on information gathered from the adversary during the operational phases of the cycle. Some of the information that is especially useful for intelligence-driven incident response includes:

- Any indicators of compromise, including IP addresses, URLs, hashes, and email addresses
- Automated enrichment for the IOCs (such as getting reverse DNS for given IP addresses or gathering WHOIS data)
- Exploit delivery samples
- Malware samples
- Common vulnerabilities and exposures (CVE) and exploits
- User and incident reports
- Communications from the adversary
- Previously identified TTPs
- Adversary objectives, goals, and motivations

It's impossible to list everything that might be useful, but analysts should collect as much information as they can about the various phases of the attack. Think through the kill chain and try to collect information about each stage where possible.

Analyze

The Analyze phase maps to (surprise) the Analyze phase of the intelligence cycle. During this phase, the idea is to assess what the collected information is telling us about both short-term and long-term implications on the activity. This is achieved through a few methods:

- Summarizing tactics, techniques, and procedures
- Putting data into models or frameworks for further analysis
- Interpreting timelines and kill chains to derive actionable recommendations

Like the general intelligence phase, the Analyze phase itself is cyclical. Malware analysis may lead to more IOCs, which themselves can be enriched, and may lead to finding more malware. The overall goal is to develop a complete picture of the actor and their TTPs, with a focus on how to detect, mitigate, and remediate their actions.

Disseminate

Intelligence is useful only when it gets to the right audience in the right format, with enough time for it to be absorbed and actioned. Dissemination is not just pushing information out—it is identifying what information is needed by decision makers, delivering it in a way that they can consume, and being available to answer questions or accepted follow-up requests for information. Dissemination of intelligence is focused primarily on the audience, not on how the individual analyst prefers to operate. Because of this, it is critical to understand the audience, which typically falls into one of the following categories:

Tactical
> The most immediate audience for the intelligence is the incident-response team, feeding back into the beginning of the next F3EAD cycle. They'll want a focus on IOCs and summarized TTPs.

Strategic
> It generally takes only one significant incident for management to start having a strong investment and interest in the incident-response and threat intelligence teams. Their interest will be in highly generalized TTPs (more focused on campaigns than individual incidents) and actions on objective. This intelligence should be useful to decision makers in future resource allocation and larger business planning (for example, informing risk assessments).

Third party
> Many organizations participate in some form of threat intelligence sharing group. Each organization has to determine its own rules of engagement for participating. Work with your leadership and legal teams to determine the best methods to do so. This may include intelligence from any level of abstraction, depending on your goals and appetite for collaboration.

Regardless of the level of intelligence or the audience you are addressing, you will want the information you disseminate to be clear, concise, accurate, and actionable.

Using F3EAD

F3EAD is one of the most powerful concepts that can be implemented to improve both the threat intelligence and incident-response side of security operations. It's also one of the most difficult. It's hard to explain why an arcane Special Forces acronym that most people don't even know how to say should be part of an IT department's standard operating procedures, but it provides a key missing piece: how operations can lead to better intelligence, and vice versa.

When thinking about what it looks like to use F3EAD, rather than focus on the details, focus on the overall concept: Security operations and incident response become an input to threat intelligence, and threat intelligence becomes an input to security operations and incident response. Whenever any part of the security operations team (whether that's a SOC, CIRT, or individual engineers) completes an incident response, all of their outputs and documentation, forensic artifacts, malware, and research should be passed on to the intelligence team. From there, the intelligence team exploits and analyzes this information. Their output, based on that incident, should be provided back to the security ops team, and then the cycle continues. This ends up forming a kind of security operations/threat intelligence OODA loop. The faster the security ops team can use this intelligence, the faster they can complete their operations tasks, which in turn drives more intelligence.

This operations + intelligence model doesn't need to be limited to the SOC and intelligence teams. This same process can be used with the vulnerability management and application security (AppSec) teams. For example, when the AppSec team finds a new vulnerability, that vulnerability can then be treated as a piece of intelligence. Nothing guarantees the AppSec engineer was the first person to find this vulnerability. Thus, the AppSec team feeds as much information as possible to the SOC, which begins looking for any indications of previous attacks against that vulnerability.

Picking the Right Model

The purpose of models is to provide a framework that can be used to interpret information and generate intelligence. Keep in mind the quote by George E.P. Box: "All models are wrong, some are useful." Hundreds of models are available for intelligence analysis, and more useful ones can be pulled from other disciplines, such as military conflict theory and law enforcement (*https://oreil.ly/ij-VH*). Some of these models are meant to be general purpose, and some have been developed for individual or specific use cases. When deciding what model to use, there are several factors to keep in mind:

- *The time available* for analysis can help determine which model is appropriate. If there is time to conduct an in-depth analysis or an incident, the Diamond Model for intrusion analysis may work well. If you have time constraints, something like the OODA loop can be used to drive decisions.
- *The type of information* may also dictate which model is most appropriate, as some models are designed to be used with certain data sources such as netflow or endpoint data.
- Finally, it may all come down to *analyst preference*. If an analyst has found that a certain model works well within their processes, then by all means continue to use that model. There may even come a time when the best option is to develop a new model.

Scenario: Road Runner

Now that we've worked through many of the key models for incident response, let's deepen our understanding of intelligence-driven incident response. We're about to launch into the practical nuts and bolts of incident response, cyber threat intelligence, and how they can work together to help you defend your organization.

The rest of the book is laid out using the joint operations/intelligence model F3EAD augmented with additional analytic models and frameworks that are especially well suited for intelligence-driven incident response. We'll work through the models and frameworks while investigating Road Runner, which is the name we have given to the election-focused activity we introduced earlier in the chapter. We believe that this is the most recent tasking of the fictitious attack group Grey Spike and that they are actively targeting our organization as well as others. Using this adversary and related activity, we will move through the F3EAD process:

Find
> The next chapter introduces how we target adversaries, both proactively and reactively, to gather the information that we need to support the rest of the F3EAD process. We will evaluate what we know about Road Runner both from

previous incidents in our organization, along with information shared from external parties.

Fix

This phase can be thought of as the investigation phase, which involves tracking an adversary in the victim's environment. Here we will actively hunt for Road Runner activity in our networks, and, who knows, we may even find signs of additional adversaries we didn't know about before!

Finish

Once all adversary activity has been identified, the Finish phase removes an adversary from the environment.

Exploit

Once the incident-response process is over, we'll start developing data that resulted from our incident-response process so that we can derive lessons and insight. We already know that the Road Runner campaign is being carried out by a well-funded and persistent adversary; we will need to actively work to prevent them from regaining access to our information. That starts with understanding as much as we can about their activities.

Analyze

Next, we'll develop that data into intelligence that can be useful for protecting our organization going forward and helping others who may be dealing with similar intrusions or the same adversary.

Disseminate

After developing the intelligence, we'll put it into a variety of useful formats for a variety of customers so that the most use possible can be derived from the process.

By the end of the book, we'll have developed a full set of products, breaking down the activity known as Road Runner.

Conclusion

Complex processes such as incident response often benefit from the use of models, which give the processes structure and define necessary steps for task completion. Determining which models should be used depends on the timeline of the situation, the data available, and in many cases the analyst's preference. The more familiar you become with these models and their applications, the easier it will be to determine which models to use in response to different incidents.

Now, let's dive into the Find phase!

## PART II

Practical Application

Once you understand the fundamentals, it is time to get down to business. processes. Part II steps through the intelligence-driven incident-response process using the F3EAD process: Find, Fix Finish, Exploit, Analyze, Disseminate. These steps will ensure that you are gathering and acting on the right information in the right order to get as much as possible from the intelligence-driven incident-response processes.

## CHAPTER 4

Find

Be very, very quiet; we are hunting wabbits.
—Elmer J. Fudd

The first half of the F3EAD cycle contains the primary operational components—Find, Fix, and Finish. *Operations* in this context means a planned, coordinated action in response to a developing situation. For us, this means incident-response operations for unauthorized network activity. During these first three phases, the adversaries are targeted, identified, and eradicated. We use intelligence to inform these operational actions, but that's not the only use of intelligence. Later in the process, the data from the operational phases will feed into the second half of F3EAD, which contains the intelligence-focused phases—Exploit, Analyze, and Disseminate.

This chapter focuses on the Find phase, which is the starting point for both intelligence and operational activities. In the traditional F3EAD cycle, the Find phase starts when the operations team identifies high-value entities to be targeted. In intelligence-driven incident response, the Find phase identifies relevant adversaries for incident response.

In the case of an ongoing incident, you may have identified or been given some initial indicators and need to dig for more, or in the case of threat hunting, you may be searching for anomalous activity in your networks. Regardless of the situation, before you can find anything, you need to have an idea of what it is you are looking for.

Various approaches can be taken in the Find phase. The method you take should be determined by the nature of the situation or incident as well as the goal of the investigation. Different methods may be combined, as well, to ensure that you have identified all possible pieces of information. The methods for the Find phase that we will cover in this chapter are actor-centric, victim-centric, asset-centric, capability-centric, infrastructure-centric, and—the method most folks end up using more often than they would like—media-centric targeting.

Actor-Centric Targeting

When there is credible information on the actor behind an attack or you are being asked to provide information on a particular attack group, it is possible to conduct actor-centric targeting.

Actor-centric investigations are like unraveling a sweater: You find a few little pieces of information and begin to pull on each one. These threads can provide insight into the tactics and techniques that the actor used against you, which then give you a better idea of what else to look for. The result is powerful, but it can be frustrating. You never know which thread will be the key to unraveling the whole thing. You just have to keep trying. Then, suddenly, you may dig into one aspect that opens up the entire investigation. Persistence, and luck, are key aspects of actor-centric investigations.

Actors Versus People

Identity is a funny thing. In many cases, when we say *they* or *them* or refer to an adversary, it's easy to assume we're referring to the people behind an attack. In some rare cases we are talking about the actual individuals (this is called *attribution*, something we'll discuss more in the intelligence chapters). But in most cases when we're referring to actors, we're referring to a persona based on the tactics, techniques, and procedures (TTPs) used together to achieve a goal. We mentally group these together and personify them, since humans understand stories told that way. This is an abstraction, because we usually don't know if it's one person or a large group. We call this abstraction of linked TTPs + goal an actor, regardless of the number of people involved.

In some cases, incident responders will go into an investigation with an idea of who the actor behind the incident may be. This information can be gleaned from a variety of sources; for example, when stolen information is offered for sale on underground forums or when a third party makes the initial notification and provides some information on the attacker. Identifying at least some details of an attacker makes it possible to carry out actor-centric targeting in the Find phase.

When conducting actor-centric targeting, the first step is to validate the information that has been provided on the attacker. It is important to understand if and why the attacker in question would target your organization. The development of a *threat model*, a process that identifies potential threats by taking an attacker's view of a target, can speed this process and can help identify the types of data or access that may have been targeted. This information can also feed into the Find phase, where incident responders search for signs of attacker activity.

A threat model can allow you to use actor-centric targeting even if you do not have concrete information on the actor by determining potential or likely attackers. Of the hundreds of tracked criminal, activist, and espionage groups, only a small handful will be generally interested in your organization. Assessing which of these groups are truly threats to you is not a perfect science, but you have to make your best guess and keep in mind that the list you come up with will not be an authoritative list but will still be a good place to start. After some time, experience will be your best guide to potential threats.

Once you validate the initial information, the next step is to identify as much information as possible on the actor. This information will help to build the *target package* on the attacker, which will enable operations to fix and finish the attack. Information on the actor can include details of previous attacks, both internal and external.

Starting with Known Information

In almost every situation, some information will be available on threat actors, whether that comes from previous incidents or attack attempts within your own environment (internal information) or intelligence reports produced by researchers, vendors, or other third parties (external information). Ideally, a combination of both types will be available in order to provide the best overall picture of the threat.

Strategic and tactical intelligence are both useful at this stage. Strategic intelligence on actors can provide information on their potential motivation or goals, where they ultimately want to get to, and what they ultimately want to do when they get there. Tactical intelligence can provide details on how an actor typically operates, including their typical tactics and methods, preferred tools, previous infrastructure used, and other pieces of information that can be searched for during the Fix stage. Both types of intelligence can help to contextualize the information that is found in later stages.

It is also useful, though difficult, to understand whether the actors tend to operate alone or whether they work with other actor groups. Some espionage groups have been known to divide tasks between several groups, with one group focusing on initial access, another focusing on accomplishing the goals of the attack, another for maintaining access for future activities, and so forth. If this is the case, there may be signs of multiple actors and multiple activities in a network, but further analysis should be conducted to see whether the activities fit the pattern of multiple actor groups working together or whether it is possible that several actors are operating independently.

Useful Information During the Find Phase

During the Find phase, our biggest goal is developing information that will be useful during the Fix portion of the F3EAD cycle. The most useful information is information that's hard for the actor to change. Incident responder David J. Bianco captured this concept, and its impact on the adversary, in his Pyramid of Pain (*https://oreil.ly/JaYTt*), shown in Figure 4-1.

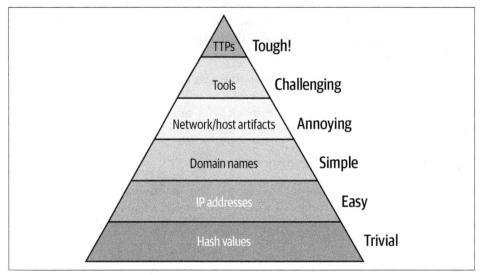

Figure 4-1. David J. Bianco's Pyramid of Pain

The Pyramid of Pain is a model depicting how various types of information are central to an actor's tool chain and objectives, which corresponds to how hard they are to change. At the bottom, you have basic characteristics that attackers can change regularly by tweaking small details of malware or network configurations such as recompiling malware (to generate a new hash) or pointing a domain name at a new IP address for command and control. At the top, you have core capabilities that are central to who an actor is, such as core techniques and methodologies.

Intelligence Versus Information

Keep in mind we are focused right now on threat *information* rather than threat *intelligence*. Intelligence is information that has been analyzed to answer a specific question, which we will get to later in the F3EAD process. At this initial stage, we are grabbing as much potentially useful information as we can find, which we will then analyze to determine whether it is something that we want to include in the remaining steps.

So how do we use this model? The Pyramid of Pain is all about understanding the relative value and temporal nature of different types of indicators of compromise (more on those in the next section!) and actor information. Are hashes useless? Not at all; they're incredibly useful in many contexts and provide a great starting place for an investigation, but they change often and easily (often just by recompiling a piece of malware). On the opposite end of the spectrum, an actor that specializes in compromising websites with SQL injection would have a relatively difficult time switching tactics to spear phishing with zero-day exploits. When it comes to threat information, we prefer, and get longer use out of, information toward the top of the pyramid. Our goal in both incident response and intelligence analysis is to move higher up the pyramid, thus making it more difficult for the adversary to evade us.

Indicators of compromise

The simplest data to gather (and thus lower on the Pyramid of Pain) is commonly referred to as *indicators of compromise* (IOCs). While IOCs can come in a variety of formats, which we'll discuss more in the next chapter, they're all defined the same way: a description of technical characteristics that identify a known threat, an attacker's methodology, or other evidence of compromise.

IOCs typically focus on atomic pieces of information at the bottom of the Pyramid of Pain. These can be subdivided based on where the information is found:

Filesystem indicators
  File hashes, filenames, strings, paths, sizes, types, signing certificates

Memory indicators
  Strings and memory structures

Network indicators
  IP addresses, hostnames, domain names, HTML paths, ports, SSL certificates

Each type of indicator has unique uses, is visible in different positions (whether monitoring a single system or a network), and depending on the format it's in, may be useful with different tools.

Behavior

Far more complex for attackers to change are behaviors, captured in the top level of the Pyramid of Pain as TTPs. This is a loose group that goes beyond tools and instead focuses on how they're used to achieve an attacker's goals. Behavior is more abstract than TTPs and can't be easily described the way IOCs can.

Behaviors can often be best understood in terms of the kill chain from Chapter 3. How does an attacker achieve each piece? Here are a few hypothetical examples:

Reconnaissance
> (Usually based on inference) The attacker profiles potential victims based on conference proceedings found online.

Weaponization
> The attacker uses a Visual Basic for Applications (VBA) macro embedded in a Microsoft Word document.

Delivery
> The attacker sends a phishing email from a spoofed industry group based on information from the conference proceedings identified during Reconnaissance.

Exploitation
> The attacker's VBA macro executes when the victim opens the attached Word document and downloads the second-stage payload.

Installation
> The attacker uses a privilege escalation exploit to install a second-stage payload, a remote-access Trojan (RAT), so it starts up at login and achieves persistence.

Command and Control
> The RAT uses connections to a micro blogging site to exchange encoded communication for Command and Control.

Actions on Objective
> The attacker attempts to steal technical schematics and emails by compressing them and uploading them through a file-sharing service.

As you go through this process of capturing behavior-based information in a kill chain format, make sure that you document any information that you find in a way that will help you remember it for use in future steps of the intelligence-driven incident-response process.

Using the Kill Chain

Actor-centric targeting is often a good place to start, partially because it has the most straightforward model when combined with the kill chain. Any information that you are given or find at the start of your investigation will most likely come from one or, if you are lucky, two phases of the kill chain. A good strategy is to use hints from the preceding and following phases of the kill chain to determine what other information to look for, so identifying where your existing information sits within the kill chain can determine where else you should look.

In the previous example, if the only information you know about the attack is that the attackers used macros in a Word document during the Exploitation phase, you could research that behavior and identify that you should look for artifacts related to privilege escalation to determine whether the exploitation was successful. Another option would be to move in the other direction on the kill chain and look for the delivery method, searching for email senders or subjects related to the original information that you received. Even if the attackers did not keep things 100% identical across attacks, similarities can be identified, especially when you know what you are looking for.

Road Runner: Building an initial kill chain

Building a kill chain for a new attacker is a great place to start when using an actor-centric approach, even if there aren't a lot of things to fill in at the beginning. One of the great things about the kill chain, even one filled with question marks, is that it provides a structure for what you need to look for next and can be easily updated as new information surfaces.

In Chapter 3 we built out a general kill chain using the typical behaviors and TTPs of an actor we know as Grey Spike. Now we will build another kill chain to enumerate a specific campaign (a series of intrusions carried out in coordination against a goal) that we refer to as Road Runner. In our case, we're starting with a private report being passed around a variety of organizations similar to ours. Although this report was generated externally, the adversary activities mirror what we have seen in our own network recently. Using this report, along with our internal intrusion documentation, we're going to start building a kill chain for Road Runner and will document what we know and what gaps we have.

TLP: Amber - Industry Advisory Report

Title: APT Group Targeting State and Local Election Campaigns

Version 1.0

Executive Summary: An increasing number of state- and national-level election campaigns with phishing emails.

Overview: Three state and local campaigns have reported receiving highly targeted phishing emails containing a weaponized PDF. The emails were similar in tone and nature, although highly individualized to the recipient. In two cases this email was opened and executed on the system. In one case the PDF would not open, and the campaign manager forwarded it to the IT staff, who identified it as malware targeting a vulnerability in older versions of Adobe Acrobat Viewer (CVE-2018-4916); see Table 4-1.

Table 4-1. Indicators of compromise

Type	Indicator	Stage
Email Address	*betty.smith@ymail.com*	Delivery
Email Address	*support.network@yoohoo.com*	Delivery
Filename	*donation.pdf*	Exploitation
Hash	b33bf51149b4a86574648351a26a846a	Exploitation

In addition, our organization, which provides operational cybersecurity support to several campaigns, has identified similar phishing emails targeting campaign managers we support. Both the dates and tactics align. Our internal report is here:

Event Summary - Road Runner Activity Targeting Campaign Staff

Beginning the week of February 14, at least three emails were sent to key campaign staff supporting a national and state election campaign in the state of Washington. These emails were not identical but had key similarities, including in the weaponization of the PDFs.

Email #1:

Subject: Following up on fundraising efforts

Sender: *charlene_abbott@yoohoo.com*

Filename: *sendingdonation.pdf*

Email #2:

Subject: Need help with anything?

Sender: *matt_albridge@yoohoo.com*

Filename: *volunteer_resume.pdf*

Email #3:

Subject: Did Donation go Through?

Sender: *tanya_smitherton@ymail.com*

Filename: *receipt.pdf*

All three attachments were opened by the recipient, although none of the systems were impacted as the version of Adobe running on each system was not vulnerable to the exploit that attempted to execute after the files were opened.

Road Runner: Developing the kill chain

Now we have an initial kill chain based on our first pieces of information about Road Runner, which came from both an external report and internal intrusion reporting. While it's obvious we have huge gaps in the structure of understanding, as we are missing several phases entirely, this activity is starting to come together. We know some of the techniques this actor might use to get into our organization, and based on previous activities of the actor Grey Spike, we have considerable information about what they might try to do once they get in. Our findings are summarized in Table 4-2.

Table 4-2. Developing kill chain for Road Runner activity

Kill chain phase	External reporting	Internal reporting
Targeting	National and State Campaign Staff	National and State Campaign Staff • Campaign Finance Manager • Chief of Staff • Social Media Manager
Reconnaissance	Unknown, but targets are listed publicly on their campaign website and have their job titles posted on social media networks.	Unknown, but targets are listed publicly on their campaign website and have their job titles posted on social media networks.
Weaponization	Macros embedded in PDFs specifically crafted to be appealing to the target receiving it.	Macros embedded in PDFs specifically crafted to be appealing to the target receiving it.
Delivery	Emails from: • *betty.smith@ymail.com* • *support.network@yoohoo.com*	Emails from: • *charlene_abbott@yoohoo.com* • *matt_albridge@yoohoo.com* • *tanya_smitherton@ymail.com*
Exploitation	CVE-2018-4916	CVE-2018-4916 (Unsuccessful)
Installation	Unknown	Unknown
C2	Unknown	Unknown
Actions on Objective	Unknown	Unknown

Throughout the rest of the F3 operational phases (Find, Fix and Finish), we're going to use the information we have to try to track and respond to the adversary and fill in some of these blanks.

Goals

The actor's goals are the most abstract of all of the information you will gather in the Find stage, because in many cases it has to be inferred from their actions rather than being clearly spelled out. However, an actor's goal is one of the things that will rarely change, even if it is identified by a defender. An attacker focused on a particular goal cannot simply change goals to avoid detection, even if they may change TTPs, tools, or indicators. No matter what technologies the actor chooses to use or how they choose to use them, they still have to go where their target is. As a result, goals are the least changeable aspect of an actor's behavior and should be a core attacker attribute to track.

Attacker Moonlighting

From time to time, attackers will *moonlight*, conducting attacks with radically different goals but the same TTPs, by taking on other types of operations with different strategic goals. Espionage groups occasionally take on criminal operations, moving from stealing information to stealing money; or a criminal group shifts from using its botnet for spam to using it for DDoS attacks. In some cases, this may be in furtherance of another operation, such as developing secondary infrastructure for another attack, or even just for personal gain.

Seeing an actor change goals is a key data point and should always be watched closely. It may signal a shift in interest or could be the setup for a new type of attack. Regardless, it gives considerable insight into attribution and strategic interests.

The goals for Road Runner are based solely on victimology. So far, the only activity we see is targeting campaign staff, indicating that their goal in this particular effort is to gain access to networks or devices associated with upcoming elections in the US. If you recall from the Grey Spike kill chain in Chapter 3, we assess that this actor is a state-sponsored group and receives targeting based on strategic needs of the state.

The goals at this point can be inferred only by looking closer at the victims that they are targeting. Next, we will pivot to victim-centric targeting to see if there is anything else we can identify about this activity that may help us in subsequent phases.

Victim-Centric Targeting

If you are dealing with an active incident, you may or may not have starting information about the actors involved in the incident, but you will almost certainly have some information about the target, or the victim, of the incident. Victim-centric targeting tries to piece together the story of what the adversary was after, how they got to a certain point in the network, and, in some cases, why they are there to begin with.

Victim-centric targeting builds off of victimology, a branch of criminology that studies the relationship between a victim and an offender by examining the causes and the nature of the consequent suffering. In criminology, understanding the victims can give investigators insight into the perpetrator. Understanding the victim's experience of a crime—for example, were they frightened or intimidated or did the perpetrator attempt to hide the existence of the crime from them—can help understand

---

motivations and even the intention of the perpetrator. In intelligence-driven incident response we tend to think of victims as the devices or servers that were targeted. Although those are very important details to capture in victim-centric targeting, the impact on the human users of those devices is also important to understanding the nature of the incident and the actors.

So how do we begin to leverage victim-centric targeting? Similar to the baseline for beginning with actor-centric targeting, you need to have access to some basic information about the victims to get started. That information can include details about the devices that were targeted, their human users, and the way the device is used. Once we have captured the basic information on the victims, you can begin to ask questions of the data: Why were these victims targeted? What commonalities (if any) do they share? Can the actors' goals or motivations be inferred from these victims?

Targets Versus Victims

During the Find phase it is important to remember that we are identifying as many investigative leads and "puzzle pieces" as we can, and while insight is helpful in moving through this phase, we are not yet analyzing the final meaning of anything we find. This distinction is especially important when it comes to referencing victims versus targets. A target is the person, device, or entity that will achieve the adversary's goal. A victim is someone or something that is impacted by the adversary's actions, regardless of whether they were intentionally identified as a way to get access to their target or were collateral damage in an intrusion gone wrong.

In many complex incidents, adversaries may end up impacting many people in the process of achieving their goal and reaching their ultimate target. As we move through victim-centric targeting, make sure to keep a mental separation between the victims that are impacted and our understanding of the adversary's goals. Victims can certainly give clues about goals, but until we get to the intelligence-focused phases of F3EAD, we will not have all of the data or the processes in place to make a solid analytic judgment.

Using Victim-Centric Targeting

In Chapter 3 we covered different models that can be used during the incident-response process—or intelligence processes in general—and one model that is especially well suited to victim-centric targeting is the Diamond Model. The Diamond Model has a vertex specifically for capturing the victims in an intrusion. One of the strengths of the Diamond Model is the ability to capture contextual indicators connecting the various vertices, which define the nature of the relationship between different components of the model. In victim-centric targeting these contextual indicators offer key insights that can help you find additional malicious activity in your network.

Victim-infrastructure connection

Adversaries must leverage some sort of infrastructure to carry out their activities, and when those activities directly impact a victim, that means there is a connection between the two. In the Find phase, this victim-infrastructure relationship can be used to find additional victims or uncover additional information about the adversary by following the link and pivoting to infrastructure-centric targeting, which we will discuss later in this chapter.

Questions to ask related to this vertex are:

- What was the nature of the connection between the victim and the adversary's infrastructure? Did it reach out to the victim, or did the victim reach out to it?
- Did any other devices interact with this infrastructure in the same way as the victim?
- Is there anything unique about the relationship here that could be pivoted on?

In our Road Runner scenario, a Diamond Model would capture the email addresses and the PDFs in the Infrastructure vertex, as they were the means by which the capability was delivered to the victim. In each case, the email address was a generic-sounding name that was not uncommon in the target's political district. In addition, the subject and the filename of the PDF that were delivered were in alignment with typical emails that the target receives—pivoting on every email about fundraising that is sent to a campaign fundraising chair would likely not be an effective use of time. One potential pivot from this relationship would be the email domain, which in this case is not a common provider.

Victim-capability connection

Similar to infrastructure, there will always be a relationship between the capability leveraged and the victim, although *victim* can be used in multiple ways. For example, a victim may be the user who clicked a phishing link, or it may be the computer that the user was on when they clicked it. Either way, the relationship can be characterized and captured.

Questions to ask related to this vertex are:

- What is it about this victim that made this capability successful (or unsuccessful)?
- Are other victims susceptible to the same capabilities?

For Road Runner, we know that the phishing campaign we identified was designed to leverage CVE-2018-4916, which exploits a vulnerability in older versions of Adobe Acrobat Reader. The attempts we know about were unsuccessful because the recipients were not running vulnerable versions of the software. This is a critical piece of information for the Find phase because we know that any devices running a vulnerable version would potentially be an appealing target to the adversary.

Victim-adversary connection

While there is typically not a direct connection between an adversary and a victim in the Diamond Model, there is the concept of a meta-feature that captures the sociopolitical relationship between the two. This meta-feature may include contextual information on why an adversary is interested in leveraging its capabilities against a particular victim or set of victims. In the Find phase, in particular, being able to describe potential relationships between the adversary and victim can help identify additional data points to search for as we try to gather as much data as possible.

Some questions to ask when digging into the victim-adversary relationship:

- What would targeting this victim help an adversary achieve? (Remember, the victim may have been the target or just a hop-point on the way to the target; explore both options.)
- Are there other victims that share similar characteristics and may have been similarly targeted?

Using victim-centric targeting, we have identified that these key campaign staff are likely to continue to be targeted as they are the best sources for the types of information that Grey Spike is after for the Road Runner operation.

Asset-Centric Targeting

While victim-centric targeting looks at the victims and victim devices that are targeted or have been impacted by an actor and uses that information to find additional signs of activity, asset-centric targeting is possible even when there is no confirmed adversary activity. Asset-centric targeting is all about what you're protecting and focuses on the specific technologies that enable operations. It can be incredibly useful for instances when you do not have specific information on an attack against your network and want to understand where and how you would look for indications of an attack or intrusion.

One of the most notable examples of this form of targeting is industrial control systems (ICS). These specialized systems, which control things like dams, factories, and power grids, require specific domain knowledge to use and thus attack. A threat intelligence team can limit entire classes of attackers based on their ability to understand, have access to, and test attacks against ICS. We are talking about not only massively complex systems but in many cases massively expensive ones as well. During an attacker's pre-kill chain phase, they have to invest incredible amounts of time and effort into getting the right software to find vulnerabilities and then getting the right environments to test exploits.

Understanding who is capable of attacking the types of systems you're protecting is key to asset-centric targeting because it allows you to focus on the kinds of indicators and tools that are useful for attacking your technology. Every extra system an attacker invests in attacking is an opportunity cost, meaning they can't spend the same time and resources working on another type of technology that needs the same level of resources. For example, a team putting effort into attacking ICS would not have the resources to put into attacking automotive technology.

Third-party research can help and hurt technology-centric attacks, either by aiding the attackers with basic research (thus saving them time and resources) or by helping defenders understand how the attackers might approach it and thus how to defend it. Most defenders have a limited need to dig into these topic-specific issues, but they provide a focused view of the attacker/defender paradigm.

Using Asset-Centric Targeting

Because asset-centric targeting focuses on the assets that an attacker would target, in most cases the organizations that will get the most out of this method are those developing a unique class of technology such as industrial control, power generation, self-driving cars, flying drones, or even Internet of Things devices. Obviously, each organization has its own specific considerations and so asset-centric targeting should be done with a similar but customized kill-chain-style approach. Robert Lee, a noted ICS expert, demonstrated building a custom asset-centric kill chain in his paper "The Industrial Control System Cyber Kill Chain" (*https://oreil.ly/6gy8Y*).

How can we use asset-centric targeting in our Road Runner scenario? So far, we have a few pieces of information that would help us, though they may seem overly broad at this point. We know the Road Runner team has targeted individuals using phishing emails designed to exploit a vulnerability in a PDF reader. While the adversary may be targeting individuals they think are vulnerable to this attack, it seems that they are just targeting specific individuals and we do not have enough information to ascertain whether they may target specific systems, or even whether they will pivot to additional systems after gaining initial access. If the adversary's goal is information gathering, there is quite a lot to be gained just by getting access to a key staff member's email account.

Asset-centric targeting is all about narrow specifics, but at this point we do not have enough information about the adversary's activity for those specifics to manifest. We will continue to gather as much information as we can for the Find phase, but what is most notable here is that we are identifying a *gap* in information. If it becomes critical to have a better understanding of the assets targeted by this adversary, we will need to come back and address this gap, but for now we have sufficient information to continue with our Find phase.

Capability-Centric Targeting

As you may be picking up on, one of the main points of the Find phase—and the reason that there are so many different approaches—is that much of this work is based on the concept of doing what we can with what we have. Over the years, as intelligence sharing has improved between different companies as well as between the government and the private sector, there have become more options for the types of information available to help with detecting malicious activity. One type of information that can be incredibly useful is information on the capabilities of adversaries.

Capabilities are the tools and methods that adversaries use to achieve their goals. While many may think of things like zero-day exploits and polymorphic malware when we discuss capabilities, it is important to remember that adversaries often use the *least* sophisticated tool that will achieve their goals. Keeping this in mind can prevent overlooking a less sophisticated method of accessing or traversing a network.

One of the most common uses of capability-centric targeting is pivoting off of a piece of malware that was found in the environment. Using tools like VirusTotal or an intelligence portal provided by an antivirus vendor, an analyst can quickly plug in a malware hash, filename, or other indicator from a compromised system and begin to identify other elements that can help in the Find phase.

Using Capability-Centric Targeting

The types of indicators that can be pivoted off of using capability-centric targeting tend to be lower on the Pyramid of Pain that we discussed earlier in this chapter—hashes, filenames, and strings. That is okay, though! The point of the Find phase is to enumerate as much as possible, and pivoting off of a capability is a good way to find additional information. It is also possible to cluster similar items to start to gather more insight and move up the pyramid. For example, look at the filenames of the attachments sent to the campaign staff:

- *Receipt.pdf*
- *Sendingdonation.pdf*
- *Volunteer_resume.pdf*

There is a clear pattern here, and while it may not be useful to search through the victim's inboxes for other attachments with receipts or resumes (they likely get a ton!), it could be something to look for in a database of malware, especially when it can be combined with other pieces of information found in the capability, such as an IP the malware reaches out to after executing, signature info, or other types of metadata. It is important to avoid going down a rabbit hole with these pivots. A general rule of thumb during the Find phase is to stop two pivots away from a piece of information that you know is relevant to the investigation. More pivoting can be taken during the later phases of F3EAD, in particular in the data Exploitation and Analysis phases, where there will be much more context to guide you and keep you from pulling on the wrong threads.

Using Malware to Identify Threat Actors

Years ago, it was common to attribute attacks to a particular group based on malware or other tools used during attacks. PlugX is a perfect example, originally believed to be created and used exclusively by the NCPH Group (*https://oreil.ly/T35aI*). Since then, PlugX has been sold or shared and is in wide use by a variety of threat actors. The time for malware-based attribution has passed, as many attack tools and RATs have been published, sold, and repurposed by a variety of threat actor groups. Rather than base attribution solely on malware, it is important to take a variety of other factors into account, including goals and motivations as well as behaviors and other tactics. Identifying previously used malware is, however, useful in the Find phase and can lead to the identification of additional pieces of information useful to the investigation.

For Road Runner, we do have some basic information about the types of capabilities that they have already leveraged against us, and as we discussed with both actor- and victim-centric targeting, we can potentially find additional information using the samples that we have access to, along with the hash that was provided in the external report we received. With the actor that we believe to be behind Road Runner, Grey Spike, we expect there to be other tools in their arsenal, as well, and can leverage information about those capabilities.

Media-Centric Targeting

This is a little bit tongue in cheek, but one of the most common targeting methodologies that occurs in many organizations is often called "CNN-centric targeting" or "media-centric targeting." This usually starts with an executive seeing something on the public news or hearing an off-handed comment from someone else that trickles down to the threat intelligence team, which then becomes tasked with analyzing the implications of the threat.

Let's set the record straight: These kinds of investigations are not always a bad thing. There is a reason even the largest traditional intelligence providers monitor news sources—journalism and intelligence are closely related. Current events can often have a dramatic impact on the intelligence needs of an organization. The key is to distill what may seem an unfocused query into something more cogent and clearly defined.

For example, a stakeholder comes to you having seen the news clip "Chinese Hackers Infiltrated U.S. Companies, Attorney General Says" (*http://cnn.it/2uK4NNV*) and wants to know whether this is relevant to your organization. There are a few key points to think about for you to answer this question:

- First, take the time to read the article and watch the video and associated media. Who are the groups and people referenced? Don't just focus on attackers, but focus on victims and third parties as well.

- This article is discussing a specific group of attackers. Do you know who those attackers are?

- What is the question being asked? Start big and then get small. It's easy, at first, to look into the names mentioned in the article or video and say "We're not any of those companies, or even related," but go deeper. The true question is likely, "Are we at risk of intellectual property theft from state-sponsored actors?"

- If possible, identify any information that will help you determine whether you have been compromised or will help you put defenses into place that would identify similar attack attempts. This is the beauty of the Find phase: You can identify any pieces of information that may be useful moving forward, regardless of what prompted the request, making it part of the formal process.

It is useful to view this type of targeting as an informal request for information, rather than as an offhanded request. The *request for information* is the process of taking investigation cycle direction from the outside. We will discuss this concept more later in the chapter. For now, though, it is important to remember that there may be key pieces of information about an adversary or activity in media reporting, including trends in activity, information about adversary goals, and other insights that may be useful. While this information may not help you tactically hunt for activity on your network, it can provide you with additional data that may help connect the dots in the future. At the very least, your responding quickly and efficiently to a request from a stakeholder can provide them much-needed support and additional insight into the role of intelligence in the organization.

Targeting Based on Third-Party Notification

One of the worst experiences a team can have is when a third party—whether a peer company, law enforcement, or someone on Twitter—reports a breach at your organization. When a third party notifies you of a breach, in most cases the targeting is done for you. The notifier gives you an actor, or at least some pointers to an actor, and ideally some indicators. From there, the incident-response phase begins by figuring out how to best use the information given, something we'll talk more about in the next chapter.

The active targeting portion of a third-party notification focuses primarily on what else you can get from the notifier. Getting as much information as possible from a third party involves establishing that you and your organization have a few key traits: actionability, confidentiality, and operational security.

Sharing intelligence in a third-party notification is largely a risk to the sharing party. Protecting sources and methods is tough work and harder when it's outside your control, such as when giving the information to someone unknown. As a result, it is up to the receiver to demonstrate that information will be handled appropriately, both in protecting it (operational security and confidentiality) and in using it (actionability).

The result is that the first time a third-party shares information, they may be reluctant to share very much, perhaps nothing more than an IP address of the attacker infrastructure and a time frame. As the receiver is vetted and shown to be a trustworthy and effective user of shared intelligence, more context might be shared. These types of interactions are the base idea behind information-sharing groups, be they formal groups like Information Sharing and Analysis Centers (ISACs) or informal groups like mailing lists or shared chats. Mature and immature organizations both gain from being members of these types of sharing groups. Just be sure your organization is in a position to both share what you can and act on what's shared with you. The more context that an organization can share around a particular piece of information, the more easily and effectively it will be to act on that piece of information.

 Many organizations struggle with getting the authority to share information. Although most organizations are happy to get information from other security teams or researchers, many are reluctant to share information back, either to individuals or to groups. This is a natural concern, but to be effective, teams must surmount it. This goes back to the childhood adage that if you don't share, no one will share with you. In many cases, this means engaging your legal team and developing a set of rules around sharing information.

Prioritizing Targeting

At this point in the Find phase, you have likely gathered and analyzed a lot of information. To move onto the next phase, Fix, you need to prioritize this information so that it can be acted on.

Immediate Needs

One of the simplest ways to prioritize targeting a request from stakeholders is based on immediate needs. Did an organization just release a threat report about a particular group, and now your CISO is asking questions? Is the company about to make a decision that may impact a country with aggressive threat groups, and they have asked for an assessment of the situation? If there are immediate needs, those should be prioritized.

Judging the immediacy of a Find action is a tough thing. It's easy to get caught up in new, shiny leads. Experience will lead to a slower, often more skeptical approach. It's easy to chase a hunch or random piece of information, and it's important to develop a sensitivity to how immediately a lead needs to be addressed. The key is often to slow down and not get caught up in the emergency nature of *potentially* malicious activity. Many experienced incident responders have a story of getting too caught up in a target that *looked* important, only to realize later it was something minor.

Past Incidents

In the absence of an immediate need, it's worth taking time to establish your collection priorities. It's easy to focus on the newest threat or the latest vendor report, but in most cases the first place to start is with your own past incidents.

Many attackers are opportunistic, attacking once due to a one-time occurrence such as a vulnerable system or misconfiguration. This is particularly common with ransomware operators or less sophisticated attackers. Other actors will attack continuously, often reusing the same tools against different targets. Tracking these groups is one of the most useful implementations of threat-intelligence processes. In many cases, analyzing these past incidents can lead to insights for detecting future attacks.

Another advantage of starting your targeting with past incidents is you'll already have considerable amounts of data in the form of incident reports, firsthand observations, and raw data (such as malware and drives) to continue to pull information from. Details or missed pieces of past incidents may be re-explored in the Find phase.

Criticality

Some information that you have identified in this phase will have a much more significant impact on operations than other pieces of information that you have gathered. For example, if, during the Find phase, you uncover indications of lateral movement in a sensitive network, that information is of a much higher priority than information indicating that someone is conducting scans against an external web server. Both issues should be investigated, but one clearly has a higher potential impact than the other: The higher-priority issues should be addressed first. Criticality is something that will vary from organization to organization, based on what is important to that particular organization.

Organizing Targeting Activities

It is important to understand how to organize and vet the major outputs of the Find phase. Taking time, whether it's 10 minutes or 10 hours, to really dig into what information is available and understand what you are potentially up against will put you in a good position to move forward. You must organize all of the information you have just collected and analyzed into a manageable format.

Hard Leads

Hard leads include information you have identified that has a concrete link to the investigation. Intelligence that is in the hard lead category provides context to things that have been identified and that you know are relevant. These leads have been seen in some part of the network, and during the Find phase you will be searching for related activity in other parts of the network. It is important to understand which pieces of intelligence are directly related to the incident and which pieces of intelligence are only potentially related. Similar to the data sources we discussed in Chapter 3, the different types of leads are all useful; they are just used in different ways.

Soft Leads

Much of the information that you have discovered in the Find phase will fall into the category of soft leads. *Soft leads* may be additional indicators or behaviors that you have identified that are related to some of the hard leads, but at this point you have not looked to see whether the indicators are present in your environment or what the implications of that are; that will be done in the Fix phase. Soft leads also include information from new reports on attacks that target similar organizations to yours, or things that have been shared by an information-sharing group that you know are legitimate threats but that may or may not be impacting you. Soft leads can also include behavioral heuristics, where you are looking for patterns of activity that stand out rather than a concrete piece of information. These types of searches, which are often technically more difficult to carry out, can produce significant results and generate a great deal of intelligence.

Grouping Related Leads

In addition to identifying which leads are hard and which are soft, it is a good idea to keep track of which leads are related to each other. The presence of hard leads, either from an active incident or a past incident, will often lead you to identify multiple soft leads during the Fix phase. This is another example of pivoting, where one piece of information leads you to multiple other pieces of information that may or may not be relevant to you. In many cases, your initial lead may have limited benefit, but a pivot could be extremely important. Keeping track of which soft leads are related to hard leads, or which soft leads are related to each other, will help you interpret and analyze the results of your investigation. In this Find phase, you are taking the time and effort to identify information related to the threats against your environment. You don't want to have to spend time re-analyzing the information because you do not remember where you got it from or why you cared about it in the first place.

Lead Storage and Documentation

All of these leads should be stored and documented in a way that will allow you to easily move into the subsequent phases and add information. There are a variety of ways that this information can be documented. Many teams still use good old Excel spreadsheets. Others have transitioned to tools such as threat-intelligence platforms (there are open source and commercial versions of these), which allow you to store indicators, add notes and tags, and in some cases link indicators together. The most important thing about documenting this stage of the incident-response process is that you find something that is compatible with your workflow and that allows the team visibility into what has been identified and what still needs to be vetted or investigated. We have seen many teams spend far more time than they need to in the Find phase because of duplicated efforts or lack of good coordination. Don't fall into this trap! Once you have identified information about the threat you are dealing with and documented it properly, you are ready to move into the next phase.

Although we won't discuss tracking incident-response activity and incident management until Chapter 7, it's important to quickly discuss lead tracking. Every incident responder has stumbled across a piece of information in a lead that they've seen before, only to fail to contextualize it. Taking the time to note your leads, even just solo in a notebook, is essential for success. Here's a solid format for saving your leads:

Lead
> The core observation or idea.

Datetime
> When it was submitted (important for context or SLAs).

Context
> How was this lead found—internal or external? Was it research-based or incident-based?

Analyst
> Who found the lead?

This approach is simple and easy but effective. Having these leads available will give you a starting point for reactive and proactive security efforts and will also contextualize ongoing incidents in many cases.

The Request for Information Process

Similar to leads, a request for information (sometimes called a request for intelligence) is the process of getting direction from external stakeholders into a team's incident response or intelligence cycle. This process is meant to make requests uniform and to enable them to be prioritized and easily directed to the right analyst.

Requests for information (or RFIs) may be simple (only a sentence and a link to a document) or complex (involving hypothetical scenarios and multiple caveats). All good RFIs should include the following information:

The request
> A summary of the question being asked.

The requestor
> Who do you send the information back to?

An output
> This can take many forms. Is the expected output IOCs? A briefing document? A presentation?

References
> If the question involves or was inspired by a document, this should be shared.

A priority or due date
> This is necessary for determining when something gets accomplished.

The RFI process needs to be relevant and workable inside your organization. Integration is key. It needs to be easy for stakeholders to submit requests and receive information, whether that be via a portal or email submission. If you or your team are frequently overrun by a high volume of informal RFIs, putting a formal system into place is one of the best ways to manage the workload. We'll discuss RFIs, specifically as intelligence products, more in Chapter 9.

Conclusion

The Find phase is the critical first step in the F3EAD process that allows you to clearly identify what it is that you are looking for. Find often equates to targeting and is closely related to the Direction phase of the intelligence cycle. If you do not know what your task is or what threat you are addressing, it is hard to address it properly. Find sets the stage for the other operations-focused phases in the F3EAD process.

You will not spend the same amount of time in the Find phase for each project. At times, the Find phase is done for you. Other times it involves only a small amount of digging. Other times the Find phase is a lengthy undertaking that involves multiple people within a team focusing on different aspects of the same threat. When faced with the latter, make sure to stay organized—document and prioritize leads so that you can move into the Fix phase with a comprehensive targeting package that includes exactly what you will be looking for.

Now that we have some idea about who and what we're looking for, it's time to dig into the technical investigation phase of incident response. We call this the Fix phase.

## CHAPTER 5

Fix

Never interrupt your enemy when he is making a mistake.
    —Napoléon Bonaparte

We do not gather intelligence just for the sake of having intelligence. At its core, intelligence is meant to enable actions, whether those actions involve strategic planning or providing support to the incident-response process. Intelligence can and should support incident response in a few key ways:

Detection
    Providing better starting points by creating improved alerting criteria

Enrichment
    Contextualizing information identified in the response process

Situational awareness
    Understanding attackers, methodologies, and tactics

The process of using previously identified intelligence or threat data to identify where an adversary is, either in your environment or externally, is called a *Fix*. In the Fix phase of F3EAD, all the intelligence you gathered in the Find phase is put to work tracking down signs of adversary activity on your networks. This chapter covers three ways to track the location of adversary activity—using indicators of compromise, adversary behavioral indicators (also known as TTPs), and adversary goals.

This chapter was tough to write, as entire books have been written about many of the items we'll cover. This discussion is not meant to be comprehensive; in fact, it should be thought of as a starting point. If you want to learn malware analysis, for example, it's not sufficient to read just a single section of a single chapter. Instead, read multiple books, learn from other experienced reverse engineers, and invest some time in the work. Additionally, many of the approaches taken in the Fix phase will be dramatically different based on the technologies in use in your organization. For example, memory analysis on Mac and Linux has similarities but is dramatically different on Windows. And, CrowdStrike's endpoint detection and response (EDR) tool Falcon is very different than Facebook's osquery. To focus on applying the intelligence we identified in the Find phase, we'll cover core concepts of incident response (focusing on the intersection of these techniques and good threat intelligence) and will call out resources for learning about the techniques in more detail. How you apply this chapter's material to your work will be up to you and your team!

Intrusion Detection

Intelligence supports intrusion detection in a variety of ways. Integrating intelligence into intrusion detection, however, is not always a straightforward process because there are various ways that an intrusion can manifest itself and various points at which an attacker's movements may be detected. Likewise, your security posture and internal visibility will also dictate where you will be able to identify attacker activity.

The two primary ways to detect intrusions are network alerting, which looks for signs of attacker communications both intra-network and extra-network, and system alerting, which looks for indications of attacker presence on the endpoint typically as the adversary moves throughout the network.

External Reflections

In addition to network and system alerting on potential intrusions, external reflections of intrusions are becoming more common. As companies become more accustomed and adept with sharing information about intrusions against their networks, external reflections become more valuable for detecting similar attempts against your own organization. In less ideal situations, the external reflections may come from places such as dark web marketplaces where your company data is for sale, or from a ransom email from an attacker that claims to have compromised your organization. In these situations, an asset-centric investigation can help to determine how (or whether) the information was accessed. Then, continue to move through the rest of the F3EAD process.

Network Alerting

Network alerting involves identifying network traffic that could indicate malicious activity. This type of alerting is most useful when the environment has been prepared to understand *expected* network activity and to engineer detection capabilities to support triage and investigation of *unexpected* activity. Several stages of the kill chain involve network communications between the attackers and the victim machine.

Attacker activities we can typically identify by using network traffic, expressed in Table 5-1 as ATT&CK enterprise tactics, include the following.

Table 5-1. ATT&CK enterprise tactic IDs and names

ATT&CK enterprise tactic ID	ATT&CK enterprise tactic name
TA0043	Reconnaissance
TA0001	Delivery
TA0011	Command and control
TA0008	Lateral movement
TA0010	Exfiltration
TA0040	Impact

Not all of these network alerting methods are equally effective, however. Let's dig into each of these activities and discuss under which circumstances they are useful and when they should be avoided.

Alerting on reconnaissance

Alerting on reconnaissance *seems* like the best place to start. After all, if you are able to identify potential attackers who are interested in your network ahead of time, you can prevent attacks outright. Unfortunately, alerting on reconnaissance is generally not worthwhile. Why? In most cases, it's a matter of the volume of potential reconnaissance events. If you've ever run a system directly on the internet without running a firewall, you know why. Aggressive scanning is going on constantly, some of it malicious, some of it legitimate research activity. Many useful security tools, including Shodan and Censys and other asset- and infrastructure-discovery resources, require frequent scanning to maintain an updated catalog of web-based assets. When defenders use scanning as a metric, they can claim extremely high numbers of cyber attacks, often citing millions of attacks in short time frames, but they're mostly referring to automated reconnaissance tools that may not be related to actual threats. In short, if you alert on every Nmap scan or DNS zone transfer attempt, you'll drown in high-volume/low-signal noise without any concrete actions to take.

This doesn't mean gathering reconnaissance information is useless. In advanced cases, reconnaissance information is an ideal place to start deception campaigns, something we'll talk about in the next chapter. For example, look at the excellent work done by GreyNoise (the company and the service) during the 2021 Log4J zero-day event. GreyNoise runs monitors for mass internet scanners (*https://oreil.ly/ 7pFui*) and was quickly able to identify systems scanning internet wide for relevant ports, including those throwing proof-of-concept or test exploits. While detecting these scanners didn't give enough information for GreyNoise to definitively identify attackers, it did give defenders a list of potential adversary systems to focus on and good examples of what to look for in the Reconnaissance phase of targeted attacks.

Alerting on delivery

The first place to focus high-signal alerting is the Delivery phase. In most cases, delivery means an email (for phishing—T1566), a website (for a drive-by compromise—T1189), or web service compromise (accessing a web application, database, or other service—T1190).

Your ability to alert on delivery depends greatly on the technologies you have available. Email is notoriously hard to alert on and often requires a purpose-built tool or heavy modifications to existing tools. The three big concerns during delivery are attachments, links, and metadata.

Attachments.   The most common form of delivery, especially for low- to mid-sophistication adversaries, in the last few years has been attachments—typically documents for commonly installed software containing exploits (although nonexploit social-engineering applications named to entice users to run them, such as screensavers, are also common). Adobe Acrobat and Microsoft Office files are common. Organizations can alert on attachments based on filenames, file types, file sizes, or inspecting content (however, this last technique can be tricky, given the various ways of embedding or compressing attachments). It can also be helpful to hook email attachments into your automated malware-analysis environment or sandbox, creating a proactive detonation environment. These can be commercial (and often come included in email-protection products) or built in-house using an automation tool like stoQ (*https://oreil.ly/xYkon*).

Links.   In some cases, malicious links in emails will lead users to a web page that is serving malware and will exploit the browser. Social-engineering attacks may also use links, sending users to fake login pages to harvest usernames and passwords for credential reuse attacks (described in the following sidebar).

Metadata.   Emails contain many types of rich metadata that organizations can alert on, but these pieces of data are often transitive. It's easy to alert on malicious email metadata, but it's also simple for attackers to change such metadata. That said, tracking information such as sender email address, sender IP address, intermediate transit servers (especially viewed as a pattern), and user agent data can all be useful for alerting.

Identifying novel or unique ways that attackers initiate their activities (aside from these common methods) means that we can come up with additional ways to detect the Delivery stage of an intrusion. This is one area where the sometimes dubious "see something, say something" approach can work in a defender's favor. Training your users to identify basic suspicious phishing techniques and report them via an email address (*phishing@company.com* for example) or a button in their mail client can often identify phishing campaigns early. Will every user be good at it? Unlikely. But, given many phishing attempts target a swath of users, there is a good chance *someone* will notice and report it. Don't underestimate using your users as detectors of intrusion; many of them will surprise you!

Credential Reuse

According to the Verizon Data Breach Investigations Report (*https://oreil.ly/gqvOl*) and everyone we've ever talked to, credential reuse continues to be one of the top ways that attackers get access to and move through your network. It makes sense, because usernames and passwords are not difficult for attackers to get their hands on. Weak passwords, password reuse, and numerous public password dumps make it easy for attackers to identify the credentials that will get them into a network. Once they are inside, getting additional credentials is even easier. Many phishing attacks are aimed at obtaining user credentials, which are then used to access the network. This ends up being a key of many "living off the land" style of attacks. Adversaries often get access to one system, monitor for password keystrokes or crack passwords, find reused accounts (especially IT or other administrator accounts), crack the passwords, and use those passwords to migrate between systems, establishing long-running persistence without having to re-exploit systems and often without triggering any detections.

Monitoring for credential reuse can be difficult; after all, legitimate users should be accessing the network so that behavior doesn't automatically stand out. If you have the proper systems in place, there are ways to detect this behavior. Methods include looking for logins from strange locations. If Alice lives and works in San Diego, a login from Italy may be a sign that something is wrong. In addition, logins at odd times or concurrent logins can also be a sign that something strange is going on. Even if you are unable to detect a suspicious login at the time of the activity, once you are in incident-response mode and you know that there is an attacker in your network, you can use logs to look for any suspicious activity and flag those accounts for further investigation and, during the Finish phase, password resets (maybe even use it as an opportunity to add two-factor authentication [2FA]).

Alerting on command and control

Eventually, the attacker needs to communicate with their systems (usually...there are a few rare exceptions). A lot happens between the Delivery and Command and Control phases of the kill cycle, but those are things most easily detected at the system level. Command and control, or C2, refers to the attacker interacting with their malware to execute actions, which by necessity results in network communication.

You can look for a few common characteristics in C2 communication:

Destination

The first and simplest of approaches. Hundreds of threat-intelligence products are dedicated to listing known bad locations, in terms of IPv4 addresses and domains. Many tools will let you blacklist and alert on known bad destinations. While you're at it, geolocation also has its uses in identifying unknown or unexpected geographic destinations (for example, "Why is our print server connecting to *X* country?").

Content

Most malware communicates by using encrypted and/or encoded messages to prevent detection. Although that does make it more difficult to know what is being transmitted, it also provides defenders the ability to search for encrypted messages where they shouldn't be. In an attempt to blend in, many pieces of malware will misuse common protocols, such as sending encrypted HTTP traffic over port 80/TCP, which is usually not encrypted. These mismatches of content and protocol can be a big tip-off. Metadata is also a fairly common class of content that attackers don't consider. For example, suspicious metadata might always use the same user agent string or common headers.

Frequency

Unless the attacker manages to take over a publicly facing server, they likely won't be able to initiate communication with their malware at will since it is likely non-routable. As a result, most malware reaches from a host on an internal network out to a command-and-control server, which we call a *beacon*. This communication usually takes place at regular intervals, as often as every few minutes (generally for operational, in-use malware) and as long as every couple of months (generally to enable reinfection if the initial malware was removed). It's often possible to identify patterns in the frequency of communication and search for that.

Duration

Most malware isn't that smart, and the messages it sends are often not that interesting. In some cases, even though the messages are encrypted, they may not have a lot to say. If this happens with enough frequency, patterns may emerge, such as a no-operation message that always has the same byte length.

Combinations

Often one characteristic isn't enough to generate a high-fidelity alert, but a combination of them may be. This takes time, recognition, and sometimes a bit of luck to develop a pattern and find a way to detect it.

Many times, it is possible to alert on indicators associated with C2, such as a known malicious IP or domain, but by better understanding the nature of C2 behavior, we can alert on suspicious traffic even when we do not know that the destination itself is malicious. This level of understanding is usually possible only via extensive reverse engineering, where the ins and outs of how the protocols work can be laid bare.

Command and control via misuse of shared resources. C2 is often subject to trends. For example, in the late 2000s, most criminal malware used Internet Relay Chat (IRC) for C2. Defenders caught on, alerting or blocking 6666–7000/TCP, the common IRC ports. Attackers then moved to running IRC on port 80/TCP, and so the cat-and-mouse game has continued, forming trends.

Today, adversaries in many cases use the same services we do, complicating these once-easy detections. The best thing an intrusion detection or hunt team can do is understand which services their organization uses and figure out which resources they should see and investigate those they don't know. Shadow IT might make this complicated, but even attacks on that infrastructure are important to investigate—shadow IT getting compromised can be just as damaging (if not worse) than regular infrastructure. Another infamous example of network intrusion, using social media, was the Russian-nexus threat actor Turla using Instagram, specifically Britney Spears Instagram comments, to execute command and control (*https://oreil.ly/TgCiT*).

One of the current and likely ongoing trends in C2 is the use of social media and software-as-a-service (SaaS) sites. Given the ubiquity of Transport Layer Security (TLS), it's often difficult to inspect this traffic, and given that the destinations aren't malicious, it can be difficult to detect and respond to. This can be complicated, particularly with platform-as-a-service (PaaS) companies where shared resources can be used in many ways, making it difficult to build generalized profiles of nonmalicious traffic and usage.

No command-and-control malware. In rare cases, malware will have no command and control at all. This is difficult to accomplish, as such malware needs to have 100% of its instructions before being delivered and must be able to accomplish its goals without any changes or updates. This is usually done only out of necessity, such as in air-gapped networks. It usually requires considerable reconnaissance to understand the lay of the land before starting. In cases like this, detection needs to focus on delivery and impact.

Alerting on impact

Similar to detection of command and control, detecting impact on the network focuses on unusual traffic patterns that indicate data entering or leaving the network or unusual interactions between internal systems. Data entering the network isn't commonly seen (though may be seen more in the future as disinformation becomes more prevalent). What is highly common is data exfiltration.

Data exfiltration is often the goal of many attacks, especially those focused on the compromise and theft of intellectual property. Each attacker will have their own preferred method of exfiltration, but in the end they all have to accomplish the same thing: get a lot of information (anywhere from a few dozen lines up to hundreds of gigabytes) from victim systems to an attacker-controlled system. How this is accomplished varies, but the end goal doesn't.

Defenders can take a few approaches to detecting data exfiltration. One is to focus on content, which is what gave rise to data-loss prevention tools. For instance, if you want to prevent the theft of credit card information, you'll search for examples of four groups of four numbers (the credit card number) followed by three numbers (the card verification value, or CVV) and then a month/year combo (the expiration date). On the surface this seems simple, but the devil is in the details. What if the credit card number is split into four sets of four numbers in one file and the dates are in another file? What if the CVVs use a letter substitution for the numbers and instead of 123 the CVV is sent as ABC? It gets only more complicated from there, such as if the attacker is using a network protocol over TLS where the encryption blocks your packet-sniffing tools looking for card numbers.

The second approach that defenders can take to detecting data exfiltration is to focus on metadata around the network connections. If the attacker stole 5 gigabytes of credit card data, they have to move 5 gigabytes of data no matter how it's encrypted (ignoring compression).

Fixing on malicious indicators from network activity is a good way to start to identify what is going on in your network and to better understand the attackers who are targeting you. It is not the only way, though. The ATT&CK techniques we've discussed, for example, are a great basis for detecting not just IOCs but the techniques in general. Next, we will discuss how to fix malicious activity from a system perspective.

System Alerting

The complement to network monitoring is system monitoring. In the same way that network alerting is focused on particular aspects of the kill chain, system alerting can be divided into the areas in Table 5-2, as expressed in ATT&CK enterprise tactics.

Table 5-2. Key areas of system alerting, aligned with the kill chain

ATT&CK enterprise tactic	Kill chain phase	Adversary goal
TA0001	Initial Access	The adversary is trying to get into the network.
TA0002	Execution	The adversary is trying to run malicious code.
TA0003	Persistence	The adversary is trying to maintain their foothold.
TA0004	Privilege Escalation	The adversary is trying to gain higher-level permissions.

ATT&CK enterprise tactic	Kill chain phase	Adversary goal
TA0005	Defense Evasion	The adversary is trying to avoid being detected.
TA0006	Credential Access	The adversary is trying to steal account names and passwords.
TA0007	Discovery	The adversary is trying to figure out the environment.
TA0008	Lateral Movement	The adversary is trying to move through the environment.
TA0009	Collection	The adversary is trying to gather data of interest to their goal.
TA0011	Command and Control	The adversary is trying to communicate with compromised systems to control them.
TA0010	Exfiltration	The adversary is trying to steal data.
TA0040	Impact	The adversary is trying to manipulate, interrupt, or destroy systems and data.

System alerting is always dependent on the operating system and the collection system. With rare exceptions, most EDR tools—open source and commercial—are focused on a particular operating system. This is necessary because most security alerting takes place at the lowest levels of the operating system, requiring deep integration into process management, memory management, filesystem access, and so forth.

As a result, you need to carefully consider the methods of integrating intelligence for system alerting, both in terms of the target operating system and the tools you'll use. For example, some string-based indicators may be useful on multiple systems, but registry keys are useful indicators only on Windows. At the same time, tools such as commercial antivirus programs may prohibit direct content integration, while open source tools such as osquery can't function without custom detection content development.

Alerting on exploitation

Companies—in fact, entire industries like the antivirus space—have been built on the idea of alerting on and blocking exploitation. Exploitation remains a natural place to alert (and disrupt) because it is where the transfer of control shifts from the defender to the attacker. The second the attacker begins exploitation, they are affecting the operation of defender resources.

Exploitation usually manifests itself in one of two ways:

- A new process begins running on a user's system, one that's created and controlled by the attacker—for example, using PowerShell to run adversary-created scripts.

- A previously running process (either system- or user-controlled) is modified and co-opted to do something new and different.

How exploitation is accomplished varies, but the result is the same: The system is executing code under the control of the attacker. The primary approach to alerting on exploitation is to track this activity in near real time, monitoring processes on a system at different points in time and identifying changes. Unexpected or anomalous activity can indicate an intrusion. This includes modification of underlying binaries, applications running from unexpected or incorrect directories, or even new processes with names meant to blend in at first glance (using homoglyphs or near homoglyphs such as *rundll32.exe* versus *rund1l32.exe* with a 1 instead of an l) to confuse analysts. Detecting unknown or previously unseen processes is a good start for alerting on a system and can leverage a variety of tools.

Alerting on installation

Installation is the bread and butter of on-system alerting. Even if an attacker can execute their own code on a victim's system during installation, it's almost never the end of the attacker's actions. An exploited process, whether modified from a normal process or created after execution, will eventually, end and after it does, the attacker will lose their foothold.

As a result, after exploitation, the next step for most attackers is to make sure they can maintain access. In a single-system phishing-style compromise, this usually means installing a second stage that maintains persistence and adds capabilities the attackers can use to execute their objectives. These capabilities are often bundled together into a modular tool, often called a *remote-access Trojan* (RAT), or a rootkit, as we've discussed. During the Find phase, we should have identified information about the tools commonly used by actors, which can help us know what to look for in the Fix phase.

Alerting on impact

Depending on the desired outcome, an attacker may need to access specific resources in order to carry out their objectives. In most cases, the impact follows the CRUD acronym:

Create
    Writing new files to disk from original material

Read
    Reading files currently on a system

Update
    Changing the content of files already on the system

Delete
    Removing files on a system, generally with extra steps to keep it from being recovered later

In some cases, attackers may do more than one action at a time, tying them together for more complex results. Ransomware-style attacks do three of these in rapid succession:

Read

The ransomware malware reads all the personal files on the machine.

Create

It then creates a new file from all the read files but encrypted with the attacker's key.

Delete

Finally, it deletes the user's original unencrypted files so the user must pay the ransom to get access to the original files.

Simple, and often effective.

Ransomware attacks are one example, but impact varies greatly from attack to attack. For instance, an attacker may read data to exfiltrate it across the network to steal intellectual property, one of the most common advanced persistent threat (APT) patterns. In another case, an attacker may simply delete all files (or key files) to render the system's resources unusable (so-called wiper attacks). Finally, an attacker may create a new application to use the system for secondary attacks, such as pivoting within a network or launching DoS attacks.

Alerting on these actions is complicated because creating, reading, updating, and deleting files are common actions that at some level are the fundamental reason we use computers to begin with. The creation of a file *can* be suspicious—or it can be a user performing an action that computers were designed to do. Leveraging this type of alerting depends on understanding the actions an attacker may want to take. If you're concerned with stealing money in a bank, monitoring actions that can access ledgers is key. If it's intellectual property the attackers are after, you may want to identify large uploads of files across the network or creation of big archives on disk. This requires a combination of creativity, experience, and the ability to think like the enemy.

By combining the information found on a threat actor during the Find phase and the information about how to detect malicious activity on our own network, we can now plan to look for signs of an attacker in our environment.

Fixing Road Runner

In Chapter 3, we developed a kill chain for the actor Grey Spike, who is carrying out the campaign codenamed Road Runner. Now we can use that information to better understand what attacker tools and activities we should look for in this phase. We identified that during the Road Runner campaign, Grey Spike uses avenues such as spear-phishing and strategic web compromises to deliver their tools and installs additional tools to maintain access and interact with the host machine, including Hikit, Derusbi, and the ZOX family of tools. We also know that they typically look for information related to economic, environmental, and energy policies, and they often compromise large numbers of host machines in a network to find the information they are looking for. Using this intelligence, we can start to build a plan of the types of activities to look for in our environment.

Network activity

Here are the types of network activity we want to look for while trying to detect Road Runner actions:

Spear phishing emails
Search email logs for senders, subjects, or attachment names that are related to Road Runner. Alerting users to the details of these spear-phishing campaigns will encourage them to inform the security team if they remember seeing any similar emails in the past and will ensure they are on the lookout for any future such emails.

Web compromises
Search web logs for any successful or attempted visits to websites that had been compromised by Road Runner. Scoping is important in this stage. If a website was compromised for only a short time before it was identified and remediated, search for activity to those sites only around the time that it was known to be compromised.

Command-and-control activity
Identifying the tools that are commonly used by Road Runner for C2 activities can help you know what activity to look for. Additional research will need to be done at this point to fully understand the actor's tools and how they function; for example, the ZOX family has been known to use PNG images to communicate with a command-and-control server.

System activity
Now that we know more about what activity we are looking for in our network, we can begin the process of investigating suspicious activity in our system, such as the following:

Exploitation
Some actors are known to exploit certain vulnerabilities over others, so understanding which vulnerabilities are targeted, and if and where those vulnerabilities exist on your network, can give you a good starting point for where to look for attacker activity. Road Runner was seen exploiting CVE-2013-3893, which is a vulnerability in Internet Explorer, so it would be useful to understand which

systems have this vulnerability present and to look for additional signs of exploitation that were identified in the Find phase.

Installation

Knowing which tools are commonly used by the actor and how those tools work allows you to build a better picture of what will be effective in your network. Road Runner uses both a 32-bit and a 64-bit variant of Hikit, depending on the victim's network topography, so understanding your network will help you know what to look for at this phase. Identify which files are generated during installation and which directories they are located in.

Impact

We know that Road Runner is looking for information on economic, environmental, and energy policies, so if we know which systems have that type of information, we can look for any signs of files being accessed, gathered, and moved off those systems. However, we also know that the actor likes to expand their presence to many hosts to look for files and potentially move throughout the network, so we can look for signs of lateral movement in the network, even on systems we would not think of as a typical target.

Now that we have a good handle on what information from the Find phase is going to be applicable to intrusion detection in our network and our system, we can move on to investigating Road Runner's activity in our networks. Doing so involves activities such as traffic analysis, memory analysis, and malware analysis, which we will deep-dive into next.

Intrusion Investigation

Separating alerting and investigation workflows requires walking a fine line because they often use the same tools, just in different ways and often by totally different teams! If alerting is about reduction (finding the smallest, most specific bit of data that will tip you off to malicious activity), then investigation is about gathering as much data as possible to get context and then reducing data again into a cogent analysis. This expansion (collection and processing) and then reduction (analysis and dissemination) workflow is common in both security analysis and intelligence analysis.

In this section, we are going to explore the key techniques and tools of intrusion investigation. That said, this is a major topic unto itself, and you could study it for multiple years. If you're new to these topics, we recommend *Incident Response & Computer Forensics* by Jason T. Luttgens et al.[1]

---

1 Jason T. Luttgens et al., *Incident Response & Computer Forensics,* Third Edition (New York: McGraw-Hill Education, 2014).

Network Analysis

The first place most intrusion investigations begin is by investigating network traffic. Unfortunately, most incidents aren't internally discovered. Many incidents begin with a third-party reporting nothing but a command-and-control IP address.

Network traffic analysis can be broken into the following major techniques based on a combination of tools and volume of traffic:

Traffic analysis
    Using metadata to understand attacker activity

Signature-based analysis
    Looking for known bad patterns

Full content analysis
    Using every single packet to understand the attack

We'll dig into each of these in the upcoming sections. Let's start with traffic analysis.

Traffic analysis

Traffic analysis is not unique to computer networks. In fact, traffic analysis largely developed from analyzing radio transmissions, and many techniques can be traced to World War I (*https://oreil.ly/wRtjp*). Traffic analysis involves identifying adversary activity based on metadata—patterns of how the adversary communicates—rather than the content of the communication itself. As a result, this technique uses the sparsest data set (a record of megabytes of full content activity may create only 100 bytes worth of metadata), tracking information like this:

- Endpoints (either IP addresses or domains)
- Ports
- Bytes in/out
- Connection length and start/end times
- Frequency and regularity

We refer to these groups of metadata as *network flows*. Even with these small amounts of information, a huge amount of insight can be gained by a trained analyst. When investigating network flows, analysts should look for the following activities:

- Connections to a known bad IP address, which can indicate command-and-control activity.
- Frequent, regular, short-duration, low-byte in/out connections, which can indicate malware beaconing, checking in for new instructions.

- A connection to a never-before-seen domain with a long duration and large bytes out/low bytes in, which could indicate data exfiltration.

- Port 445 connections from a known compromised host to other internal hosts, which could indicate data collection (445/TCP is Microsoft SMB file sharing).

All these and far more can be discovered based on investigating limited network traffic metadata.

A variety of methods are used to collect data for traffic analysis. Network flow data (NetFlow being the Cisco-specific implementation, not the generic term) is often available from various networking equipment. This data is often easy to collect because it's useful for both the security team and the network team, allowing for dual use and split infrastructure costs. Another security-specific method for collecting network flow data is Bro, a network security monitoring tool that focuses on deeper metadata than basic NetFlow, including protocol information and signature-based detection (we'll get to that later). Carnegie Melon's Computer Emergency Response Team Coordination Center (CERT/CC's) SiLK (*https://oreil.ly/66Gi7*) and QoSient's Argus (*https://oreil.ly/kjCdN*) are other open source tools for capturing traditional network flow information. Other systems that can generate flow information include network proxies and firewalls.

Tools for analyzing flow information can range from very general to very specialized. Logging and full-text search tools like Splunk are often used to great effect. Purpose-built tools like the slightly dated but still highly relevant FlowBAT (*https://oreil.ly/ NanFm*) add flow-specific operators. It's also possible to build custom tools using graph databases like Neo4J (*https://neo4j.com*), NetworkX (*https://networkx.org*), or even Synapse (*https://oreil.ly/pnaB8*) (more on that one later).

Another advantage of flow-based data analysis over signature-based or full content analysis is the density of information in flow. Since only the metadata is kept, storage per record for flow information is low, making it both less expensive to store and faster to process. This means that while keeping and searching more than a few months of signature-based information can be cost-prohibitive, keeping significantly longer flow-based data may be possible. Although flow data cannot completely answer all network security questions the way full content can, the information density and long-term storage make it a valuable capability. Add to that the ease of collection and analysis, and it's clear why traffic analysis is such a high-value data source.

Applying intelligence to traffic analysis. The most common application of intelligence to traffic analysis is using traffic data to look for connections to known bad resources (e.g., IPs, domains) or to identify patterns of anomalous activity by trusted systems (such as scanning, lateral movement, or beaconing). While simple techniques, they are often effective and easily automated. The danger of using traffic analysis exclusively is that it may result in false positives based on a lack of content understanding, such as dual-use IPs and domains that are malicious for only short periods of time such as web services that store arbitrary text or files (*https://oreil.ly/-pOG0*).

Another way to apply intelligence to traffic analysis is to look for traffic patterns that indicate malicious activity, such as short and repeated communications, communications during nonworking hours, or communications to newly observed domains, which are domains that have only recently become active. Most users do not visit a domain mere hours after it has been created. This can be a sign of command-and-control activity. Combining passive DNS monitoring and network flow analysis makes it possible to automate hunting for those domains.

Gathering data from traffic analysis.   It may seem counterintuitive, but traffic analysis is often a great source for generating leads. By looking for top talkers (hosts generating or receiving the highest frequency or amount of traffic) or bottom talkers (hosts generating or receiving the smallest frequency or amount of traffic), you can often identify important leads. Detecting rare hosts (hosts with very little communication to or from your network) is especially important because attackers will generally use new infrastructure to avoid bad reputations, but don't underestimate looking at large traffic amounts (top talkers) as well. It's important to discern whether a system sending gigabytes of traffic on a Sunday morning is doing offsite backups or exfiltrating data.

Signature-based analysis

Between the sparseness of network traffic data and the comprehensive full content monitoring is signature-based analysis. While traffic analysis is purely focused on metadata around connections, signature-based analysis is monitoring for specific content. Unlike traffic analysis, which can be pulled from a variety of sources and tools, signature-based analysis is the realm of purpose-built systems called *intrusion detection systems*.

Intrusion detection systems (IDS) combine network capture, a rules engine, and a logging method. The rules are applied to the network traffic, and when one matches, a log is generated. A wide variety of IDS are available, in both commercial and open source options. At the same time, one ubiquitous standard exists for signatures: the Snort signatures (*https://oreil.ly/ukKnO*). Here's an example of a Snort IDS signature:

```
alert tcp any any -> any any (msg:"Sundown EK - Landing";
flow:established,to_server;
content:"GET";
http_method;
pcre:"\/[a-zA-Z0-9]{39}\/[a-zA-Z0-9]{6,7}\.(swf|php)$";
http_uri;
reference:http://malware.dontneedcoffee.com/2015/06/\
   fast-look-at-sundown-ek.html;
```

```
class-type: trojan-activity;
rev:1;)
```

Let's explore a subset of these keywords and actions for Snort signatures (Snort has a lot of options; check out snort.org (*https://snort.org*) to find more!). This example signature breaks down as follows:

```
alert
```

The first word specifies the action to take if the signature matches. Snort has a variety of actions (though other IDS that use Snort's signature format (*https://oreil.ly/4C8sp*) may implement only a subset of them), summarized in Table 5-3.

Table 5-3. Variety of Snort actions

Action keyword	Action definition
alert	Generate an alert using the selected alert method, and then log the packet.
log	Log the packet.
pass	Ignore the packet.
activate	Alert and then turn on another dynamic rule.
dynamic	Remain idle until activated by an activate rule, and then act as a log rule.
drop	Block and log the packet.
reject	Block the packet, log it, and then send a TCP reset if the protocol is TCP, or an ICMP port unreachable message if the protocol is UDP.
sdrop	Block the packet but do not log it.

By far, the most common action is alert, but the others can be wildly powerful in the right situation:

```
tcp any any -> any any
```

This next clause in the example Snort IDS signature specifies many of the same characteristics from traffic analysis and applies them as limiting factors. The first word specifies the protocol (most likely TCP or UDP). The rest of this clause is key and takes the following generic form:

```
SOURCE_LOCATION SOURCE_PORT -> DESTINATION_LOCATION DESTINATION_PORT
```

Locations can be a few different things. It's perfectly valid to use an IP address or domain name for a location, but Snort allows for lists of multiple locations as well.

Inside the parentheses (starting in our example with msg) is the bulk of the rule. There are a wide variety of configurations for describing network connections, far more than we can cover, but here are some core options to know:

```
msg:"Sundown EK - Landing";
```

The msg is the alert name. This is what comes through in logging (along with a bunch of other content):

```
content:"GET";
```

The content field finds regular ASCII strings in packet content:

```
pcre:"\/[a-zA-Z0-9]{39}\/[a-zA-Z0-9]{6,7}\.(swf|php)$";
```

Snort signatures can also contain Perl Compatible Regular Expressions, or pcre, a way of specifying patterns instead of explicit content:

```
reference:http://malware.dontneedcoffee.com/2015/06/fast-\
    look-at-sundown-ek.html;
```

Finally, the reference field includes links to information that gives details on the threat that a signature looks for.

Being able to understand and work with signatures is the key to implementing and using signature-based detection successfully.

Applying intelligence to signature-based analysis.   Once an IDS is in place, the key to applying intelligence is twofold. The first is in signature creation. An obvious direct way to apply intelligence is to create new signatures based on intelligence you've received or developed. Applying intelligence well requires understanding your IDS capabilities, as well as experience creating and tuning signatures.

Second, effectively applying intelligence to signature-based analysis requires not just creation of signatures, but also modification and removal. Having inaccurate or nonactionable signatures slows incident response, forcing teams to waste time on fruitless investigations or analyses. It takes experience to develop an understanding for when a signature is losing usefulness and when it should be modified versus removed.

Gathering data from signature-based analysis.   Signature-based analysis is a limited but important technique, given signatures must be based on known (or strongly suspected) bad patterns. It's difficult to write signatures for purely hypothetical activities, but it can be done with practice and good engineering. To that end, building signatures is only part of engineering good signatures. In addition, you'll want large corpuses of known good traffic (to test for true positives) and known bad traffic (to test for false negatives). Even more useful is the ability to do limited deployments, sometimes called *canary deployments*, to test new signatures against real-world traffic within your environment, such as deploying to one or two sensors rather than all of them. Lastly, analysts and engineers benefit from having the ability to deploy and remove signatures quickly, which allows them to test new signatures and remove bad ones before there is impact.

What signature-based analysis can do is key you into the patterns and content of past attacks, including bad sources and destinations, so when a signature triggers against a certain endpoint, that endpoint may be a good place to start investigating. You may need to investigate another data source, either traffic or full content, but chances are you may find a plethora of information with signature-based analysis.

Full content analysis

On the opposite end of the spectrum from traffic analysis is full content—literally capturing every bit and byte sent across the network. From there, information can be searched, reassembled, and analyzed in a wide variety of ways. Unlike traffic or signature analysis, which cannot be reanalyzed after real time since it's metadata, the huge benefit of full content is that it can be reanalyzed or analyzed differently as long as the traffic is still stored (including regenerating metadata after the fact). The downside of full content analysis is the storage requirement. Full content monitoring literally requires keeping a copy of every bit of network traffic, which for most enterprises means storing immense amounts of data. This has become an increasingly head-scratching task in recent years; in the 2020s the vast majority of data is encrypted, which means it doesn't compress well (too much entropy) and it can't really be searched beyond traffic and signature analysis. It's tough to justify storing terabytes of opaque data that may or may not ever be useful or readable.

At the most basic, full content analysis lets you look at every single element of a piece of network traffic in a way that no other technique allows. Using a tool such as Wireshark (*https://www.wireshark.org*), you can dig into every element at every level of the open systems interconnection (OSI) model. This is often the basis for creating IDS signatures. Raw network traffic like this also allows you to look for specific items that other tools might not detect.

Full content analysis allows analysts to rerun traffic and signature analysis after developing new intelligence. For example, if you create a new signature for C2 traffic after an investigation, full content will allow you to rerun that new signature against earlier network traffic. In this way, full content essentially acts as a network time machine, allowing you to use new intelligence on old network traffic. Raw packets also allow engineers to apply new or different tools when doing network analysis, even the same tools with different configurations, retroactively.

Finally, using full content is the only way to do full user activity re-creation. For instance, if a user triggered an alert for data exfiltration via FTP, it might be useful to look at everything else that endpoint was doing at that time. This could reveal secondary but important information, such as the C2 mechanism controlling that exfiltration. This type of full content analysis requires specialized tools such as NetWitness (*https://www.netwitness.com*) or Arkime (*https://oreil.ly/mdzNY*) (formerly aol/moloch) to re-create the many levels of most network packets.

Applying intelligence to full content analysis. As you might expect, application of intelligence is particularly flexible with full content analysis. All the techniques from traffic analysis and signature analysis apply to full content, as well as a few unique options:

- At the packet level, tools such as Wireshark allow filtering based on a variety of characteristics, including IP addresses and other characteristics you can get from intelligence or even other network-monitoring tools.

- Intelligence can also be applied by rerunning new intelligence against old network traffic.

- Using intelligence at the full content re-creation layer allows for hunting for secondary activity.

Gathering data from full content analysis. Where full content really shines is in gathering data. Full content analysis is the easiest and most comprehensive source for gathering data and developing further intelligence. Actual packet data allows you to pivot from information about bad endpoints to information about bad data. This makes things possible that metadata cannot allow such as developing signatures, extracting files, or even looking into protocol anomalies or errors that some tools may miss, such as C2 that works by deliberately causing errors in network protocols.

 In a world of TLS, alerting on network traffic content has become more and more complicated. It is possible, through a variety of means, to decrypt TLS sessions and extract contents, but this comes with a variety of risks, and different organizations may take different approaches to this. On one hand, TLS decryption is expensive; in most corporate settings it takes commercial solutions that require configuration. On the other hand, TLS decryption comes with significant privacy ramifications, both legally and policy wise. It's an invasive procedure that, if not configured correctly, risks exposing users' medical, financial, and other personal data. Be sure to work with policy makers and legal counsel if you're considering decryption TLS.

Learning more

There are a number of great places to learn more about network analysis. For example, check out *The Practice of Network Security Monitoring* by Richard Bejtlich[2] or *Practical Packet Analysis* by Chris Sanders.[3] Want something more hands-on?

---

2 Richard Bejtlich, *The Practice of Network Security Monitoring* (San Francisco: No Starch Press, 2013).

3 Chris Sanders, *Practical Packet Analysis: Using Wireshark to Solve Real-World Network Problems*, Third Edition (San Francisco: No Starch Press, 2017).

Consider enrolling in the SANS courses Network Monitoring and Threat Detection In-Depth (*https://oreil.ly/PNZzn*) or Advanced Network Forensics: Threat Hunting, Analysis, and Incident Response (*https://oreil.ly/211xB*).

Live Response

Live response is analysis of a potentially compromised system without taking it offline by dynamically collecting state information. Most forensics analysis requires turning the system offline, losing system state information such as active processes. It also risks tipping off the attacker and is widely disruptive to users as well.

Live response pulls the following information:

- Configuration information
- System state
- Important file and directory information
- Common persistence mechanisms
- Installed applications and versions

Although they do not always provide everything necessary to investigate a system, most live responses at least provide enough information to determine whether more thorough analysis is necessary.

In the beginning, live response tools were commonly built with scripting technologies such as Perl, Python, or PowerShell, and as a result, many were open source. Classic examples, now largely deprecated, include Yelp's OSXCollector (*https://oreil.ly/HpZer*), Loki (*https://oreil.ly/4ojqL*) and Fenrir (*https://oreil.ly/YefBC*) by Florian Roth (*https://oreil.ly/WZFeE*), Dave Hull's Kansa (*https://oreil.ly/WlXHs*), Sekoia Lab's FastIR tools (*https://oreil.ly/sScCt*), and Nextron System's THOR (*https://oreil.ly/PEabZ*).

So how do you integrate intelligence into live response? Live response tools are typically built to collect a set group of artifacts without any configuration, making their use repeatable and fast. Intelligence integration is generally focused on the backend and is going to be dependent on tools.

For example, OSXCollector (now deprecated but still one of the best examples of these tools) outputs a JSON blob with system information. This is meant to be analyzed using another Yelp project, osxcollector_output_filters, which can be integrated with multiple intelligence sources, including custom indicators and intelligence services like OpenDNS. This post-processing approach is common for complicated collections and can be seen in other tools such as Mandiant's Redline (which straddles live response and memory analysis).

You may be asking why so many live response tools have been deprecated. Well, in short, they've been subsumed into other tools. Most live response tools are highly manual, requiring an analyst to put hands on keyboard. In large incidents, this quickly becomes untenable. It didn't take long until engineers started trying to automate the deployment and use of these tools, but we'll discuss that more in "Enterprise Detection and Response."

Memory Analysis

Similar to live response, memory analysis focuses on collecting volatile system state in memory. Given that every process on a system requires memory to run, this technique provides an excellent vantage point to gather information, especially from tools that attempt to run stealthily with limited system footprint.

Comparable to some live response tools, memory analysis almost always has a clear break between collection and analysis, grabbing everything first and then focusing on processing results and applying intelligence after the fact. Mandiant's Redline memory analysis tool (*https://oreil.ly/a50ij*) always collects system memory first but uses OpenIOC later at analysis time.

Redline is one tool for memory analysis and is great as an all-in-one solution that's able to do collection and analysis together, but one of the best aspects of the split between collection and analysis is the opportunity to mix and match collection and analysis utilities. A great example is the Volatility toolkit.

Volatility (*https://oreil.ly/aDKE6*) is a Python-based, open source memory analysis framework. Volatility does not gather memory itself the way Redline does. Instead, it reads the memory formats from a variety of collection tools that run on a variety of operating systems. Volatility provides a framework and set of scripts for analyzing memory, detecting malware running in memory, extracting cryptographic keys—in fact, anything you can find a plug-in to do.

Integrating intelligence into memory analysis is obviously very tool-dependent. Volatility makes it easy to use Yara signatures to scan memory for specific artifacts. Additionally, Volatility is highly scriptable, making it possible to automate hunting for specific processes, memory artifacts, cryptographic primitives, and so forth. Volatility's ability to parse out everything from basic strings to very high-level information like certificates means you can apply indicators from other phases to memory analysis. Using Redline instead? Redline will accept indicators in the form of OpenIOC, which can then be applied directly to an individual memory capture. To learn more about memory analysis, check out *The Art of Memory Forensics* by Michael Ligh et al.[4]

---

4 Michael Ligh et al., *The Art of Memory Forensics: Detecting Malware and Threats in Windows, Linux, and Mac Memory* (Indianapolis: Wiley, 2014).

Disk Analysis

Traditional disk forensics (sometimes called *dead disk* or *dead system forensics*) typically involves using specialized tools to extract filesystem information from the raw bits and bytes on a hard drive. The information on a hard drive is unintelligible at first glance. It contains endlessly nested structures at the hardware, filesystem, operating system, and data-format level, similar to the OSI model. Peeling through these layers is a process called *file carving*.

Carving works from the very lowest levels, building up the various data structures until files, data streams, and other operating system artifacts become available. This isn't done by hand, but by using specialized tools such as EnCase, FTK, or Autopsy. Once the data is carved, analysis can begin. From there, these tools make it possible to browse the system much like being on the system itself. An analyst can export specific files and look through logs and operating system–specific constructs like alternate data streams and registries on Windows. The forensics software may have extremely powerful search, even allowing for searches across specific types of files such as email.

The power of an experienced forensic analyst is their understanding of exactly where to go looking, based on what's being hunted for. For instance, if you have a compromised machine, a forensic analyst should be able to look at common persistence mechanisms, identify any malware running, and then acquire any artifacts the malware dropped. Additionally, the analyst may pull secondary pieces of data, such as logs that took place around the time frame of malware installation or activity. This is often an interim step, and the forensic analyst will usually pass much of what they collect to other analysts (such as passing malware to a reverse engineer, which we'll get into later in this chapter).

Like network traffic, disk forensic analysis often runs into encryption. While a difficult-to-configure add-on a few years ago in modern operating systems, strong end-to-end disk encryption has become the default. This means even successful forensic collection may not lead to meaningful data. Forensic engineers often build password-cracking systems to try to find user passwords, which allow them to extract the logical filesystems after decryption. In more recent years, computer manufacturers have countered this by tying more encryption to hardware modules, making the user password only one of the necessary decryption primitives. While in some environments this may be worth continuing to attack, most enterprises have moved to EDR tools that operate while the system is live and leave encryption in place while still allowing file carving.

Applying intelligence to disk analysis

Applying intelligence to disk analysis isn't terribly common. While some tools may allow searching for certain strings or indicators, in most cases this is more easily done in logging tools or network-wide systems like IDS or endpoint-detection systems. Typically, the goal of disk analysis is to carve out useful artifacts to be analyzed by others. After specific files are extracted, such as a potential malware artifact or phishing email, intelligence can be applied more directly.

Gathering data from disk analysis

System disks, especially of compromised machines, are a treasure trove for investigators and in many cases hold answers that are difficult to discover with other means. Disk analysis is also less volatile than other methods and more stateful. In memory analysis or live response, by contrast, the analysis takes place at a single point in time, so it's possible that an important artifact might not be observable or that analysts would ask a different question based on what they've learned during the investigation.

With disk analysis, the analyst can collect what they think they need to start, say, a piece of malware. Then, after further analysis, they may realize they missed an important configuration file. Because of the time-dependent nature of disk analysis, that file is likely still on disk, and the forensic engineer can go back and collect it.

The most useful sources of disk information for investigation and intelligence are as follows:

- Persistence mechanisms
- Temporary files
- Hidden files and data streams
- Files located in unallocated space
- Malware and configurations
- Indications of impact

Enterprise Detection and Response

You may be saying to yourself at this point that there seem to be a whole lot of tools built for analyzing various pieces of host compromise such as live response, memory, and disk. Heck, even antivirus tools. It sure would be a lot easier if someone just *combined all of these* into a single enterprise system that could do everything!

As you might have guessed (and likely already use in your enterprise), they did. Enterprise detection and response (EDR) tools combine as many investigative tools as possible into singular packages aimed at doing everything a security team needs to do on a host including:

- Proactive detection of threats
- Proactive detection of anomalies

- Investigative actions including host interrogation, system state collection, even memory and network capture
- Post compromise remediation such as removing malware
- Remote system management, running scripts, and many other management tasks

Basically, EDR tools can provide anything and everything an analyst could want for identifying, blocking, and remediating a system compromise. The goal in most of these systems (such as SentinelOne, CrowdStrike Falcon, Carbon Black, even Facebook's osquery depending on configuration) is to be a one-stop shop for analysts no matter which portion of the investigation.

Given how good that sounds, what's the issue? Well…combining a lot of systems rarely leads to perfect coverage, and trying to do everything often means trade-offs will be made. That's not good or bad, just the reality of building a complicated system. The result is each EDR system tends to have aspects it's better at and aspects it doesn't do as well. For example, Mandiant's early EDR solution MIR parsed most things based on the memory state of a device, which meant certain malware was far easier to spot, even with aggressive anti-disk forensic techniques. But, it inherently didn't capture certain system states as well as a tool like osquery, which didn't have any memory analysis capability early on. Some EDR agents are also very good on certain platforms, often Windows, but lacking on less popular platforms like macOS, and may have only limited support for certain Linux variants. Integrations also vary, whether the system stores logs on its own (often useful for deeper investigation) or shuffles them off to your SIEM/logging platform (often useful for improved data fusion). Another variable is how the system integrates with various SOAR platforms or tries to do automation by itself.

What does this mean for network defenders? Well, it means you need to really take the time to work through your needs and balance them against your system capabilities. As much as certain analyst firms would like to convince us they can pick the "best-in-class" solution, the EDR system that will work best for your organization depends a lot on the organization, network architecture, systems architectures, threats commonly faced, etc. As so many things in the intelligence space, the answer is (the often correct but rarely satisfying): "It depends." No matter which system you choose, success may start with product selection, but it isn't achieved until the system is integrated into other data sources and workflows, analysts are trained, and processes and procedures are established to make the best use possible of chosen systems features. This is rarely a "set it and forget it" process. While initial setup may take months just to get to initial operating capacity, it's never done. This is a key point to keep in mind while building, staffing, and managing EDR solutions.

Malware Analysis

In most incidents, the most deeply technical analysis that takes place is analyzing any of the malware samples involved. Sometimes this analysis is as basic as reading over a shell script, and sometimes multiple reversers pour over thousands of lines of code with extensive anti-analysis capabilities. Few areas of information security require quite so much breadth and at the same time depth of understanding. In advanced or mature organizations, a threat intelligence team may have a dedicated reverse engineer focused on analyzing malware, but there's still plenty even a nonexpert can do.

Two basic sets of techniques are used for understanding malware: static analysis and dynamic analysis. The ability to perform basic static and dynamic analyses is a skill every incident responder and intelligence analyst should have. Advanced static analysis skills are usually limited to dedicated malware analysts.

Basic static analysis

The easiest form of malware analysis is *static analysis*. Basic static analysis is the process of gathering metadata about an unknown binary. This includes gathering information such as the following:

File hashes
> Common hashes such as SHA1 and SHA256, which are useful for comparing files, including looking them up in other malware resources such as VirusTotal. Fuzzy hashes such as SSDeep that allow samples to be compared to each other later. This is especially useful for tracking campaigns, as small edits to files that change their SHA hashes often won't change the SSDeep significantly.

File type
> Not just the extension. File extensions can be easily changed, inaccurate, or mistaken. The easiest way to detect the real file type is by using a tool like `file` to invoke libmagic, which classifies files. You can also use MIME type (*https://oreil.ly/KddZV*) detection or even look directly at so-called magic bits that make up unique signatures for specific types of files (*https://oreil.ly/wkIu1*).

File size
> Useful along with other data for identifying similar files. Always be sure to specify units—50kb is a lot different than 50mb.

Strings
> Some binaries have useful information including IP addresses and authentication tokens in plain text. Strings are also useful for soft grouping, similar to soft hashes.

The ultimate goal of malware analysis is developing intelligence that can be used in wide-ranging detection-and-response systems and to track the evolution of campaigns. Static analysis metadata is also useful for comparing or even basic clustering. Basic static analysis also helps develop intelligence from outside your organization, such as vendor reporting.

File selectors: Yara.   One of the singular most useful ways to describe, track, classify, and detect file information (among others) is using Yara. Yara describes itself as, "The pattern-matching Swiss knife for malware researchers (and everyone else)." It allows you to describe files in a variety of ways, from specifying bytes to building advanced patterns to even identifying particular structures within specific files.

Basic dynamic analysis

In most cases, the next step after basic static analysis is basic *dynamic analysis*. In dynamic analysis, the analyst runs the malware in a controlled, heavily monitored environment to observe what it does. The key to dynamic analysis is having a safe environment to execute the malware that's collecting good telemetry. Both parts of this are key; if the environment isn't properly controlled, you run the risk of an out-of-control self-infection (which is exactly what the adversary wants anyway), and if the environment isn't configured for collection, you will miss out on the primary value of dynamic analysis.

The most common technique for dynamic analysis is using a sandbox. A sandbox typically manages running a sample on a purpose-built system, often in a virtual machine, isolated from the internet. The sandbox imports the sample to the virtual machine, executes it, and then monitors the behavior of the system to see what the malware does. Typically, this analysis focuses on changes to the system, such as new processes, new files, changes to persistence mechanisms, and network traffic. Just as in static analysis, the goal of dynamic analysis is to gather indicators useful for identifying the malware in your environment.

Dynamic analysis has a few downsides, especially with sandboxes. Building a safe environment that can collect proper telemetry is difficult and carries some risks; it also needs to mirror your environment, including common software. In addition, some malware samples may do things to detect they're in a sandbox, such as looking for evidence of a virtual machine or trying to reach network services. While there are ways to fool malware under dynamic analysis, the complications they present are important to consider and address. Tools such as INetSim (*http://www.inetsim.org*) and FakeNet-NG (*https://oreil.ly/w8I1X*) can help.

Advanced static analysis

Finally, when analysts need to fully understand a piece of malware, they resort to what most people think of as full-on reverse engineering. Another form of static analysis (the malware is analyzed without running it), advanced static analysis focuses on understanding malware at the code level by using multiple tools, most notably a disassembler.

A disassembler works by breaking down a compiled binary application into the machine-code instructions that a victim host would run. This is an incredibly low-level set of instructions that take experience to understand. What makes disassembly so effective is that, to an analyst who can understand it, the entire binary and all its capabilities are laid bare. By tracking every code path, it's possible to understand all the functions a piece of malware has, even ones that wouldn't trigger during dynamic analysis. IDA Pro (*https://oreil.ly/r3Pko*) is the gold standard that most reverse engineers use for this process, but the newcomer to the field is the NSA's Ghidra Software Reverse Engineering framework (*https://ghidra-sre.org*). Both tools assist reverse engineers in digging into malware or exploits to understand how they work.

Many reverse engineers also lean on custom tools, whether it's IDA scripts, custom mocking tools faking server responses, or many others. It's safe to say development experience is an essential for reverse engineering; analyzing software requires under-standing how software is put together and also understanding how to build tools. Malware authors specifically go to great lengths to make tools difficult to understand, especially by blue teams. It's often necessary to build custom tools to undo or mitigate these anti-reversing features. Reversers also build their own tools just to speed up their workflows and improve consistency. Some even release their tools as open source (*https://oreil.ly/xJSV5*) to help others!

The downside to advanced static analysis is the level of effort necessary. Understand-ing a sample, depending on its size, complexity, and anti-reversing measures, could take hours or even days. As a result, comprehensive reverse engineering is usually saved for new or especially prolific samples where indicators aren't enough, but there is also a need to understand all capabilities that a piece of malware has. Even in those cases, reverse engineers are usually hired only in very high-end security teams, such as those at vendors like CrowdStrike or very large platform providers like the Microsoft Threat Intelligence Center. So, what if your team doesn't need that level of engineer on a day-to-day basis? Well, in many cases you can work with firms on retainer to get access to reversing capabilities when necessary.

Applying intelligence to malware analysis

Other intelligence and analysis can often key a reverse engineer into useful avenues of investigation. If prior analysis suggests C2 based on encrypted HTTP, reverse engineering might want to focus on looking for the encryption keys. If there is an indication that information was stolen and never stored on the computer but discussed near the computer, it might make sense to focus analysis on alternative information collection capabilities such as using the microphone or camera.

Gathering data from malware analysis

Malware analysis is one of the most data-rich types of analysis that a team can undertake, in addition to being one of the most difficult to exploit fully. Malware analysis reports result in a wide variety of exploitable types of data, including indicators, tactics, and capabilities that lead to the impact available to an attacker, even sometimes indications of who the attacker might be. Malware analysis leads to useful information for detection and alerting on both the network and on hosts. That said, in the same way that good intelligence can help a reverser, it's also helpful when an intelligence analyst can give specific requirements to a reverse engineer so they can focus their efforts. Reverse engineering means many different things to many people, and without a focus, reversers may find themselves going down rabbit holes that may or may not ultimately be useful. So, if you're primarily interested in network connectivity around C2 or persistence mechanisms, be sure to call that out early so your reverser doesn't spend days working on how a specific keystroke-logging behavior works.

Learning more about malware analysis

Malware analysis is one of the toughest skills to learn in information security. It requires a deep understanding of general computer programming concepts, operating system concepts, and common malware actions. *Malware Analyst's Cookbook and DVD* by Michael Ligh et al.[5] teaches most of the basic static and dynamic analysis techniques necessary for incident responders.

If you're interested in developing a comprehensive reverse engineering skill set, including understanding assembly, you'll want to work through *Practical Malware Analysis* by Michael Sikorski and Andrew Honig.[6]

More interested in taking a course? SANS Reverse-Engineering Malware (*https://oreil.ly/24C2i*) course goes in depth on a variety of static and dynamic techniques. While it's impossible to "learn reverse engineering" in a week, this course provides the basics to get started. Ultimately, reverse engineering is never fully learned and will always require growth and exploration.

---

5 Michael Ligh et al., *Malware Analyst's Cookbook and DVD: Tools and Techniques for Fighting Malicious Code* (Indianapolis: Wiley, 2010).

6 Michael Sikorski and Andrew Honig, *Practical Malware Analysis: The Hands-On Guide to Dissecting Malicious Software* (San Francisco: No Starch Press, 2012).

Scoping

Throughout the period of alerting and investigation, one of the most important pieces of information you're trying to determine is the *scope* of the incident: which victim resources (e.g., systems, services, credentials, data, users) are affected. This leads directly into later workflows, such as determining the impact and methods of response.

Say, for instance, a piece of malware is found on one computer. Your reaction would be different if, after scoping, you found that piece of malware on only one computer versus dozens of systems in your network.

Another important part of scoping is determining patterns among affected resources. Are all the infected systems related to a specific type of user or department? This data could be important for understanding the attack at a deeper level (something we'll get to in the Analyze phase of F3EAD). This type of understanding requires good inventory management and collaboration with IT management teams. One of the most important, and often frustrating, aspects of incident response is having to ask, "What does this system do?"

Scoping can be done at both the network and host levels. In either case, it starts by using previously established data, either IOC (yes, this is a case where certain IOCs can be highly useful) or patterns of behaviors, and applying it to your systems. For example, consider a piece of malware that moves between systems by using the EternalBlue exploit. In that case, you would use network tools to look for systems attempting connections on common SMB ports.

Hunting

Until now, our discussion of incident response has focused on *reactive* incident response: what to do after we know a security control has failed and trying to understand it. Hunting is different. *Hunting* occurs when we *proactively* search for IOCs without any alert or notification of a security control failure. Detection is far from perfect, especially signature-based detection. Security controls can fail silently. For any number of reasons, attacks could be ongoing with no indications.

To people outside the security team, hunting looks like lucky guessing (in fact hunting teams often get accused of that, at least this author's teams have), but it's far from that. Hunting is based on a combination of planning, process, instinct, experience, and good intelligence. Ultimately, these add up to what hunting really should be: a science in service to either prove or disprove the existence of adversary behavior inside an environment.

Much like traditional hunting, it's limited by your tools. If you have limited network telemetry, this will limit your ability to hunt on the network. It's best to focus hunting on the deepest and widest pools of network and host telemetry and then pivot into less strong sources. If you have considerable application logs, start there, but correlate odd activity against network or host traffic after you have a lead. Hunting is all about developing hypotheses and then testing them (confirming or denying the theory).

Developing Hypotheses

For most teams, the toughest part of getting started with hunting is knowing where to start. The easiest way to think about starting points is to develop a series of hypotheses, just like an old-school detective story. So, where do these hypotheses come from? A combination of intelligence, instinct, and imagination:

- Look at past incidents to spot patterns or trends. Have past attackers commonly used a given ISP for C2? Did you read about a group of attackers using Compiled Help files?
- Build hypotheses around activities that are out of profile for your organization. With the exception of huge organizations, it may be odd to see connections to certain countries or at certain times of day, especially at a high volume.
- Build hypotheses off the results of vulnerability assessments or red team penetration testing. Did the simulated bad guys attack a specific host? Take the time to see if nonsimulated bad guys did the same.

The list goes on and on. The exercise of developing hypotheses is one of those "there are no bad ideas" kind of brainstorming exercises: write it down, no matter how crazy.

Testing Hypotheses

Just as with alerting, it is possible to generate a high volume of noise or false positives when hunting for indications of an attacker. Because of this, it is a good idea to test any hunting leads before you deploy hunting detection methods across your environment. You can conduct this testing in several ways. One way is to run a query with the information from your leads against a single, known good host to ensure that you are not bringing back a high volume of data that is related to normal operations.

Another option is to run the query against a sample data set, such as a day's worth of proxy logs, again to ensure that the query will not bring back an overwhelming number of results. A high number of results can either indicate that your system is massively compromised (which we hope is not the case) or simply that the lead needs to be refined or reevaluated. It can take some time to develop good leads for hunting, but once you have mastered the practice, you will be able to identify potential badness even without a specific signature.

Conclusion

Integrating intelligence into alerting, investigation, and hunting allows us to improve processes, deploy or modify tools, and, most important, train people to understand how everything fits together. Alerting is boiling down what you're interested in knowing to the most essential aspects. Once you've identified an important alert, the process moves into a wider collection to gather context. Investigation is gathering a wide variety of information and then distilling it into a cogent understanding. Once you master these aspects of reactive tasks, it is possible to move on to hunting—proactively applying the lessons and techniques of alerting and investigation to look for undetected malicious activity.

The goal of all analyses in this phase is to understand the scope of the incident and make a plan for response. Once you have that plan, it is time to act on it and remove the threat. We call this next step Finish, and we will discuss how to accomplish it in the next chapter.

## CHAPTER 6

Finish

It's not so important who starts the game but who finishes it.
—John Wooden

Once you have identified the threats that you are facing and investigated how those threats have accessed and moved through your network, it is time to remove them. This phase is known as Finish and involves not only eradicating the footholds that malicious actors have put in your network, but also working to remediate whatever enabled them to get access in the first place.

Finish involves more than removing malware from a system, which is why we spend so much time in the Find and Fix stages. To properly finish an attacker's activity, it is critical to understand how that threat actor operates and to remove not just malware or artifacts left behind by an attack, but also communications channels, footholds, redundant access, and any other aspects of an attack that we uncovered in the Fix phase. Properly finishing an adversary requires a deep understanding of the attacker, their motives, and their actions, which will allow you to act with confidence as you secure the systems and regain control of your network.

Finishing Is Not Hacking Back

Finish does not mean hacking back. That is because, unless you are a government department or agency with the proper authority, hacking back—as we discussed earlier—is a very, very bad idea! Why, you ask? There are several reasons:

Attribution is rarely perfect.
> You don't always know what you will end up hacking. Attackers will rarely attack you directly from their infrastructure. They will pivot through other victim machines to get to you, which means that if you take action against the machine you think is attacking you, it might end up being a hospital or your grandmother,

or a computer in another country, introducing all sorts of new complications because you just violated that country's laws and probably your own.

You don't know what will happen when you take action.

You may think you will just be ending a session or removing some files, but unless you know exactly how the target system is set up as well as the intricacies of network operations (which, let's face it, we often don't even know this about our *own* systems), it is difficult to know exactly what will happen when you take action. In military operations, including the traditional F3EAD cycle, understanding the exact actions you are taking and any potential for collateral damage requires practicing the operations against a simulated environment by using information from the Find phase. In intelligence-driven incident response, all of the Find activity takes place inside your own network, so you don't develop a picture of the attacker's networks. Developing that picture, which is needed to carry out a successful offensive operation, is also most likely a violation of law.

You don't know who you are messing with.

Even if you have done extensive research on the attackers in your environment and think you have a good idea of their motivations and intentions and know how to stop them, you may find yourself facing an adversary who does not take kindly to your operations. This may result in additional attacks against you. In the most extreme cases, where you may find yourself hacking back against a nation-state adversary, your actions may have national security implications, causing problems not just for you but for other organizations or agencies that had nothing to do with the original attack.

It is probably illegal.

According to 18 U.S. Code § 1030 (*https://oreil.ly/XEOmW*), "Fraud and related activity in connection with computers," and similar laws in many other countries, make it illegal to gain unauthorized access to protect systems. Even if bad actors are using those systems, they are still considered protected computers under US law, and accessing them can be a violation of the law.

In short, please do not take anything we say as a call to offensive action. The Finish phase focuses on resources *you* control, whether those be your users, endpoints, servers, or cloud providers and services.

Stages of Finish

Finishing an attacker in your network can encompass many different actions over a variety of timeframes, leveraging many different stakeholders. The things that dictate the best way to remove an attacker and to keep them from returning are the nature of the activity that is identified during the Find phase, your organization's sophistication and tolerance for risk, and the legal authority that you have (even partnerships and relationships you can lean on).

The Finish phase has three stages: mitigate, remediate, and rearchitect. These stages acknowledge that you can't do everything at once. Even after a comprehensive investigation, some tactical response actions can take place quickly, but many strategic response actions, such as system and network hardening, will take longer (often much longer, spanning multiple incidents). We will discuss the three phases next.

Mitigate

During an incident, the defensive team—which can include the incident-response team, security operations team, threat intelligence teams, and other security teams (e.g., the blue team)—will often have to mitigate the issue. *Mitigation* is the process of taking temporary steps to keep an intrusion from getting worse while longer-term corrections are taken.

Ideally, mitigation should take place quickly and in a coordinated fashion to avoid giving the adversary a chance to react before you have cut off their access. Mitigation takes place at several phases of the kill chain, including delivery, command and control, and actions on objective.

Tipping Off the Adversary

When an incident-response team moves from the Fix phase to the Finish phase, it is important to consider the adversary's potential response to your finishing actions. Although the investigation process is largely passive (collecting and analyzing information), a response is, by necessity, active. This can tip off the adversary, causing them to change tactics or take new actions. To avoid this adversary response, you need to plan your actions and then execute the plan as quickly as possible, taking care that the adversary can't leverage their access to stay in the environment.

Mitigating delivery

It is critical to try to limit the adversary's ability to reenter the environment. Blocking an adversary's way into networks and systems involves using the information gathered during the Find phase (which can tell you how this adversary typically operates), as well as information gathered during the Fix phase (which will tell you how the adversary got initial access to your network). Mitigating delivery can involve blocking email addresses or attachments used for delivery or cutting off compromised credentials used to log in to the environment. Mitigating delivery is usually the least likely type of mitigation to be detected because it doesn't impact active sessions but only future attempts to gain or regain access.

Mitigating command and control

If the adversary is using some form of command and control, cutting off this access is one of the most important actions before moving on to remediation. The overall key of mitigation is to keep the adversary from changing the environment as you are trying to regain control of it. The easiest way for an adversary to do this is to use the connection they have already established to set up an alternative means of accessing the system. One example is an attacker installing a secondary RAT with different characteristics in addition to their primary RAT, but with a much longer communication interval that may not be detected as readily. In a situation like that, the attacker may allow their primary tools to be removed, knowing they will be able to come back later.

Revoking Sessions

Unfortunately, many online systems such as email don't automatically revoke sessions when a compromised user password is changed. This can result in a situation where you think you have removed access, but the adversary remains logged in. This can be devastating to mitigation and remediation efforts, because the adversary may be able to reestablish complete control over a resource the incident-response team believes has been fixed and can monitor additional responder actions and adapt to them. Few things feel worse to a defender than being compromised again via a vector you thought was fixed. Revoking sessions is important when changing account passwords.

In addition, don't forget application-specific passwords as well. Many services use one-time passwords for desktop clients or third-party services. These rarely change and may be used by an adversary for long-term access even when the victim regularly changes passwords.

Mitigating actions on objective

Mitigating actions on objective is something that stakeholders will often want done immediately. Knowing that there is an adversary in your environment who is potentially accessing sensitive information or manipulating critical systems is not a thought that makes anyone, especially executives, feel comfortable or safe, especially as ransomware incidents have gone from a hypothetical to everyday news. Reducing the consequences or severity of an adversary's actions while going through the process of securing your network is a balancing act aimed at protecting information without allowing an adversary the opportunity to change tactics and find alternate ways to achieve their goals.

Mitigating actions on objective focuses on limiting access to sensitive information or operational systems, reducing network transport options to prevent exfiltration, stopping malware before it takes actions on the system (*https://oreil.ly/vFR9E*), or shutting down impacted resources altogether. Remember that stealing information is not always the adversary's goal. They may be using your network as a hop point to reach another victim, to conduct DoS attacks against other targets, or to manipulate data in place. These actions may be remediated with network access controls or by limiting outbound connections as necessary, but they may also require on-system response.

Mitigating Road Runner

In the past two chapters, we have focused on finding out how the adversarial campaign, Road Runner, operated—both in general by finding external information on related activities (including from our suspected actor behind the campaign, Grey Spike) and more specifically by understanding how the activity was able to successfully compromise our systems and what actions were taken after the compromise occurred. Now that we understand this campaign, we can begin the Finish phase by mitigating their activities.

We identified that Road Runner activity accessed our networks via spear-phishing emails. In the Fix phase, we were able to identify email subjects, attachments (which were campaign-support themed and targeted at staff members and volunteers who open attachments like that every day in the course of doing business), and senders. To mitigate the risk of the attackers trying to reestablish access using the same or similar methods, we will reroute any similar emails to a sandbox for analysis, which has signatures targeting both Road Runner's and Grey Spike's common IO, as well as signatures focused on their common TTPs like ATT&CK T1547.015 - Boot or Logon Autostart Execution: Login Items on macOS. We will also talk with all campaign staff to let them know of the threat to raise their awareness while understanding that opening emails from unknown senders is part of their day-to-day tasks. We plan to include additional threat information to volunteers as part of their onboarding. The goal is not to stop them from doing their job (a non-starter in any organization) but to enable them to do their jobs safely.

To mitigate command-and-control activity, we will block traffic at the firewall (for in-office employees) and system level via EDR (for our remote employees) to the identified command-and-control servers. We will either block or monitor for other command-and-control-methods that we identified have been used by Grey Spike or as part of Road Runner, including ATT&CK T1102.001 - Web Service: Dead Drop Resolver (*https://oreil.ly/EZcHK*), via a legitimate social media website. We know that the adversary may switch tactics after they realize that their activity has been detected, so we want to be prepared for any changes they may make to retain or regain their foothold.

Finally, we will force a password reset across the environment, including service accounts, and will revoke all sessions to online systems and applications that are used in the environment, knowing that the attackers almost certainly have captured both user and system credentials (ATT&CK T1078 - Valid Accounts (*https://oreil.ly/vbSbr*)). We know the types of information Road Runner activity is likely to look for on our network, but we have assessed that this information is widely distributed through the network, including on users' systems, mobile devices, and email. We will increase monitoring on databases, file shares, wikis, and other places where large amounts of information are stored, and we will focus on how to better track and protect sensitive information in the rearchitecture stage of Finish.

Once mitigation steps have been taken to stop or limit the damage being done by an adversary, it is time to move into remediation, which will have a more permanent impact on the attacker.

Remediate

Remediation is the process of removing all adversary capabilities and invalidating any compromised resources so that they can no longer be used by the adversary to conduct operations. Remediation generally focuses on a different set of kill chain phases than mitigation does, most notably exploitation, installation, and actions on objective, which we will break down in this section.

Remediating exploitation

In most cases, remediating exploitation means patching. Every exploit relies on a vulnerability, and so the top ways to keep an exploit from being used to compromise a system in the future is either to make the exploit target unreachable (by putting a system behind a firewall or other security appliance using access-control processes) or to correct the flaw. If a patch is already available, it is a matter of prioritizing patching of vulnerable systems and identifying why this wasn't done before, but in some cases a patch may not be available. In those situations, remediation involves working with the software creator, who may or may not be aware of the problem. During the sometimes-lengthy process of creating a permanent fix, it is possible to put other mitigations in place, such as isolating a vulnerable system or enforcing and monitoring strict access controls.

Many organizations have plenty of custom code around, and in some cases, you may not need to reach out to a vendor but instead to the responsible team. If your organization relies on custom tools or code, it is a good idea to develop a process for working with internal application development teams when security issues arise.

Remediating installation

On the surface, remediating installation seems simple: You need to delete anything created during exploitation and installed at that point and revert anything the adversary has changed to its original state. Even though the concept is simple, remediating installed malware can be difficult and time-consuming.

We've discussed malware several times in the book, but what is it, exactly? Typically, *malware* is one or more executable files, possibly some libraries, and a persistence mechanism that makes sure the first executable file runs on a system in the case of a reboot or an error. At exploitation time, the attacker has control of the system and may take a variety of actions. Fully understanding malware requires a deep understanding of the system and considerable investigation. This topic is even more complex as more and more adversaries are "living off the land," using built-in system tools and utilities. In reality, this is nothing new, but it's taken on a new shape as these techniques and tools have been enumerated by websites like LOLBAS (*https://oreil.ly/iEQSR*), GTFOBins (*https://oreil.ly/a0gEh*), and WTFBins (*https://wtfbins.wtf*), as well as being enumerated by multiple ATT&CK techniques such as T1053 - Scheduled Task/Job (*https://oreil.ly/gAff4*) or T1090 - Proxy (*https://oreil.ly/-t0Ph*).

Given that complexity, how do you successfully and completely remove malware after installation? It's not always as simple as just deleting the files. This leads to a fundamental argument between responders over whether the best approach is to remove malware or reformat the system and rebuild it completely. Antivirus works under the expectation that malware can be removed successfully, but many incident responders have found that that is not always the case. The decision on how to handle things is up to each incident-response team. Complicating this decision is the low, but not impossible, chance of low-level malware persistence, such as BIOS rootkits. While these are exceedingly rare and seldom deployed, even by the most sophisticated actors, the possibility of their presence may influence a team's decision. Given the near impossibility of introspecting to that level, the only viable remediation option, if you suspect firmware-level compromise, is junking the system entirely, not just reformatting and reinstalling the operating system.

Remove Malware or Reformat the System: Our Opinion

This is normally the place we'd give a charming anecdote or humorously suggest you need to make the decision on your own (which you do), but instead we'll give you our standard advice: *Just reformat the system!* Although your factors may differ and you may need to make a different decision, we always recommend reformatting. It's the only way you can be 100% certain that any malware is gone and attacker system actions have been fully mitigated. On some specialized systems, such as control systems, this may not be possible, but when it is possible, it is the best way to know that you have not missed anything. One challenge teams face is understanding their own processes. IT teams may opt to simply reinstall rather than reformat first, which may leave malware directories unchanged. In other cases, organizations restore not just their data from backup but sometimes the adversary's tools as well. This is why fully understanding the adversary during the Find and Fix phases is so critical, not just to clean up the malware, but also to be able to verify the fix worked before a critical system goes back into production.

Remediating actions on objective

Not every Actions on Objective phase can be remediated, but it's always worth considering. The ability to do so may be limited by your telemetry as well as the actions the attacker takes.

For data theft, it's usually difficult to do much more than determine what information may have been taken and develop an assessment on the damage done, though it highly depends on which data. For example, in 2013, Bit9, a security firm, was compromised specifically so attackers could steal the company's code-signing certificates. Software signed with these certificates was inherently trusted by the Windows operating system. As a result, the best way to remediate the attack was to issue a certificate-revocation request, which invalidated the certificate and thus any software signed with it.

Not all malware is built the same, though; ransomware has become a greater and greater problem in the last few years. General remediation actions with ransomware can be determined by answering a few key questions:

- What is the specific family, and what are its unique characteristics? Not all ransomware acts the same, targets the same files or network targets, etc.
- How long did the ransomware run before getting detected and remediated? While there's an easy assumption that ransomware works instantly, it turns out

that's not true. The Splunk SURGe research team (*https://oreil.ly/cu0Ki*) did some excellent work looking at how long some processes have to run. Early detection makes a huge difference and may make remediation much easier.

- Does the organization have good backups available for the affected systems? This will depend a lot on the system itself; in some organizations, a domain controller is more likely to have good backups than a random graphic designer's computer. In other organizations, it'd be the opposite.

- Is the organization willing to allow the affected systems to be destroyed or unsuccessfully remediated? Ransoms work only on the expectations that customers want the data back.

- Lastly, is the organization willing to pay the ransom? Consult your legal team.

While these are complex and unique considerations and it may seem impossible to prepare, the best solution is to rehearse your response ahead of time. This special case is a topic unto itself, and if you work at the kind of organization that's at risk of experiencing ransomware attacks, it's worth spending the time to study and prepare (*https://oreil.ly/HB3Yp*).

Other examples of remediating actions on objective could be blocking outbound network activity for a DDoS bot, invalidating stolen credit card numbers by reporting them to the credit card providers, changing passwords or other stolen credentials, or even initiating full source-code reviews for stolen software. It's almost impossible to predict everything that could be done until the situation presents itself, but good remediation of actions on objective often requires deep investigation of a root cause of the problem and attacker goals, collaboration with those who work with the compromised resource, and a little bit of creativity.

Remediating Road Runner

We know that the group behind Road Runner is sophisticated and often uses malware, including GoldMax, a C2 backdoor written in Go. Remediating compromised systems involves rebuilding those machines when at all possible. Doing so is not always possible, however, and although our plan is to rebuild all the compromised hosts, some of the compromised servers must be handled differently.

In the case of our domain controllers, the downtime associated with rebuilding the servers is not acceptable because of the many systems that rely on them, and therefore we must take a different approach. In this situation, we have decided that, after we take appropriate steps to mitigate the adversary's ability to access the systems using stolen credentials or command-and-control communications, we are going to build a new system, this time with specific allow-lists for known good activity and alerting on anything that is not known to be good. We have high confidence, based on reporting, that Road Runner will attempt to get back into the network and, while we do not know exactly how they will accomplish that, we know to remain vigilant for any activity that is outside the normal. Once the new systems are properly configured and additional security measures are in place, we will replace the compromised systems all at once.

We have also identified that Road Runner used CVE-2018-4916 against some of our hosts, so we will need to partner with the information security team to identify and patch any systems using an outdated version of Adobe Acrobat Viewer. We have already enforced credential changes as part of the mitigation process, but we have decided that we will monitor attempts against several previous accounts to identify any adversary attempts to regain access using credentials.

Rearchitect

One of the most effective uses of intelligence-driven incident-response data occurs during an advanced form of remediation: when the incident-response team looks at past incident trends, identifies common patterns, and works to mitigate these at a strategic level. These mitigations are generally not small changes and may range from small things like tweaks to system configurations or additional user training to massive shifts in tooling such as the development of a new security tools or even complete network rearchitecture.

Often, these massive changes occur after a single large breach, but don't underestimate the ability of an organization to identify trends with smaller intrusions or even failed intrusions and use the information on what vulnerabilities or weaknesses are being targeted as a driver for change.

Rearchitecting Road Runner

We have identified several architecture- and process-related issues that contributed to the opportunity the Road Runner activity had to compromise our system. These issues include the fact that many systems are old, some volunteers occasionally use their own systems, and a vulnerability from 2018 was not remediated on several hosts. Because patches are usually installed as part of a larger package that addresses several vulnerabilities, we know that other vulnerabilities existed on those systems as well. We need to better understand why the process did not work in this case and make any changes that are needed.

We have also identified several issues with the way that authentication and access are controlled in our environment. Road Runner activity was able to use legitimate accounts to move through our environment, and nothing was in place to identify suspicious activity on these accounts. Addressing this problem requires additional investments that we will not be able to make immediately. The mitigation and remediation steps we take will secure and protect the network while more lasting architecture changes can be planned and implemented.

Taking Action

The act of finishing adversary activity requires strategic and operational planning as well as tactical action. When a cohesive plan is in place and all responsible parties know what actions need to be taken and when, it is time to act. The alternative is chaos, missed opportunities to collect data, and the distinct likelihood that some aspect of the adversary's infrastructure will be overlooked. Missing a single compromised machine or stolen credential can be worse than doing nothing at all given the false sense of security when an adversary still has a foothold.

In Chapter 3, we discussed some of the most common actions on objective by attackers: deny, degrade, disrupt, deceive, or destroy the systems or networks that they target. In the Finish phase, we can use those same five Ds to determine the actions a defender can take to remove the attackers from the network. Once again, it is important to note that with all of these options, the actions that are being taken all occur *inside* your network and should never be directed outside the systems that you control.

Deny

Deny is one of the most basic response actions to take, and in almost all cases it will be the initial response to attacker activity. Attackers want access to your network. They want access to your information. They want to be able to move freely from system to system to find what they want and take it. The goal of Deny is to remove their ability to do any of these things.

The attackers got into your network somehow, and after they were able to get in, they likely installed backdoors or dumped user credentials to make sure that they could retain their access. Ideally, you have identified these activities during the Find phase, and in Deny you can focus on removing that access in a way that will completely deny the attacker access to your network. Here are some ways to deny attackers access or movement:

Credential-based access
> If the attackers used stolen or default credentials to get access to the network, the best approach is to change those credentials or remove old accounts to deny the attackers that avenue of access. It's also critical to look for accounts that the attackers created for themselves using stolen access.

Backdoors and implants
> In Chapter 2, we discussed backdoors and implants—how they operate, how attackers use them, and how to efficiently and completely remove an attacker's ability to leverage those tools to access your network. The process of denying access requires that you understand how the backdoor was installed in the first place. Often you will have to make sure you not only remove the attacker's tools,

but also change credentials because the two usually go hand in hand. Either an attacker used credentials to gain access and then installed the backdoor, or they dumped credentials after they had access.

Lateral movement

Denying access is not just about keeping an attacker from getting into your network from the outside; it also means making sure that they do not have the ability to move laterally through your network. As we mentioned, Finish is not just about kicking one attacker out of your network. This phase is about making sure that you deal with the things that allowed them access in the first place, and that means denying their ability to move throughout the network. During the Find and Fix phases, you likely identified methods that attackers used to move through networks—both common methods as well as methods specific to your incident and your environment—and it is important to address the issues that allowed those methods to work.

All of the information you gathered in the Fix stage will help develop a plan that ensures you can completely deny access. However, sometimes denying access is not enough, as access is something determined attackers will try to immediately regain. It is important to also take steps to disrupt attempts to regain access to the network or gain access to information and to disrupt an attacker's ability to get that information out of your network.

Disrupt

In traditional operations, it is often impossible to deny an adversary's ability to take action. The goal then becomes to force an attacker to take *ineffective* actions and to diminish their ability to conduct operations. *Disrupt* and *degrade* are approaches to take with an advanced attacker when simply attempting to deny access is not likely to be successful.

Many organizations experience repeated breaches, often by the same attackers, because permanently denying access is a difficult thing to do. An attacker who is determined to get into a network will likely find a way, especially if that network has users who can be targeted to circumvent technical security measures.

Just because an attacker is able to get back into a network does not mean, however, that they will be able to get the information that they are after. To deny attackers access to the information that they are looking for, it is important to identify what it is they are targeting (which should have been determined in the Find and Fix stages) and then restrict access to that information. This may mean setting up additional access-control measures around critical information and setting up alerting to detect when someone is attempting to discover or access that information, or it may mean requiring additional authentication when accessing shared resources. These steps can be taken only if you understand the information attackers are after and also know where this information is located in your network.

Degrade

Where the Deny and Disrupt actions are somewhat binary—the adversary's activity is either stopped or not (before it begins for Deny and midway through for Disrupt)— Degrade isn't yes or no, but a matter of degrees. For example, if you were denying a command-and-control protocol, you'd block the protocol overall. If you were disrupting it, you'd cut the communication midway through. If you were degrading it, you'd slow down the communication to a crawl by throttling the adversary's bandwidth for C2. This doesn't mean making it useless; this means making it less useful.

Deceive

Deception is the practice of trying to throw off an attacker by providing false or misleading information. In many cases, this focuses on actions on objective, for example, trying to get an attacker who is focused on intellectual property to take a version of widget plans with the wrong type of metal that could cause failure. The idea is to devalue attackers' collection efforts and ideally force them to focus elsewhere.

Another common type of deception technique is the use of honeypots, which we introduced in Chapter 2. These are systems set up to look like a common system in the environment but that are secretly set up to provide enhanced telemetry. A good example is a system set up to look like a database server with all the right listening services on the right ports—maybe even deliberately set up with an inviting hostname like "ma-contracts-db" ("ma" in this case suggesting "mergers and acquisitions"). An attacker in the environment might look for hosts, see a tempting target where there might be useful data, and then attempt to access it. Given that those who should be in the environment know that there's nothing useful on this system, the only attempts to access it can be attributed to attackers. By identifying attempts to access this system, the defenders can be tipped off. Honeypots don't just have to be systems; the technique can be used in other contexts such as social networks or user personas.

Hypothetically, this sounds great. In practice, deception techniques can be useful, but they're hard to execute effectively. Most deception relies on a *dangle*, a lure that entices the attacker. The dangle has to walk a fine line. Not enticing enough, and the attackers won't bother attempting to access it. Too enticing, and the attackers may smell deception and avoid it. Even if you pick the perfect level of enticement, deception can still be a challenge, and authenticity is important. Say you want to identify phishing by using a fake persona on a social network. Even if the profile setup is perfect, it will quickly fall apart if the picture is pulled from a source that the attacker could find or if a user has too few connections.

Deception is hard. It's a challenge to get everything right and still be useful. It can often result in high rates of false positives as well. It can be useful but should be reserved for sophisticated shops that can put in the time and effort to make it effective.

Destroy

Destroy means to cause some sort of physical damage to a system and is not usually a good response because we are talking about actions you take against your own network. You may discover an antiquated system that was compromised and, while *removing* it from your network may be a good option, you would not necessarily *destroy* it.

To be absolutely clear, we are not talking about the destruction of any system owned or operated by the attacker. As we mentioned, all of these actions take place within *your* network.

Organizing Incident Data

During—but most importantly, after—an incident, it is critical to record details of the investigation and the actions taken. These details should focus on the following:

- Initial leads, sources, and outcomes
- Details of the attacker kill chain, including both indicators and descriptions of tactics, techniques, and procedures (most likely in ATT&CK notation)
- Information about compromised hosts, including their identifiers, vulnerabilities, configuration, owners, and purpose
- Details on actions on objective, how the compromise impacted users, and what was stolen (especially important when/if you engage law enforcement)
- Response actions taken on which hosts by which responder (important if you have to track down what went wrong)
- Follow-up leads or ideas for long-term actions

You may need to record additional information based on individual organizational needs. The ultimate goal is to develop a single source of truth, a place where all responders can share what they've found and keep everyone coordinated. There are many ways to approach this, and in the end the key is not exactly how the information is stored, but that everyone works together, follows the process, and gets the job done.

Tools for Tracking Actions

A variety of tools are available to track your incident data and the actions that have been taken. This section covers ways to organize data, using both publicly available and purpose-built tools. When you are just getting started with incident response and do not have existing systems in place to track information and actions, it is often best to start small and grow into increased capability and functionality. It's easy to get overwhelmed by adding complex ticketing systems with aggressive required fields and end up doing very little. The worst possible outcome is an incident-tracking system that analysts don't want to use, making it more difficult to track information about an incident. Fortunately, there are several easy places to start tracking incident information.

Personal notes

In almost every case, incident management starts with analyst notes. Good analysts will realize (or have it drilled into them) that they need to take notes for both formal investigations and casual observations. As a result, many analysts get in the habit of writing down whatever they stumble across throughout a shift in the SOC or day of hunting.

These notes can be invaluable to analysts and are frequently their primary reference when writing up formal reports but are often less useful to the rest of their security organization. This is largely due to formatting. Analysts who write personal notes typically develop a personal style and format for their own investigations. This starts with the medium: paper notebooks or text files. From there, analysts do a wide variety of things, including using different structures for dates (12-1-16 versus 20161201) and creating written narratives, bullet points, or drawn graphs.

The tough part about individual notes is that they're difficult to exploit (not hacking exploitation but intelligence exploitation—more in Chapter 7). If they're written, it's basically impossible, short of using some form of handwriting recognition. If typed, opportunities for exploitation may exist, but not without a lot of lost context (and often quite a lot of difficulty getting these notes from different analysts for aggregation or summarization across the whole team).

The result in most cases is that personal notes stay personal, for the analyst who wrote them, and the team works together with a shared format for tracking information. A key exception may be situations where an investigation goes to litigation (this is not legal advice, just things folks who do legal things have shared). Juries supposedly like these personal notes, especially handwritten. Confer with your lawyers as necessary.

The Spreadsheet of Doom

In most cases, when a team starts tracking information together, the first attempt starts as a spreadsheet, jokingly referred to by analysts as the *Spreadsheet of Doom* (SOD) because its content is sprawling and generally unwieldy to work with.

The SOD benefits from being easily structured, though. Typically, it's made up of multiple spreadsheets or tabs on a single spreadsheet, capturing the following information:

- Indicators of compromise
- Compromised resources (e.g., systems, services, data)
- Response actions (e.g., planned, taken)

Figure 6-1 shows an example SOD.

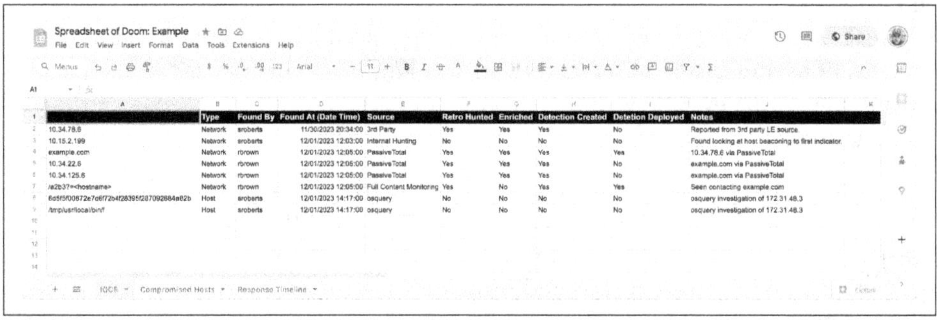

Figure 6-1. Using Google Sheets for a Spreadsheet of Doom

How the SOD is set up, what fields it has, where it's stored, and how people collaborate on it is up to each organization and will evolve over time. What is important is consistency and an agreed-upon format and conventions around names, dates, and categories. The need for consistency is important because the big advantage of the SOD versus personal notes is the ability to exploit spreadsheets easily.

Spreadsheets can be exported as comma-separated values (CSV) documents. These are easily read and written to by many tools and with a wide variety of scripting languages, making it easy to do more with a CSV than you could with other text-based documents, such as automatically resolving the reverse DNS of all IPs or checking hashes against VirusTotal. This type of automation can be invaluable. The other side is true, too. Automations can write data into your SOD, including automatically populating host details pulled from your EDR or references to other systems such as IT tickets.

It takes discipline to use the SOD effectively and follow convention. There's no default validation of any kind (and even building your own can be tricky), and there's nothing to keep bad data from polluting otherwise valid information. As soon as this falls apart, the SOD itself fails.

Third-party, non-purpose-built solutions

There are, of course, alternatives to using what is publicly or commercially available, and many teams have adapted their own tools for managing incident response and collecting incident information. This is a team decision and may be a stopgap or long-term solution. When evaluating a third-party, non-purpose-built tool like a Kanban board, a semi-structured flat file format like Markdown, a wiki, or a generalized IT ticketing system, consider the following needs:

Analyst usability
> Responders will be working with these systems directly, especially before automation is set up, and these systems need to be analyst friendly, easily understood, and fast.

Ability to automate
> The big advantage of having a data structure is the ability to build tools to automate common tasks.

Integration with typical team workflows
> Teaching new technologies is tough, especially when expecting those tools to be used in high-stress situations.

Once a tool is decided upon, the best approach is to use it and evolve your processes to get the best use out of the tool. Given that relying on a new tool in an incident-response situation is dubious at best, it is highly recommended to put new workflow tools through their paces with multiple tabletop and sample exercises. Running into problems is common, but it is better to sort them out in practice than during an incident.

Purpose-Built Tools

Personal notes and apocalyptic spreadsheets are great, but eventually even the most seat-of-their-pants incident-response and intelligence teams want a purpose-built solution. This turning point will often arrive after they have spent too much time chasing down a mistyped or mistaken IP address or after they discover that confusion exists about whether a new detection was applied. The result is that most teams end up deploying or creating an incident-response platform.

Purpose-built incident-response systems provide important characteristics out of the box that we've discussed before. They're often easy to integrate with. Most provide a variety of integration points, often including email (for sending and receiving information sent as email) and an API used for connecting directly to other tools.

One of our favorite purpose-built tools is FIR (*https://oreil.ly/6FWrV*) (Figure 6-2), short for *Fast Incident Response*. Built by the computer emergency response team at Société Générale, the third largest bank in France, FIR is an open source ticketing system built from the ground up to support intelligence-driven incident response.

Figure 6-2. FIR

FIR is an ideal starting tool for teams looking for a dedicated platform to support their incident-response and threat-intelligence operations. One challenge of dedicated systems is striking a balance of utility and customizability. Too few options and the system ends up being so generic it may as well be a SOD downloaded off the internet. Too much customizability and the analysts suffer from analysis paralysis, unsure which of a wide set of options to choose. FIR strikes a balance by having an opinionated workflow and set of defaults but also allowing considerable customization .

Assessing the Damage

One important point of discussion that comes up at the end of every incident is how to assess the damage. In some cases, this can be tied directly to dollars lost (such as events that impact retail operations, destruction of tangible resources such as physical hardware, or even the cost of incident-response services or internal incident-response time). In many cases, determining damage requires working with impacted business units, IT, and sales. Take special care to work with your insurance team, as they may have special insight into impact and costs since cybersecurity incident insurance (*https://oreil.ly/ymvJ4*) is becoming more and more mainstream.

Being able to put a dollar figure on incidents is often key for engaging law enforcement. In many cases, law enforcement will get involved only when incident costs that affect organizations reach a certain minimum. The exact figure depends on your jurisdiction.

Monitoring Lifecycle

The last big piece of the Finish phase is managing the monitoring lifecycle. In the heat of an incident, it's easy to generate a wide range of signatures. These signatures need to work through a lifecycle, and the end of the Finish phase is an ideal time to review them. The monitoring lifecycle usually involves the following steps: creation, testing, deployment, refinement, and retirement.

Creation

The first stage is creation of the signature, which occurs when an analyst takes an observable and uses it to create a way to monitor for signs of that observable on internal systems. These are often rough and either too specific (such as looking for a specific combination of a single IP and port) or too generic (like using a string found in a binary before realizing its programming language boilerplate common to every Golang binary, not just the cross-platform backdoor the adversary used in your environment). Too far in either direction can make you remarkably unpopular with your intrusion detection team, which is why you need testing.

Testing

This is the most commonly skipped step, and if you skip it, you will pay for it elsewhere. The obvious form of testing takes place during the preceding step, creation, where a detection is applied against known bad observables or, even better, a variety of known bad observables. Testing, however, should focus on known good observables, hoping to identify false positives. One way to achieve this is to put the detection into production as "monitor only," set to generate statistics but not alerts (such as using Snort's log action instead of the usual alert). This method is often effective and reflective of the real world, but time-consuming.

Another testing method is having a corpus of known good data to test against. This technique is especially useful in an incident where deployment of alerts is often more important than false positives. The upside is that the results are much quicker, but not usually as thorough. In many cases, the ideal solution is combining both techniques.

Deployment

Once a detection is ready (ideally after testing), it gets deployed. While some teams treat this step as the end of their responsibilities, that is a quick way to anger SOC analysts or intrusion-detection team members. Working with the detection team and getting feedback is critical at this stage, because you will use that feedback during the next step: refinement.

Refinement

Based on the feedback gained during deployment, the detection goes back to the drawing board for refinement. This can yield a variety of improvements:

- Overly specific detections can be broadened. This is especially useful when new, related samples are identified.

- Overly broad detections are tightened up. Everyone who has spent time building detections has had an unexpected string that triggers on a common network service. Often this is discovered only after being in place.

- Refinement is often based on performance as well. Depending on the telemetry source, a given signature (especially in the case of intrusion-detection systems) not only can run slowly, but can also have significant impact on the entire system. Often signatures need to be reviewed and optimized for performance, either speed or memory. It's key to work with your detection engineering team to ensure sensors and signatures are performing optimally.

Retirement

Eventually, a signature stops being useful, either because the threat has been mitigated (such as a signature that detects a vulnerability after the vulnerability is patched) or the tool, technique, or infrastructure falls out of favor. In some cases, it's useful to put a signature back into logging-only mode, allowing continuous gathering of statistics (assuming the impact on performance is acceptable).

An interesting topic originally explored by Jeremy Johnson of Ford at the SANS CTI Summit 2017 was the idea of using seemingly less useful (high false-positive) indicators of compromise more effectively. In his talk "Using Intelligence to Heighten Your Defense" (*https://oreil.ly/WOnyL*), Johnson explained ways of taking noisy indicators and improving them not by refinement of the indicator itself but by judicious application to high-risk populations. For example, if the detection team has a very general indicator for an adversary C2, one that causes too many false positives across the entire network, it may still be useful in an IDS on a network for research and development or executives.

Conclusion

As the active stage of incident response, Finish is one of the most important phases to focus on. If done effectively, an incident-response team can throw an adversary out, learn from the attacker's actions, and ensure a more secure network. If done poorly, it can tip off an adversary, allowing them to dig in, hide, and avoid being completely removed from a system. Taking the time to understand your mitigation and remediation options and how they fit in your response plans will make your team more effective in the long term. Finally, finding methods for managing all the output will set your team up to move into the next phase—Exploit, which is the first phase of the intelligence portion of F3EAD. The intelligence portion is where we will make sure that we learn from the attacker's actions and ensure a more secure network moving forward.

## CHAPTER 7

Exploit

If you focus solely on the enemy, you will ignore the threat.
—Colonel Walter Piatt

After the Find, Fix, and Finish phases, it is common for the final incident-response report to be delivered and the responders to move on to the next matter requiring their attention. But that is not where this book ends. Throughout the course of the investigation, incident-response teams gather a lot of data on attackers, look for additional information from within their networks, and take actions that have an impact on the attacker's operations. Now, we need to gather all of that data, analyze it for intelligence value, and integrate it into not only detection and prevention methods but also more strategic-level initiatives such as risk assessments, prioritization of efforts, and future security investments. You now have to engage the intelligence portion of the F3EAD cycle: Exploit, Analyze, and Disseminate.

It is no secret why most security teams stop short of completing the F3EAD cycle: It's hard enough to generate intelligence, but managing it is a whole new series of headaches. Dealing with processes, timing, aging, access control, and formats is enough to make anyone's head spin. And yet, as undeniably complex as these problems are, they have to be addressed head-on. Properly extracting and capturing information about an incident and ensuring that it is followed up on can mean the difference between truly remediating an adversary's access to your network and simply delaying their return and eventual success. Exploiting the intelligence that you have generated during the incident-response process ensures that all of the time and energy that went into identifying, understanding, and remediating the incident further supports network defense and response processes across the board—for your own organization and ideally many others. This chapter describes the various tasks you should do in the Exploit phase of F3EAD and will make the process a little less daunting and, dare we say, maybe even a little exciting.

> ## What "Exploit" Means in F3EAD
>
> We've discussed the occasional difficulties between military jargon and common information security vernacular, and *exploit* happens to be particularly complicated. In information security, we tend to almost exclusively use the term *exploit* to refer to the exploitation of a vulnerability that will give an adversary system access or information. By contrast, in military terms, exploit more broadly means "to take advantage of" and is used not only in the context of system vulnerabilities but in many other contexts as well. In the context of F3EAD, it refers to extracting information that has been collected during pre-operations. When lined up with the traditional intelligence cycle, the Exploit phase can be considered a combination of collection (though, usually more of an aggregation of internally gathered information) and processing to get that information into a usable format so that it can be analyzed.

Tactical Versus Strategic OODA Loops

In Chapter 2, we introduced the OODA loop model and discussed how it applies to incident response. To review, OODA stands for Observe, Orient, Decide, and Act. The general rule of thumb is that the first side to get through the OODA loop will gain a competitive advantage by acting on complete information first. In the first three phases of F3EAD—Find, Fix, and Finish—we moved through an OODA loop aimed at giving incident responders a *tactically competitive advantage*. In the second half of F3EAD—Exploit, Analyze, and Disseminate—the goal is to gain a *strategically competitive advantage*. In short, we want to understand the adversary so well that their usual tactics and techniques will no longer work against us. The adversary will have to take a step back, regroup, and try to come up with different ways to carry out their tasks—all things that will take time and make their tasks, and lives, more difficult. They will also give us more time to continue to build defenses and resiliency against them.

Depending on the structure of your team, which we will discuss in Chapter 10, you may actually be running these two OODA loops at the same time. The incident response portion of your team may be heads-down fighting in a tactical OODA loop while your intelligence team begins gathering the information they need for their strategic OODA loop. If those functions are one and the same, the tactically focused OODA loop may take priority and you will complete Find, Fix, and Finish before ever beginning to execute the Exploit phase. Either method is fine; the important thing is that you do actually move into the second phase of operations because a tactical advantage may last for a few days or weeks, but a strategic advantage will have a long-lasting impact and give you the time you need to prepare for future intrusions, which undoubtedly will come.

In a strategic OODA loop, the Exploit phase covers both the Observe and Orient steps. In these steps, you begin to sift through the mountain of data that has been gathered during the incident-response operation, gathering or aggregating additional information from previous incidents or external sources related to the incident, and capturing what this information means to your organization in the past, in the present, and potentially in the future. This can seem like a daunting task, so it is helpful to know where to start.

An Aside from a Hungry Intelligence Analyst

In many ways, developing intelligence is a lot like cooking. There are lots of ways to do it and lots of potential products. These can look like a peanut butter and jelly sandwich (like a single-page TIPPER) or an elaborate multi-course dinner (like a major multi-page intrusion-intelligence product). What's important in the Exploit phase is how you begin "cooking." For certain types of products, you can make it up as you go along; just throw things in a pot. For others, more preparation is necessary. In cooking terms, exploitation is the meal prep phase, what chefs call putting together your *mise en place*, literally "put in place" in French. Well before they start cooking, chefs set things up—cutting veggies into the right sizes, partially cooking items that take exceptionally long to cook, making sure tools from knives to towels are ready, and making sure every bit is within reach, in the right place.

A chef's goal in setting it all up is that once service starts, especially when it gets extra busy (being "in the weeds"), everything is already prepared and ready to go. It's easy to make one dish, but to make dozens of dishes a night, especially complex ones, it's not just nice to be set up ahead of time, it's essential. In many ways, the Exploit phase is the intelligence analyst building their *mise en place*. Writing an intelligence product when you're "in the weeds" is much easier when you have already set up your environment correctly, making sure you have the data you need, in the formats you need, in the places you need to get access quickly.

What to Exploit

When F3EAD is not properly implemented or is not carried out completely, you will likely find yourself dealing with the same intrusions or types of incidents time and time again, and likely not too far down the road. This is not only a waste of time but may cause additional scrutiny if the intrusion results in the loss of sensitive customer data. In September 2017, the credit reporting company Equifax experienced an intrusion that resulted in unauthorized access to highly sensitive information of 147 million people. In 2019, the US Federal Trade Commission filed a complaint claiming that Equifax failed to properly address a known vulnerability in their web application system, resulting in the breach. This claim set the stage for future companies to have their security practices, including their incident-response processes and follow-up, closely evaluated following an incident. Focusing on the Exploit phase will allow you to more easily identify additional risks and call out actions needed in order to completely address an incident.

In the previous Find, Fix, and Finish stages of the cycle, we focused on a specific attack, a specific adversary, and the specific actions needed to deal with that particular incident. If you happen to identify or mitigate an attack by an adversary leveraging similar tactics, it is a happy coincidence but is by no means intentional. By the end of the Finish phase, we identified a large amount of information around the Road Runner intrusion, the actors behind it, and how they operated. But even though that information is organized in a way that facilitates the rapid-response nature of incident response, that doesn't necessarily mean it is in the right format for follow-up intelligence analysis.

In the Exploit phase, we begin the process that ensures we not only address but learn from the incident. We focus on the threat, and not just the enemy. Because of this, it is important that we not only extract technical indicators related to the particular attack, such as malware samples and command-and-control IP addresses, but also the overarching aspects that led to the intrusion and allowed the attackers to be, at least to some degree, successful. This includes information about the vulnerabilities or weaknesses that were targeted in the attack, the information or systems that were targeted, and the process weaknesses that may have prevented us from identifying and acting sooner. We are not just trying to protect the network from a replay of the exact same attack, but to understand the various factors such as policies, technical vulnerabilities, or visibility gaps that led to the successful intrusion and to develop protections or detections for them as well. Because of this, we believe that there is very little information that should *not* be exploited and analyzed—but this, of course, makes managing that information complex.

To make this process a little more manageable, we like to break information down into the following categories:

Technical indicators
> This includes IPs, domains, hashes, and certificates, as well as their contextual information.

Tactics and techniques
> How the adversary carried out their operations, most often captured using VERIS or ATT&CK, which we will describe in detail later in this chapter. CVEs or CWEs can also be captured in this category.

Supporting information
> This includes non-technical or tactical details of the intrusion—who was targeted, what was going on in the company (or in the world) that may have motivated the intrusion. What was the impact?

Links or references

> This refers to information related to the incident or the adversary that was shared, publicly available, or used as a reference in the course of the investigation.

Internal actions taken or request made

> One very important aspect that should not be overlooked is what was done in response to the incident, and what requests for additional action were made for the future. For example, if the incident-response report called out that more frequent monitoring of company credentials on underground forums would prevent similar attacks in the future, that recommendation (or possibly commitment!) should not be lost in the aftermath of the incident.

After deciding what information should be exploited, it is necessary to extract that information from incident data, standardize it, and store it for future analysis and reference. This will require a process—ideally one that is documented and can be shared with others so that it can be repeated and improved upon moving forward. Processes will vary from team to team; however, there are a few key components that all Exploit-focused processes should have: gathering information, storing information, and managing information.

Gathering Information

If your organization is anything like most of the ones we have seen, at the end of the investigation you have an official Spreadsheet of Doom (plus 5 or 6 non-official versions); 13 files of notes; several photos of whiteboards; and a Slack channel full of hypotheses, links to external documents, and various "let's follow up on this in the future" comments. The difference between this and some of the best process-driven teams we have seen is that the more advanced teams clean things up periodically along the way—we have yet to see, meet, or even hear about a team that doesn't have somewhat messy, creative, but effective processes in the middle of an intense incident. If you are staring at a mountain of disorganized data in as many different structures as you have team members, do not fret. The Exploit process will help you get things in order so that you can learn and adapt moving forward.

Depending on how you manage your incident-response data, it is entirely possible that the most difficult part of the Exploit phase will be finding the important bits of intelligence from the investigation. When it comes to gathering incident-response data, we have seen it all—from elaborate systems to Excel spreadsheets to Post-it® notes with IP addresses stuck to a whiteboard. There is no wrong way to gather that data, but if you want to be able to extract it so that it can be analyzed and used in the future, there are certainly some ways to make the process easier.

When you are dealing with exploiting information from a previous incident, the data available to you is often limited. One of the goals of intelligence-driven incident response is to ensure that the incident-response process captures the information needed for intelligence analysis, but if you are just beginning the process of integrating operations and intelligence, you may not have been able to influence what information was gathered (yet). A good starting point for the Exploit phase is to understand exactly what you *do* have available. We have found that the available information usually falls into one of two categories: high-level information, and technical details such as malware analysis.

If you have only high-level information in the form of a narrative about the incident, you will be looking at extracting strategic-level details. If you have access to detailed malware analysis, you can extract tactical-level details about the malware's functionality. Initially, you may have access to only one level of information or the other, but, ideally, as you implement this process in your organization, you will be able to gather both the technical details of an incident as well as the strategic information on what was targeted and the impact. Being able to combine information across both levels is one of the things that makes intelligence so powerful.

Information-Gathering Goals

The first thing to consider when gathering data, no matter the source, is your goals. There may be a variety of goals, but the most common are:

Indicators of compromise
> Many say indicators of compromise aren't useful anymore, but even the best adversaries don't always change everything. While there may be more durable methods of tracking adversaries, you'd be making a mistake not to pull even the IOCs at the bottom of the Pyramid of Pain and add them to your pile of threat data.

Signatures
> While not always available, depending on the product, you may be able to pull out even more advanced compound indicators in the form of signatures. Snort and Yara are most common, and it will often depend on your tech stack, but even product-specific signatures can be translated into other tools.

Tactics, techniques and procedures
> While not quite as atomic as ATT&CK, another common approach is to pull out how an adversary operates in the form of TTPs.

Strategic data
> This is a bit fuzzier, but in a lot of cases (especially reading third-party data), it's the non-technical data that is most interesting. Information about attribution and adversary motivation can be harder to capture but is often very high value.

So where do we pull this data from?

Mining Previous Incidents

If you are reading this book with the intention of understanding how to start integrating operations and intelligence, it is important to note that you don't have to start with the next incident; you can go back through previous incidents and exploit that information. In fact, this type of activity is a great way to familiarize people in your organization with the F3EAD process and help them feel comfortable with it as you build your threat profile. Digging through and analyzing previous incident data can give you a great idea of the types of threats facing your network and identify the visibility or information gaps you may need to address as you move forward. Whenever possible (and ideally it is always possible), include dates and date ranges when mining information from previous incidents.

Gathering External Information (or, Conducting a Literature Review)

In addition to gathering internal information about previous incidents, we can also gather considerable information about adversaries from external sources. While you are a beautiful and unique organization, your adversaries probably aren't just focused on you exclusively. Chances are, you're not the first organization that they have targeted. And you're likely not the first organization to share information about tactics, techniques, or other organizations that were targeted. It is important to remember that attribution based off things that "seem similar" is often not useful for creating an exact roadmap of what your organization should do or how you should respond to an incident. However, such attribution can help provide additional context or situational awareness. It can be helpful to understand what is similar with other known incidents and what is different, where different actions or analysis may need to be made.

In this sense, gathering external information can be similar to a literature review in academic research. A literature review involves researchers looking at what previous studies, papers, or analyses have been conducted, what conclusions they drew, where they are similar, and where they are dissimilar to your own research. The goal of a literature review is twofold: to identify the unique aspects of your research that fill in gaps in previous research and to build upon and further the overall understanding of a topic. In intelligence-driven incident response, we want to build upon our own knowledge and, if sharing is possible, further the collective understanding of threats to help the entire community grow stronger and more resilient. Whatever the scope of your knowledge-furthering, it is important to understanding what has been reported externally about the actors, indicators of compromise, or other information related to your own incident. However, as with a literature review, remember that information found during this process should not be directly mixed with your own data and findings without a clear citation. In many cases, this "literature review" should be kept in a separate section and referred to during the next step of F3EAD, the Analysis phase.

Extracting and Storing Threat Data

At the end of an investigation—whether immediately following or six months after the fact—you will likely have a plethora of data. Your task in the Exploit phase is to take that information, whatever it may look like, and structure it into a format that can be analyzed and used moving forward. While there are many different ways an organization may go about this task, we have found that it is typically done in one of two ways: mostly manual or platform based. We will walk through these two different approaches using two specialized tools—the common spreadsheet and the more exotic graph-based centralized intelligence platform—but first let's talk about standards.

Standards for Storing Threat Data

No discussion of threat intelligence would be complete without a discussion of the various data standards. Many debates have been had—both on Twitter and in hallways at security conventions—about which standards are the best, which are just fads, and which ones are experiencing "a comeback." These debates aside, the standards you choose are (more than anything) based on the unique needs of your organization. What you choose may look different than what someone else does. We are about to dive into the details of the various data standards, details that may make you never want to talk about them again, but please stick with us. Data standards will make your life a lot easier once you find the one that works for you. If it helps, think of yourself as a chef planning your *mise en plate,* determining which style of knife cut and which containers are going to make for the easiest meal service.

Data Standards and Formats for Indicators

There are several groupings of data standards that are commonly used to store and share technical threat data. No one magical standard rules them all—despite the industry's best efforts—so the best approach is to understand what standards exist and determine whether one of them will work for you. For example, if you are part of sharing organizations that use STIX/TAXII to share data, that may be a good choice for you to store your own data. If your organization has already invested in security tools that use a specific format such as OpenIOC, that may work best. If there is more than one standard that you need to work with (which we see quite often), the next best approach is to make sure that you understand the fundamentals of the various standards and be prepared to do data field mapping, because you will likely deal with information in one of these data formats at some point.

OASIS suite (aka STIX/TAXII)

Structured Threat Information eXpression (STIX™) was initially created in 2010 as a way to standardize the information that was captured about cyber incidents and to facilitate the automated sharing of information between organizations. It was originally maintained by the MITRE Corporation on behalf of the Department of Homeland Security. The Oasis Cyber Threat Intelligence (CTI) technical committee, a component of the Oasis open standards organization, took over MITRE's role in supporting the CyBox, STIX, and TAXII data formats. These standards are some of the more well-known standards, in part because the US government has adopted this suite. Because of this, many of the threat-intelligence platforms have integrated STIX—either STIX 1 or STIX 2.X along with TAXII, which is the transport mechanism for STIX data.

STIX 1. The original version of STIX 1 was built with building blocks called CybOX™, aka Cyber Observable eXpression. CybOX is made up of observables, which are *defined objects with stateful and measurable properties.* There are multiple use cases for CybOX, ranging from event management to malware analysis and information sharing. There are many CybOX objects for capturing observables, although they're not all directly relevant to incident response.

In STIX 1, CybOX are the basic units but the "STIX" portion of the standard allows for more contextual detail to be added to the CybOX objects. This enables further analysis and is a huge benefit when sharing threat data. These additional context fields include Threat Actors, Campaigns, Victim Targets, and TTPs. This allows you to take individual observables that are captured through CybOX and chain them together and add more context. This is when threat data can truly begin to become threat intelligence. Although it is good to know that a certain file is malicious, it is more useful from an analytic perspective to know that the file was used in a particular campaign targeting victims in a specific sector and that, after execution of the file, the actors attempted to exfiltrate intellectual property.

While it is interesting to look at STIX 1 in terms of how systems developed, STIX 1 wasn't really meant for people to *use* it, but instead to be tightly integrated with a specific set of tools. As the need for information exchange and sharing expanded beyond just a small group of similarly minded organizations, the data standard needed to evolve as well. And evolve it did.

STIX 2.X.   STIX 2 was introduced with several improvements that made its adoption easier for many practitioners. One major change was that STIX 2 used JSON rather than XML. STIX 2 also reduced the complexity by merging the two data standards (CybOX and STIX) into one standard called STIX Cyber observables. STIX 2 also introduced two top-level Relationship objects—Relationship and Sightings—which more clearly define the association between different observables.

When STIX, or any standard, is used fully, it can be a great tool for analysis, but just remember that work is required to get all of the information captured! STIX is built into many cyber threat intelligence platforms, making it relatively easy to use, but it is still important to have a solid process for determining what gets captured in this format and for making sure that information on insights from an incident is not lost because it never makes it out of the notebook and into the platform.

TAXII.   Trusted Automated eXchange of Indicator (TAXII) is a transportation and sharing framework that comprises four services: discovery, poll, inbox, and feed management. TAXII enables STIX to be shared between entities or organizations. TAXII has three primary transport and sharing models:

Subscriber
> In this model, one central organization shares information with partner organizations, without the partner organizations sending any information back. This is the model most commonly seen with threat-intelligence providers, either commercial or open source, who send information to customers.

Hub and spoke
> One organization or source serves as the central authority for information sharing. It pushes information to other organizations, and when those organizations want to share back, they send information to the central organization, which redistributes the information to the group.

Peer to peer
> This model can be used by any two or more organizations that want to share information directly without going through a centralized organization. Several mesh networks utilize this model as well.

In most cases, TAXII is used as a top-down distribution (subscriber) model, such as from an ISAC. If the other models are in use, we haven't seen them.

MILE Working Group

In addition to the Oasis suite, another set of data standards is actively maintained and updated by the Managed Incident Lightweight Exchange (MILE) Working Group, which includes the following:

Incident Object Description Exchange Format (IODEF)

RFC 5070 (*https://oreil.ly/icwTa*), first published in 2007, defines IODEF as: "A data representation that provides a framework for sharing information commonly exchanged by Computer Security Incident Response Teams (CSIRT) about computer security incidents." IODEF is an XML-based standard and is used by groups such as the anti-phishing working group and ArcSite. It includes tags for sensitivity and confidence level.

IODEF—Structured Cybersecurity Information (IODEF-SCI)

This extension to IODEF provides a framework for capturing additional context around incident data. RFC 7203 (*https://oreil.ly/D8pkO*) defines the standards for IODEF-SCI and was first published in 2014. IODEF-SCI provides a structure for embedding additional contextual information into IODEF documents, including MITRE's Common Attack Pattern Enumeration and Classification (CAPEC), Common Vulnerabilities and Exposures (CVE), Common Vulnerabilities Scoring System (CVSS), and several other standards.

Real-time Inter-network Defense (RID)

Just as STIX has TAXII to facilitate the exchange of information in STIX format, IODEF and IODEF-SCI have RID. The goal of RID is to allow different organizations with incident data to share that information in a secure, easy-to-manage fashion. RID is defined in RFC 6545 (*https://oreil.ly/C96QV*), and RID over HTTPS is defined in RFC 6546 (*https://oreil.ly/JNjv2*). Similar to TAXII, RID has several options for information-exchange models, including direct peer-to-peer, mesh peer-to-peer, and client-to-subscriber.

OpenIOC

As we discussed previously, the term *IOC*, or indicator of compromise, was popularized by Mandiant. In addition to coining the term, Mandiant developed a standard for capturing IOCs, which is called OpenIOC. This is an XML-based schema (you may have picked up on a trend here) designed to capture and categorize forensic artifacts from compromised hosts as well as network indicators related to malicious communications or other malicious activity. Mandiant identified more than 500 possible artifacts that can be documented using OpenIOC. However, the framework also allows for customization and the creation of new fields as needed by organizations using OpenIOC. It is interoperable with STIX, and documentation has been published on how to transfer between the two standards (*https://oreil.ly/hF4KO*).

You will likely find yourself needing to convert data from one standard to another as you share and receive both threat data and intelligence. It is important to be aware of the various fields and components of the standards, because as you move between them (for example, from STIX to OpenIOC), you could lose or gain certain data fields. If you are unaware of the differences between the standards, you may find yourself searching for something that you *know* you had captured but that did not make it across in the conversion. When converting from one data standard to another, be sure to identify the important fields within the current standard, and then identify the equivalent field in the standard to which it will be converted.

While OpenIOC was an ambitious program, it has largely been deprecated at this point. Mandiant merged with FireEye, combined tech stacks, and broke them up again as the companies separated. Beyond Mandiant, OpenIOC never really gained enough traction to become an industry standard and eventually lost out to STIX 2.

Data Standards and Formats for Strategic Information

As we mentioned, indicators that can be captured using the preceding formats are only half of the picture. Indicators are extremely useful for detection and response, but it is also important to gather other contextual information that will support strategic analysis. Although that information can be stored by using formats such as STIX, standards for capturing technical information are not often the best fit for strategic information. Often such information ends up being stored in documents or PowerPoint slides, if it is captured at all. Not as many options exist for storing strategic information as for storing technical information, but frameworks can be used to avoid losing this critical component of an incident. We will explore three of the primary standards for storing strategic information: ATT&CK, VERIS, and CAPEC.

ATT&CK

We have mentioned ATT&CK several times already in this book because it truly has taken the threat intelligence community by storm over the past few years. As the cry was made to move on from just IOCs to actor tactics (and thus up the Pyramid of Pain) and techniques became louder and louder starting around 2018, MITRE's ATT&CK was ready to answer the call.

MITRE's Adversary Tactics, Techniques, and Common Knowledge (ATT&CK) (*https://oreil.ly/bCUDO*) was created in 2013 with the goal of categorizing attacker behaviors throughout the attack lifecycle. The standard was originally focused on attacks against Microsoft Windows. It focused on tactics (which were described as short-term, tactical adversary goals of an attack) and techniques (which were the means through which adversaries achieved their tactical goals). It has grown to include attacks against Linux and macOS, along with additional matrices describing pre-exploitation activity (PRE-ATT&CK), mobile platforms (Mobile ATT&CK), as well as Industrial Control Systems, cloud systems, even containers like Docker and Kubernetes.

The ATT&CK object structure includes tags, fields, and relationships. Tags are data points that can be used to filter or pivot off of; fields are used for free text to describe different tactics or techniques; and relationships are fields that define the relationship between different entities.

The model and its relationships can be seen in Figure 7-1. Adversary Group, Technique, Tactic, and Software have their own fields that can be used to capture additional relevant information, making ATT&CK a model that can be used to capture both tactical and strategic information.

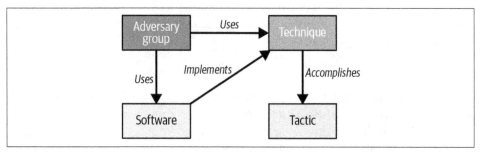

Figure 7-1. MITRE's ATT&CK model relationship

VERIS

The Vocabulary for Event Recording and Incident Sharing (VERIS) is a JSON-based standard that is well-known for supporting the Verizon Data Breach Incident Report (DBIR). The VERIS framework captures information that falls into four categories, known as the four As: Actor, Action, Asset, and Attribute. All four categories answer a question about the incident:

Actor
> The Actor field answers the question, "Whose actions affected this asset?" This field captures high-level information about the actors responsible for an incident. The data schema enumerations for Actor include whether the actor is an internal, external, or partner actor, as well as the actor's motivation.

Action
> The Action field answers the question, "What actions affected the asset?" Action includes things such as how the attackers were able to get access, including the use of malware, hacking, or social engineering. It also includes the specific vector, such as exploiting a known vulnerability, or using phishing emails.

Asset
> This field answers the question, "Which assets were affected?" This is an incredibly important question to answer from a strategic perspective. The enumerations include information about the type of asset affected, as well as its accessibility and management.

Attribute

> The Attribute field answers the question, "How was the asset affected?" It uses the traditional Confidentiality, Integrity, Availability triad.

VERIS also captures information about the timeline and impact of an incident. These fields provide places to capture how long it took to identify, contain, and remediate an incident and how severe the impact is for the organization affected. The primary use case for VERIS is not generating rules or alerts, but for helping organizations understand the risks that they face. Therefore, the information is not as detailed nor as technical as that which is captured in STIX or other formats mentioned previously. However, the information VERIS captures can be used to tell a more complete story of what happened in a particular incident.

CAPEC

The Common Attack Pattern Enumeration and Classification (CAPEC) framework was originally designed to help with the development of secure software. The concept behind CAPEC is that if software developers understood the common ways in which attackers targeted and exploited software, they could design and build software that is not susceptible to those attacks. Rather than just capturing specific technical details, CAPEC attempts to capture the entirety of an attack as an attack pattern, which includes information on attack prerequisites, related weaknesses, related vulnerabilities, and attacker steps.

An organization can learn a great deal from an attack when a clear picture of what happened is available and is captured in CAPEC. An analysis of attack patterns over time can provide an understanding of the way attackers operate, the way they adapt to security measures, and any additional measures required to protect an organization.

Process for Extracting

Once you have identified the format you want (or need) to capture data in and where you will store it, it is important to develop a process for extracting all the relevant information. This is the part of the Exploit phase where the rubber meets the road. While we wish we could spend this section outlining the exact step-by-step process that you should use, the truth is that like everything else in cyber threat intelligence, there are unique components to every CTI program that will make these processes vary case by case. We are instead going to outline the process for developing a process, with the goal of helping you outline something that will work for you long term but that can easily be modified if your needs change.

Step 1: Identify your goals

Be as specific as you can be here. Don't just say, "Our goal is to manage the data from the incident," although that can be a good start. A clear goal would include the intended outcome of the Exploit phase, who it will be supporting, and the intended impact. For example: *"Capture all information—including IOCs, TTPs, target information, and strategic information—in a spreadsheet with an executive summary of the incident so our current team of five intelligence analysts can further analyze and make additional recommendations for detections and mitigations."* Written out like this, a goal becomes a roadmap for the process that you will follow.

Step 2: Identify your tools

We use the term *tools* very lightly here. A tool is anything that is going to help you achieve the goal(s) outlined in step 1. Some organizations have threat-intelligence platforms (or TIPs, covered later in this chapter), which may have built-in functionality like automated indicator extraction and categorization. If you don't have a TIP, there are still many other resources that can be used to help, including scripts, spreadsheets, non-TIP databases, and productivity and collaboration tools. In this step, you should also call out whether you have the right tools to achieve the goal(s) you laid out. For example, if the goal involves sharing information with a team of five analysts, you will need some sort of collaboration tool(s). If you do not have any tools that will facilitate sharing of information, then you will have a difficult time meeting that goal.

Step 3: Identify the system or process you will use

This can be the most diverse step out of all because there are many different ways an analyst can get data into the tools needed to achieve the Exploit goals identified in step 1. Approaching this undertaking in a systematic, ideally documented, fashion is the best way to make sure that it is done completely and there isn't information missed or overlooked. One process may involve the following tasks:

1. Identify the location of all data sources that will be aggregated as part of the Exploit process.

2. Create a checklist of all sources to keep track of what has been exploited.

3. Based on your tools, complete the necessary logistical steps to prepare them for exploitation—whether this means creating a new file based on a template, identifying the tags that will be used when entering data into a database, or beginning a new wiki page that will house all of the information from this incident.

4. Working down the checklist of data to be aggregated, begin moving data from disparate sources into your tool of choice, checking off each source once it is complete.

Having a clear process to get from a pile of data post-incident to a structured, comprehensive set of information ready for analysis is one of the best ways to set yourself up for success. The system you develop may involve multiple people focusing on different functions within the system, or it may just be a process for yourself. You may add timelines or milestones into the process to keep you on track and accountable, or you may find that every incident is so different that timelines don't matter as much as just moving through the steps. The important thing is to document how you will move through the data extraction process and to be comfortable updating or revising the process as goals, tools, or needs change.

Step 4: Launch and iterate

This where you dive in. This can be the hardest part of the whole process—even if you have the right tools and a solid process to start working through the steps in a systematic way. Try things out to see what is working and where you are running into hurdles. Don't be afraid to change your process up, start identifying new tools you may need, or new skills that would make the process easier. If you find a method or approach that is especially useful, make sure to document it for future analysts (or for future you).

Managing Information

Managing information is not simply capturing the individual IOCs or artifacts from an investigation. A great deal of additional information needs to be captured as well so that you know how to manage and handle all the types of information moving forward.

Some key things are critical to capture in order to help manage information:

Date
> When was this piece of data or information seen? This will help with analysis as well as support expiration or retirement of data, essentially determining when data is still good to act on and include in analysis and when that data is no longer valid.

Source
> Few things are more frustrating than not knowing when and where a piece of information came from. Capturing the source of the information will help if you ever need to go back to get more information or if you want to assign the confidence of that piece of information, both of which will be useful during the Analysis phase.

Data-handling information
> Often data will need to be handled differently based on the sensitivity and the source. We recommend using DHS's Traffic Light Protocol (TLP), which dictates

how information can be shared. The TLP standard was updated in August 2022. Additional information can be found here (*https://www.first.org/tlp*).[1]

TLP: CLEAR

- Publicly available information that can be shared with anyone using any method.

TLP: GREEN

- Information that can be shared with peers and partners, but not using publicly available channels, such as posting it on a blog or tweeting it to journalists. Seriously, don't do that.

TLP: AMBER

- This information can be shared with people within your organization and its clients, but not outside it and not using public channels. TLP v2 helped to clear up some confusion about the use of TLP:AMBER by specifically including client of an organization and introducing the new caveat TLP:AMBER+STRICT, which means that the information must stay with the organization with whom it is shared and cannot be shared with external parties, including clients. TLP:AMBER and TLP:AMBER+STRICT information should not be shared using public channels.

TLP: RED

- This is extremely sensitive information, usually related to an ongoing incident or investigation. It should not be shared outside the specific recipient, not even within the recipient's organization, without prior approval. Often TLP:RED information will be reclassified as Amber or Green once the situation has been resolved.

Duplicate data

It is important to make sure that you are not duplicating data by accidentally capturing the same incident data or threat report more than once. However, at times you will receive the same information from more than one source. When that happens, it is important to capture. Receiving the same indicators from multiple places, such as from an internal investigation *and* from a threat report from the FBI, can have serious implications. But if you are not able to capture the details around both sources, you can seriously hinder the analytic process, which you will be moving into next.

---

1 This is a chocolate cake recipe (*https://oreil.ly/ZXWzq*) Rebekah originally linked instead of the TLP documentation.

Keeping these things in mind as you begin to store and manage your data will make using and maintaining it much easier.

Threat-Intelligence Platforms

As you can probably tell—considering our coverage of standards and the numerous requirements for managing all the information that you have exploited during an investigation—capturing and analyzing all of this information is no trivial task. A threat-intelligence platform (TIP) is often used to simplify that process and make gathering, storing, and searching this information easier.

A TIP is a database and user interface specifically designed to handle threat information. Various types of TIPs exist—some that specialize in information sharing, and some that focus on the storage and management of large quantities of IOCs. Most TIPs can ingest information in the tactical formats described earlier and capture the additional details needed to manage the information as well. Using a TIP will significantly reduce the amount of work that needs to be done in the Exploit phase of F3EAD. Several popular open source platforms are available and a variety of commercial solutions as well. We will discuss those options next.

MISP

The Malware Information Sharing Platform (MISP) is a free option for managing malware-based threat data. MISP was created by a group of developers in conjunction with NATO's Computer Incident Response Capability (NCIRC). MISP includes a database with a user interface that enables organizations to store both technical and nontechnical data related to attacks to facilitate correlation and sharing of information on threats. MISP can export information in OpenIOC, plain text, CSV, MISP XML, and JSON formats to support intrusion detection and prevention. MISP also has a robust sharing capability, enabling users to share with other MISP users or groups. You can get more information on MISP on GitHub (*https://oreil.ly/Rxjiy*).

CRITs

Collaborative Research into Threats (CRITs) is another open source tool for managing and sharing threat data. CRITs was developed by MITRE and therefore was designed to work with STIX and TAXII. CRITs stores threat information and includes the ability to add confidence and severity to the indicators that have been captured. It integrates with TAXII services to facilitate sharing and is therefore a good choice for many organizations that receive or exchange information with the government or other organizations using STIX/TAXII. CRITs can export data into CSV, STIX, and JSON formats. Information and documentation for installing and using CRITs can be found on GitHub (*https://oreil.ly/s7VX_*).

YETI

Your Everyday Threat Intelligence (YETI) platform is a threat-intelligence management tool that was released for public use in March 2017. YETI was designed to enable analysts to organize and analyze the various components of threat intelligence in one place. It supports observables, IOCs, TTPs, as well as general knowledge on threats. One of the great aspects of YETI is that in addition to storing information that you have already found about threats, it can also perform some indicator enrichment, including domain resolution and WHOIS lookups, as well as any additional integrations you want to configure. YETI can ingest data from MISP instances, JSON feeds, XML feeds, and various malware sandboxes. YETI was specifically designed to support the many challenges that threat-intelligence analysts have identified in recent years and to be flexible—many analysts often need the same information but have different processes or workflows. YETI has a GitHub repository (*https:// oreil.ly/O_cAj*) where you can find more information on installation as well as documentation.

Commercial solutions

A variety of commercial solutions are available for threat-intelligence management as well. Most of the commercial solutions include similar features to MISP, CRITs, and YETI, but also manage system configuration, take responsibility for setup and hardware management, and offer support for troubleshooting or feature requests. Commercial solutions can be ideal for organizations with limited development resources that want something easy to set up and maintain.

All of the TIPs, whether open source or commercial, have many of the same features and functionality but may have been designed with a particular use case in mind, whether that is malware-based threat information, specific information sharing, or supporting and enabling analytic processes. One of the best things about starting with open source TIPs is that you can find the best fit for your organization. If installation and support of the tools are a problem for your organization, you can explore commercial solutions once you identify the best overall type of platform for your organization.

Conclusion

Information that is gained from an investigation should not be forgotten after the engagement is over—whether that investigation occurred at your own organization or happened somewhere else and you are fortunate enough to have access to the data. That information needs to be analyzed and disseminated so that organizations can learn from and adapt to threats. Analysis and dissemination are not possible, however, without first going through the critical exploitation phase where information is gathered, processed into a usable format, and stored for analysis.

As you learned in this chapter, you have many options for processing and storing this information, from the format in which it is stored to the actual database in which it is kept and the interface used to access it. Take time to explore your options and find a system or combinations of systems that will work well for you. Once the Exploit phase is completed, it will be much easier to move into the next phase of the F3EAD cycle: Analyze.

## CHAPTER 8

Analyze

If you do not know how to ask the right question, you will discover nothing.
   —W. Edwards Deming

All of the information that you have gathered has been exploited and is now sitting—formatted and standardized—in a database or a threat-intelligence platform. Now what? The information sitting there does little good until it is analyzed. The Analyze phase of F3EAD is one of the hardest to articulate but also one of the most important. This is the phase where we take data and information and process it into intelligence. This chapter covers the basic principles of analysis, models such as target-centric and structured analysis, and processes to assign confidence levels and address cognitive biases.

The Fundamentals of Analysis

To properly analyze the information you have, you must go through another (thankfully, smaller) version of the intelligence cycle. You must decide what your requirements are or, in other words, what questions you are going to answer. To get started, you first need to collect the information that you will use to answer those questions. Most of that information was gathered throughout the investigation and standardized in the Exploit phase, but other information will be needed to enrich or augment that data so it can be properly analyzed. Therefore, you may need to continue to collect more data as you move into the Analyze phase. The Analyze phase of F3EAD captures the entire intelligence cycle, pictured in Figure 8-1.

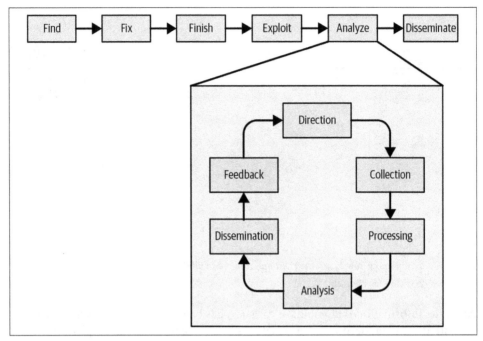

Figure 8-1. Analysis within F3EAD

During the response to the Road Runner intrusion, we identified domains and IP addresses that were used in the Exploitation and Command-and-Control phases of their operations. That information helped us in the Fix and Finish stages and will continue to help us as we analyze the intrusion. Rather than only identifying the technical details of the attack, to respond and remediate, we can analyze those same domains and IPs to identify patterns that can help us better understand the attacker's tactics and predict future behaviors. This process involves gathering additional information about the domains and IPs, including who they were registered to and how the attacker used them. This new information is then analyzed, intelligence gaps (critical pieces of information that are needed to conduct analysis) are identified, and more information is gathered as needed.

Dual Process Thinking

You may be picking up on the fact that things have slowed down a bit by this phase of the F3EAD cycle. That doesn't mean these subsequent steps are any less important or significant. It means that the mental processes required here—especially in the Analyze phase—require both significant cognitive efforts and significant cognitive rigor that cannot be accomplished by using the "fast thinking" often employed in incident response. Instead, we need "slow thinking," though probably still on a deadline (often even short deadlines).

The concept of thinking fast and slow was popularized by Daniel Kahneman in his book by the same name, *Thinking, Fast and Slow*;[1] however, the theory of the dual process of thought has been studied for decades. The general idea states that there are two modes of thinking. The first mode is fast thinking, also known as *system 1 thinking*, which is a quick, automatic process often based on association and experience, relying heavily on pre-existing mental models. This type of thinking can get us out of a jam when time is short and action is needed quickly. When using this system, the mind makes an assumption that the risk associated with minor flaws in intuitive judgment is less significant than the risk of not acting fast enough. The flaws associated with system 1 thinking include cognitive biases and misapplied mental models, which may not be that serious when outrunning a tiger but could cause a lot of problems when making decisions that will impact you long term.

The second mode is slow thinking, or *system 2 thinking*, which is a deliberate process of reasoning that aims to counter the impulsive biases that are so effective with system 1. With system 2 thinking, not only do you need to take the time to counter things like biases, but you also need to make sure that you have a firm grasp on the context of the different pieces of information that you are analyzing. You need to ensure you are thinking through second- and third-order effects—things that may not be immediately apparent but that have the potential to have significant impact on the future. Understanding complex networks and situations takes time and, without the time to think things through, it is very likely that you will have at least some faulty judgments.

In this chapter, we will focus on the system 2 (slow) mode of thinking as a way to help generate greater insights that can be clearly articulated, defended, and shared with others who will be able to follow the reasoning and come to more or less the same analytic conclusion. This is not an easy task; however, throughout the chapter we will present different approaches, methods, and frameworks that can be used to support this type of analysis. We will also cover some additional mental models that can put analysts in the right frame of mind for *thinking about thinking*, or metacognition, a concept that has been discussed and debated since at least the time of Greek philosopher Aristotle.

Deductive, Inductive, and Abductive Reasoning

When thinking about approaching a problem, we don't usually think about how we *think* about problems. It's a little bit like driving a car; it's easy to just pick a "normal" way to go and head the same way no matter what. But it's not always that easy, is it? Sometimes there's traffic, sometimes there's construction, sometimes you need to stop

---

1 Daniel Kahneman, *Thinking, Fast and Slow* (New York: Farrar, Straus and Giroux, 2013).

by the store, sometimes you just want a different view. In these cases, you may take a different route to get to the same place. Reasoning can go the same way.

It's important to know that reasoning, like so many things we do, follows the typical intelligence axiom. When you ask which type of reasoning is the best, the answer is: it depends. Like your trips in the car, which type of reasoning you use depends on what you're trying to accomplish. The issue is when you don't know *why* you chose a given approach (kind of like when you drive somewhere on mental autopilot). In a lot of cases, analysts (both intelligence and security) do the same thing. So, take a step back, and let's think about how we solve problems and why we should consider different approaches.

Deductive reasoning

> Deduction: the deriving of a conclusion by reasoning specifically: inference in which the conclusion about particulars follows necessarily from general or universal premises
>
> —Merriam-Webster's Collegiate Dictionary, 11th edition (definition 2a)

Made famous by everyone's favorite detective, Sherlock Holmes, deduction isn't usually what people think it is. In short, a deduction is always based on universally accepted premises. Another way to think about it is starting with an idea, making an observation or series of observations on causes, and then making a conclusion about the expected effect.

Deductions are often very direct and simple, not what we think of in investigations. For example, think back to high school geometry. One rule of geometry is that the internal angles of all triangles add up to 180 degrees. If you have a triangle with two 45-degree angles, then you can deduce, based on the 180-degree rule, that the third angle must be 90 degrees (you could go one step further given another rule that any triangle with a 90-degree angle is a right triangle and say this must be a right triangle as well).

While the Baker Street resident sleuth likes to reference it a lot, most detectives aren't deducing their cases. In most examples of deduction, there are both simple premises and nearly perfect information. Deductions are often useful for understanding basic life but not for investigations. We rarely have enough perfect information and can rarely make universal rules.

Inductive reasoning

> Induction: inference of a generalized conclusion from particular instances.
>
> —Merriam-Webster's Collegiate Dictionary, 11th edition (definition 2a)

The first, and most commonly seen, reasoning method in most investigations is induction. *Induction* is a circumstance where you start with a pile of data, maybe a singular example, maybe a few different examples, and work out a rule that fits all the data. You could simplify this further—induction is the process of using a specific set of cause-and-effect relationships to build a generalized rule.

Inductive reasoning is often a shortcut. For example, say you have a new coworker who has a peanut butter and jelly sandwich for their lunch on their first Monday. They have the same peanut butter and jelly sandwich on Tuesday, Wednesday, and Thursday. So, what about Friday? Well, inductive reasoning may lead you to say, "Obviously, they eat peanut butter and jelly sandwiches every day, so clearly they'll eat a peanut butter and jelly sandwich on Friday as well." And maybe they do, but your new coworker asks others if they want to go out to lunch on Friday.

Inductive reasoning always benefits from more information as it makes it possible to further refine the theories you're matching against. These inductive theories are only as good as the data available, but this imperfect data also makes it possible to come up with generalizations that aren't 100% correct, such as assuming our coworker would follow four days of one lunch with a fifth. After the first week, we might refine our theory to assume they always eat out for lunch on Fridays, but after a second week, that could change again if you find they went out only that first Friday to meet coworkers. So, you might need to refine your reasoning again. This often manifests as "correlation doesn't equal causation."

The more data, the better the theories will be, but this is a challenge in security investigations. It's impossible to know how much data we have, whether we can see 10% or 100%. It's impossible to know how good our theories are, and it's dangerous to assume they're too good. We see this happen a lot using link analysis tools such as Maltego. People will often throw data on a force-directed graph and start making inductive theories. This can often be something as simple as looking at network flows in a graph and assuming the node with the most connections must be the most important. Is it? Well...sometimes it is, but ask any malware analyst how many pieces of malware reach out to *google.com* or *microsoft.com* to verify internet connectivity. Does that mean those are bad websites? Clearly not.

Abductive reasoning

> Abduction: a syllogism in which the major premise is evident but the minor premise and therefore the conclusion only probable.
>
> —Merriam-Webster's Collegiate Dictionary, 11th edition ('Deduction' vs. 'Induction' vs. 'Abduction')

At this point, you might have guessed that abductive reasoning is what we end up using most often in security investigations. Abductive reasoning is in some ways a combination of the other two reasoning types (and mostly what Sherlock Holmes is actually referring to). *Abduction* is the process of taking information that's available, applying past rules and facts, and coming up with a plausible set of causes. This differs from induction, where we're trying to create these basic rules rather than apply them, and it differs from deduction, where you're taking a set of cases and rules and using them to predict an effect.

Abduction is always the best way to think about our investigations because, unlike both induction and deduction, it takes into account that we rarely have perfect information and can rarely come up with universal rules based on the information we do have. In addition, our usual goal in investigation is to discover the cause. For example, if you said, "Our website is down with too much traffic" (an effect) and "DDoS for ransom is a common reason for too much traffic" (a rule), then you could come up with a cause: "We're being DDoS'd for a ransom."

What's the reasoning for talking about reasoning?

Our most common issues and challenges within cybersecurity come down to bad reasoning about problems and bad fundamental assumptions. One example is attribution of malware to specific threat actors. For many years, it was often assumed the Winnti malware family was being used by only a single threat actor, and the threat actors and malware were used interchangeably—in this case, a bad rule. This is an example of induction gone wrong. As a result, this bad rule was applied many times and led to confusion around who was really attacking an organization, as the adversaries' actions didn't match the original Winnti threat actor. If you look at the MITRE ATT&CK Winnti Group (*https://oreil.ly/t9SUL*), the confusion is clear. They call out overlaps with Axiom, APT17, and Ke3chang.

In short, if you don't know how you're approaching a problem and why you're approaching it that way, it's easy to introduce mistakes that could lead to confusion or even failed analysis further down the line. The first analyst who saw the Winnti malware and associated it with a single actor may not have been wrong, but how their reasoning was accepted became a problem for many organizations later. The Key Assumptions Check—a structured analytic technique—is meant to help you challenge and avoid these kinds of mistakes, but the best thing possible is to consider how you're framing your thoughts to begin with and avoid making assumptions before it becomes a problem!

Case Study: The OPM Breach

One of the most significant breaches, which is likely still impacting countless people and entities today, was the breach of the US Office of Personnel Management (OPM) (*https://oreil.ly/_cpzJ*). This breach resulted in the loss of personal, highly sensitive information about more than 20 million individuals who had undergone a background investigation for a security clearance. In addition to the size and sensitivity of the information that was stolen, the OPM breach is notable because of the multiple missed opportunities for the attack to be identified and prevented. The intrusion was a complex campaign that spanned years and included the theft of IT manuals and network maps, the compromise of two contractors with access to OPM's networks, as well as OPM directly. Even when the individual intrusions were identified, no one connected the dots to identify that a larger threat needed to be addressed.

Even before the attackers began their campaign, opportunities existed to take what we know about attackers and how they operate and apply this to defense. It is possible to identify that a government agency with access to highly sensitive, highly actionable personal information on every American with a security clearance was a high-value target for nation-state attackers.

The complete timeline of the breach is a lesson in how analysis, if done properly and in a timely fashion, can prevent or reduce the devastating impact of a successful campaign. It also shows just how bad it can be when incident responders, managers, and executives fail to connect the dots and see the bigger picture. The OPM breach was a classic and disheartening example of a failure to analyze, even when all of the information was available.

Analytic Processes and Methods

In incident response, experience with networking, intrusions, and other cybersecurity fundamentals is key to making quick and accurate decisions, recognizing patterns of malicious activity, and identifying how to mitigate them. As we learned in the chapters on Find, Fix, and Finish, using the kill chain and the Diamond Model can help us organize both our thoughts and the data surrounding an incident. With analysis, we rely on a separate set of skills that tie into our knowledge and experience around network intrusions and cybersecurity, but that are unique to intelligence analysis. These can be thought of as cognitive skills that underpin any particular area of content-based expertise. Cognitive skills include memory, cognitive processing, logic and reasoning, attention, and cognitive flexibility. These skills, which are helpful in all aspects of life, can be applied to a given subject by a set of processes and frameworks. In intelligence-drive incident response, we use Structured Analytic Techniques (SATs) and analytic frameworks such as target-centric analysis and victim-centric analysis to help guide our analysis processes (more on these later).

The processes and methods described in this section are common approaches to analysis and can be used on their own or combined. In intelligence analysis, it is not our experience with a particular subject that will make the most difference, but our experience with the overall process of conducting *intelligence analysis*.

Structured Analytic Techniques (SATs)

One of the best primers on SATs is the book *Structured Analytic Techniques for Intelligence Analysis* by Randolph H. Pherson and Richards J. Heuer, Jr.[2] While SATs are relevant for all types of intelligence analysis, there are some techniques that are more applicable to intelligence-driven incident response, so we will focus on those.

The goal of using SATs is to give analysts a (more or less) step-by-step approach that is repeatable, explainable to others participating in the analytic process, and reproducible. SATs are specifically designed to counter the type of system 1 thinking flaws we discussed at the beginning of the chapter—cognitive biases and misapplied mental models. *Structured Analytic Techniques for Intelligence Analysis* breaks SATs into six families:

Getting organized
> Techniques in this family help an analyst at the beginning of the analytic process, when they are staring at a pile of data without a solid idea of where to begin. It includes methods such as sorting, ranking, and checklists. Fortunately, with intelligence-driven incident response you are not starting from a blank slate—you have been gathering, sorting, and organizing data throughout the incident-response process and are often not starting from zero. If, however, you decide to spend some time going through old incident data that has not been fully analyzed, it could be useful to begin with methods from this family.

Exploration techniques
> Techniques in this family help an analyst come up with new approaches, rethink previously held beliefs, or begin to push the boundaries of the biases that tell us something *isn't possible*. Exploration techniques focus on methods such as brainstorming and creating mind maps, often focusing on the relationships between different elements.

Diagnostic techniques
> This family of techniques is used frequently in intelligence-drive incident response—in fact, we deep dive into one of its most commonly leverages methods, Analysis of Competing Hypotheses, in the next section. Diagnostic techniques most closely mirror the scientific method that many of us learned when we were younger, with the caveat that in intelligence analysis we almost never have the complete picture and it's typically not possible to fully test any hypothesis that is generated. Other methods in this family are Multiple-Hypothesis Generation, Diagnostic Reasoning, and Deception Detection.

---

2 Randolph H. Pherson and Richards J. Heuer, Jr., *Structured Analytic Techniques for Intelligence Analysis*, 3rd edition (Thousand Oaks: CQ Press, an imprint of SAGE Publications, Inc., 2020).

Reframing techniques

These techniques are a key staple in any analyst's tool belt. They are specifically designed to help identify when biases or misapplied mental models could be impacting analysis. Many of the "contrarian techniques" covered later in the chapter, including Red Hat Analysis and What If? Analysis, are considered reframing techniques. These techniques are best done with a group to better identify flaws in mental models that an individual may have; however, they can be done even by individual analysts, such as through a Structured Self-Critique exercise.

Foresight techniques

"Predictive intelligence" is something that every security manager and CISO wishes that their teams could generate regularly. While it is unfortunately not possible to perfectly predict the future, there is a set of SATs—foresight techniques—designed to help identify driving forces that may indicate a future outcome and to prepare to monitor those forces to anticipate changes. One method that is particularly useful in intelligence-drive incident response is Indicator Generation, Validation, and Evaluation, which we will cover in the next section.

Decision-support techniques

There are times—many times in fact—when an analyst is not conducting analysis to help determine their own next steps, but to know what to present to a senior leader or decision maker to help *them* make a decision. And, fortunately, there is a family of techniques that help think through information and structure it in a way to support decision making. These techniques include heavy hitters also used in business intelligence, such as SWOT Analysis, which we will cover in Chapter 10.

Here are a few steps that will help you decide which SAT to use and identify who else should be part of the process:

1. Determine what question you are going to answer, ideally using specific requirements from your leadership. You can conduct multiple iterations of structured analysis in order to answer multiple questions, but just as you should not try to test multiple variables within a single experiment, it is best not to try to answer several questions with the same analysis. Even if the processes are only slightly different, it is ideal to keep them separate to avoid clouding your judgment or contaminating your conclusions. If time constraints are present, focus on the most pressing question/requirement and begin to work on that.

2. Identify the nature of the question you are trying to answer through analysis. Is it future looking? If so, perhaps you should review techniques from the foresight family. Are you attempting to describe how a recent intrusion fits into the overall pattern of threats that your organization has dealt with? If so, a diagnostic

technique may be more beneficial. Capturing not only the question but the *nature* of the question will guide you to the right path.

3. Review your exploited data to determine whether you have all the information that you need to generate a hypothesis, or several hypotheses, to answer your question. This involves going through the information you gathered from the investigation and may require collecting additional enrichment information, which we will discuss later in the chapter.

4. As we mentioned, structured analysis can be done by an individual analyst, but many of the techniques are most effective when done by a team, so think about who on your team should be here. If you already work on a team of dynamic analysts, then this may be easy—and you are very fortunate! If that is not the case, there are still others you can include in the analysis. Key incident-response personnel, malware analysts, red teamers—all of these groups are used to thinking analytically, and one of the benefits of using SATs is that it provides a step-by-step process that allows you to leverage unique experiences and perspectives, while also addressing biases that may come with that experience.

In addition to the families of techniques, which can make it easier to narrow down the list of SATs that could be helpful in a given situation, authors Heuer and Pherson designated several individual techniques that fit into different families. These are considered *core techniques* and are often useful with intelligence-driven incident response. The core techniques we will cover in the next section include Key Assumptions Check, Analysis of Competing Hypotheses, and Indicator Generation, Validation, and Evaluation. We will also cover some very helpful Contrarian techniques to help address biases, which can seriously hinder analysis.

Key Assumptions Check

A Key Assumptions Check is a systematic approach to identifying the assumptions that are being used to fill in key information gaps and determining whether these assumptions are valid and should remain part of the analytic process. Ideally this is done at the beginning of an analytic undertaking because, as we will see as we move through other common structured analytic techniques, it's critical to have a firm grasp of assumptions and preconceptions that are part of the analysis.

Key Assumptions Check is one of the most leveraged SATs, and for good reason. As we discussed previously, our brains look for shortcuts wherever they can. They often look for assumptions that then typically become the basis of our analysis, whether they should or not. And to be fair, sometimes they *should*, but it is important that we are intentional about understanding the fundamental beliefs we have of our situation. For example, with our Road Runner intrusion, we made an assumption that because we were passed information about a threat from another campaign, when we found some of the same indicators in our network, it was *because* we were a campaign.

While this is a reasonable assumption and it certainly seemed to help us during the Find, Fix, and Finish phases, that does not mean we should never question that assumption. A Key Assumptions Check supports that questioning process.

Heuer and Pherson outline a process for conducting a Key Assumptions Check:

1. Gather the group who will participate in the Key Assumptions Check. This should include those who are familiar with the project or topic, along with some respected analysts who are not intimately familiar with the issue and can provide a fresh set of eyes.

2. Begin the session by identifying the specific topic to be discussed and ask each participant to silently write down the assumptions that they have about the topic. For Road Runner, this could include things such as "election campaigns are targeted by sophisticated actors," and "the information passed to us from the sharing group was a legitimate intrusion and not a false flag or misinformation operation."

3. Collect each participant's responses and write them on a whiteboard or, if conducting the session virtually, on a collaboration document or via screen sharing.

4. As a group, review the assumptions that have been identified and start brainstorming additional assumptions. One good question to ask to get this part moving is, "What assumptions are so basic and fundamental that we would never even think to question them?"

5. Once you have a solid list, go through each assumption and ask key questions about it such as, "Why do we think this is true?" or "How much evidence supports that this assumption is true?" or "If this was true in the past, why do we think it is still true?" It is also helpful to propose counter assumptions—not necessarily the exact opposite of the assumption, but an alternate assumption that would significantly change the perception of a situation.

6. For each assumption, evaluate as a group whether it is a sound or solid assumption, whether it is supported but with some caveats, or whether it is unsupported or questionable. Heuer and Pherson suggest using these three categories; however, other practitioners use a 1 to 5 scale to rate confidence in an assumption, with 1 being totally unsupported conjecture, and 5 being an assumption with significant evidence supporting it. A 3 or less for any assumption should include a plan to gather additional information to help determine whether that assumption should remain part of the analysis—these are known as "key uncertainties" rather than key assumptions.

7. One additional suggestion, especially if there are several key assumptions low on the confidence scale, is to assign each key assumption a place on a 2 x 2 matrix measuring high and low certainty and high and low potential impact (Figure 8-2). Once they are all assigned a spot, based on group consensus, the

low certainty/high potential impact assumptions are the ones to start trying to address most urgently.

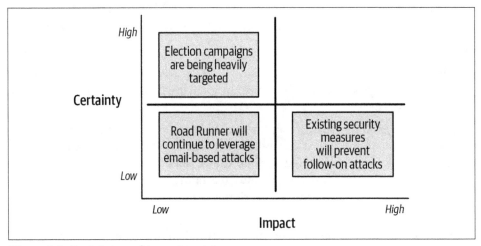

Figure 8-2. Certainty and impact matrix

It is important to note that you cannot do a Key Assumptions Check at one point in time and then hold the position that the assumptions will always remain valid (or invalid, based on your findings). A Key Assumptions Check does not turn an assumption into a fact or a piece of evidence; it remains as assumption, which means that at some point additional information may make it more or less valid. It is important to recheck your key assumptions periodically, for as long as they remain central to your analysis.

Analysis of Competing Hypotheses

Analysis of Competing Hypotheses (ACH) is a method developed by Heuer that is used to evaluate multiple alternate hypotheses and identify the most likely hypothesis based on the evidence. ACH is an eight-step process that aims to force an analyst to consider all possibilities and look for evidence that supports a hypothesis, rather than to identify a hypothesis based on intuition. The eight steps are as follows:

1. Identify the possible hypotheses to be considered. Heuer recommends using a group of analysts with different backgrounds and different perspectives to brainstorm the possibilities. It is also important to differentiate between an unproven hypothesis and a disproven hypothesis during this step. An *unproven* hypothesis is one where there is no evidence that it is correct, whereas a *disproven* hypothesis is one where there is evidence that the hypothesis is incorrect. Include an unproven hypothesis, no matter how improbable, in the ACH process, but do not include disproven hypotheses.

2. Make a list of significant evidence for and against each hypothesis. If you have already gone through the process of evaluating key assumptions, this step should be relatively simple; you already have the key pieces of evidence that contribute to the various hypotheses.

3. Create a matrix with hypotheses across the top and evidence down the side and evaluate whether each piece of evidence supports or refutes each hypothesis. See Table 8-1 for an example of this matrix. There are several approaches to filling out the matrix. Heuer suggests listing whether each piece of evidence is consistent with the hypothesis by inserting a *C*, if it is inconsistent with the hypothesis by inserting an *I*, or if it is neutral or not applicable, in which case you would insert *N/A*. Others suggest using a weighing scale such as a plus sign (+) if a piece of evidence moderately supports a hypothesis or two plus signs (++) if it strongly supports a piece of evidence, and so forth.

Table 8-1. Completed ACH matrix template

	H1	H2	H3	H4
E1	C	I	I	C
E2	C	I	I	C
E3	N/A	N/A	N/A	N/A
E4	C	C	I	I
E5	I	I	I	I
E6	C	C	I	I

In the matrix in Table 8-1, we can see that H3 is not supported by any piece of evidence and therefore would be removed from the matrix. Likewise, E3 is not applicable to any of the hypotheses, and E5 is inconsistent with every hypothesis, so the analyst would need to go back and reevaluate those pieces of evidence to make sure that they are both relevant to the analysis and are accurate. It is possible for a flawed or biased piece of evidence to make it through the evaluation stage, and this is another opportunity to identify whether something should be considered in the analysis.

4. Conduct initial analysis to refine the matrix. After step 3, the matrix should show a few things: Some hypotheses may have inconsistent (*I* or -) assessments for every piece of evidence. Although this doesn't disprove a hypothesis, if there is no evidence to support it, then it should be removed from the matrix. Similarly, if a piece of evidence has an *N/A* assessment for each hypothesis, the analyst should either remove it from the matrix or, if it truly is a key piece of evidence, reevaluate whether there is another hypothesis that needs to be considered.

One thing that incident responders may run into from time to time is evidence from a separate, unrelated intrusion ending up in the analysis, simply because it was identified around the same time as the other evidence. When something does not match up with any other evidence, it may be best to remove it from the current analysis and analyze it on its own.

5. Draw initial conclusions about the likelihood of each hypothesis. Focus on disproving the hypotheses rather than proving them to be correct. After the matrix has been initially refined, you can reevaluate the likelihood of each hypothesis based on how much of the evidence supports it. In the example in Table 8-1, H1 has the most supporting evidence, and if it is deemed by the analyst that E5 is not a valid piece of information, then there is no evidence that contradicts this hypothesis. H1 would therefore be considered the most likely hypothesis. H2 and H4 both have evidence that supports them, but also have evidence that is inconsistent with them; therefore, they are less likely. If any of the evidence that was marked as inconsistent proves that those hypotheses are incorrect, they would be considered disproven hypotheses. It is easier to disprove a hypothesis than it is to prove that a hypothesis is absolutely true.

6. Analyze how much of your conclusion is dependent on a single piece of evidence. Re-analyze the information that led to your judgment of the most likely hypothesis or led to a hypothesis being disproven. Was there a single piece of evidence that weighed most heavily? If so, how confident are you in that piece of evidence? This will help determine the overall confidence in a judgment. If multiple pieces of evidence from various sources strongly support a hypothesis, there will be higher confidence in the assessment than if the judgment was based on one or two key pieces of information from a single source.

7. Report your conclusions on the likelihood of all the hypotheses, not just the most likely one. It is important to record and report all the hypotheses that were considered, as well as the evidence that led to the final judgment. This is especially important if the analysis is going to go through a red cell analysis process, which we will discuss later in this chapter. It can also help to identify whether the analysis needs to be reevaluated if new information is provided, which brings us to the final step of the ACH process.

8. Identify situations in which the analysis would need to be reevaluated. Heuer writes that all analysis should be considered tentative and that it is always possible for new evidence to be presented that will require a new analysis. If any intelligence gaps are identified or if any information is currently missing but has the potential to change the judgment, these should be documented to assist in future analysis. An example in the Road Runner intrusion would be the addition of information from another organization that experienced a similar

intrusion, or information that the attacker's activity was detected in the future due to additional security measures that were put in place. In those situations, you would have access to new log information. If either of these things happened, you would need to revisit the judgment.

The concept of setting predetermined criteria on when a judgment should be reviewed and potentially revised is a key component of the final core SAT that we will discuss.

Indicator generation, validation, and evaluation

In traditional cyber threat intelligence vernacular, indicators are equated with IOCs, which we covered quite a bit in the first half of this book. In structured analysis, an indicator does not just mean an IOC, although in some cases they are useful in this technique. Instead, *indicator* in this context refers to a set of observations that are used to track events, identify trends, or provide warning that something unexpected is occurring or about to occur. In fact, there is an entire discipline around this called Indications and Warnings Intelligence, which is worth studying on its own if you find yourself frequently leveraging this SAT. Indicator Generation, Validation, and Evaluation is an SAT that can be incredibly helpful in intelligence-driven incident response and involves generating a list of indicators for the activity being analyzed and then validating and evaluating them before moving on to the actual analytic process.

Prepare an indicator list.   The first step in this technique is to generate a list of the indicators that are used to identify the patterns that indicate a particular activity is or is not occurring. With Road Runner, we can capture the following list of behaviors that, when combined, show us that our organization is being targeted:

- We are engaged in an activity that has historically been targeted by a variety of malicious actors.
- Malicious emails are identified that mimic activities unique to our operations, such as offering donations or volunteer support.
- Adversaries rely on exploit mechanisms that require user-interaction.
- Members of our organization who are publicly identified are targeted more heavily.
- Similar tactics that we have seen are also used against other organizations similar to ours.
- We receive warnings from government and other sharing groups about targeting.

This list of indicators describes the status quo for our current operations, and a change in any of these behaviors could mean a change in the threats that we are facing. For example, a change in the type of suspicious or malicious emails we receive could indicate that something in the threat landscape has changed, either our adversaries are switching to a new tactic that we should be on the lookout for or we are being targeted by different actors that we should strive to understand.

For each indication demonstrating the status quo, it is possible to generate an indicator that would let us know that something is changing, either internally or with an adversary. These would be indicators to actively look for. As an example, our indicator list could look like this:

- The campaign ends and we are no longer engaged in an activity that is heavily targeted.
- Malicious emails are identified with novel subject matter.
- Adversaries we have seen targeting us begin leveraging vulnerabilities that do not require user interaction.
- We see more widespread targeting of employees, including those who are not publicly affiliated with us.
- Other organizations, governments, or sharing groups begin reporting novel tactics and targeting we have not previously identified.

This list can be as detailed as you would like it to be and can include specific tactics being used or vulnerabilities being exploited, as long as you have a plan to monitor for them. An added bonus of generating an indicator list is that it can help to establish collection requirements for future monitoring efforts. Regardless of whether you prefer to monitor for the status quo remaining the same or for direct indications of things changing, the indicators that you generate need to be validated and evaluated before operationalizing them.

Validate and evaluate indicators. One area where Indications and Warning Intelligence and IOCs overlap is in validation. The criteria of what makes a good indicator are relatively the same between the two. The indicators need to be something that can be observed, either directly or indirectly; otherwise, they will be useful only retrospectively. The indicators also need to be reliable as a sign that something either is remaining consistent or is changing. If its presence or absence can be influenced by various unrelated factors, then it is probably not a good thing to monitor. Finally, indicators should be specific and point to one thing that can be monitored or observed, rather than a combination of factors that may change independently. For example, we listed that malicious emails mimic expected campaign activities as one indicator, and the exploitation requires user interaction as a separate indicator. While these two indicators both describe the phishing emails that we received, they are two different factors that could change independently and should be monitored individually.

Similar to ACH, indicators can be evaluated by the previous criteria and categorized as either ideal indicators (highly likely to identify activity in the situation or scenario that they were designed for and are highly unlikely to indicate alternate activities) or non-diagnostic indicators (which could be observed in many unrelated scenarios). Many indicators will fall somewhere in between, and alternate scenarios or possibilities should be carefully captured and recorded to support analysis if needed.

After you have done all of the indicator generation, validation, and evaluation, it is important to remember that you are NOT DONE. You need to develop a process to monitor for these indicators on a regular basis, whether that is weekly, monthly, or some other regular interval. As with all of the core techniques we have covered, you should also schedule some time to evaluate your findings regularly, ensuring that this analysis technique remains valid and useful. When reevaluating, it can be helpful to leverage some of the SATs specifically designed to test previously established findings and seek to disprove them. When you have already established a viewpoint on something, you may need some additional tools to avoid biases and remain objective. Contrarian techniques provide those tools.

Contrarian techniques

The final type of SAT to cover includes methods that are considered to be *contrarian*, meaning they seek to deviate from the existing standards or norms by providing a different view of the situation. In some cases, the initial analysis is conducted using contrarian methods. In others, contrarian techniques are used to question an existing judgment to ensure the analysis stands up in all possible situations. This type of analysis is not required in every case but is strongly recommended for analysis in which a wrong judgment would have serious consequences, or where the judgment is expected to be contested.

Devil's advocate. Devil's advocate is used to challenge a widely accepted analysis of a situation by taking an opposing viewpoint and evaluating whether the available evidence truly disproves the alternative point of view. The devil's advocate approach does not truly intend to prove that the alternative viewpoint is correct and the accepted analysis is wrong. Instead, it looks to expose any weaknesses in the original analysis, uncover any biases that were not accounted for, and help the original analysis stand up to intense scrutiny.

"What if" analysis. This type of analysis attempts to introduce new variables into the situation to see how they would change the analysis. For example, "What if this key piece of evidence is part of a deception campaign by the adversary?" or "What if this log data has been tampered with?" Again, this type of analysis does not attempt to directly disprove a hypothesis and in fact can help with assessing confidence in an overall judgment by determining whether the analysis is sound even when certain pieces of intelligence are called into question. This technique can be useful in step 6 of the ACH process, as the analyst determines how much of the analysis relies on one or two pieces of evidence.

Red team analysis.   Red teaming is a well-known concept in the information security industry. This technique seeks to analyze how an adversary would think or act in the given situation. The analyst tries to put themselves in the mindset of the attacker and asks questions such as, "What is important to me in this situation?" and "What actions would cause me to deviate from the plan?" When conducting red team analysis, it is critical that an analyst take on an adversary's persona. This technique can help counter mirror-imaging or mirroring bias by forcing an analyst to identify when an adversary's mindset would differ from their own. Red teaming helps to identify additional factors that an analyst may not have initially considered. It is important to know that this type of analysis relies on an understanding of an adversary, including their social, political, and cultural tendencies, as opposed to some red team exercises that take a "just do whatever works" approach.

Futures Wheel

One of these authors had a professor who described history as, "And one thing led to another." It's a simple way to think about it but has a lot of elegance to it. In most cases, a decision doesn't just have a singular outcome, but leads to multiple outcomes. The Futures Wheel technique is a forecasting technique aimed at not just asking, "What are the possibilities?" but "What could happen if this happens?" It works by creating an outline from an event, real or predicted, and then creating branches of hypothetical possibilities. The key is to consider what each of those possibilities entail and restart the process, taking each possibility and creating a new set of hypothetical possibilities. This spanning lets you see how one set of decisions could lead to unexpected possibility. To better choose your decision, consider third, fourth, or nth level effects!

Target-Centric Analysis

SATs are incredibly useful for giving analysts detailed, often step-by-step, methods for working through different analytic problems. Just like the different models we have presented throughout this book, they can be leveraged on their own or alongside other analytic methodologies. Let's discuss another methodology that is useful in intelligence-driven incident response: target-centric analysis.

In the book *Intelligence Analysis: A Target-Centric Approach*, author Robert M. Clark presents a new take on the traditional intelligence cycle that focuses on analyst-customer and analyst-collector relationships.[3] By emphasizing these relation-ships, the process attempts to build and maintain a collective mental model of the situation to make it easy for customers to ask questions and easy for analysts to provide actionable intelligence. Clark writes:

> The target-centric process outlines a collaborative approach for intelligence collec-tors, analysts, and customers to operate cohesively against increasingly complex opponents. We cannot simply provide more intelligence to customers; they already have more information than they can process, and information overload encourages intelligence failures.

He further articulates that recent intelligence failures are rarely failures of not having the right information; they are primarily the result of failure to share information, failure to analyze information objectively, and failure of customers to act once intelli-gence has been shared. Most analysts have experienced each of these three things at some time in their lives, and they tend to leave a lasting impression. Target-centric intelligence aims to address these failures by removing silos between roles and reduc-ing the time between each step of the traditional intelligence cycle.

An example of the target-centric intelligence analysis process is shown in Figure 8-3.

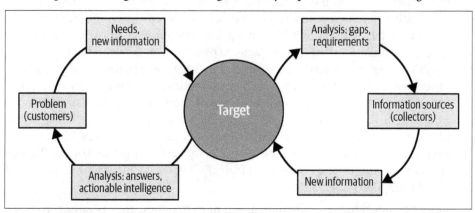

Figure 8-3. Target-centric intelligence analysis process

Unlike SATs, which detail specific methodologies, target-centric analysis at its core is a conceptual model built around an entity that is being analyzed. A *conceptual model* is a representation of a system that helps others understand what the system entails and how it operates—many of the models that we discussed in Find, Fix, and Finish are conceptual models, including the kill chain and the Diamond Model. The goal of a conceptual model is to build an accepted representation of what is being modeled

---

3 Robert M. Clark, *Intelligence Analysis: A Target-Centric Approach*, 4th edition (Thousand Oaks: CQ Press, an imprint of SAGE Publications, Inc., 2012).

so that it can be discussed among different stakeholders and support collaboration. Since those are two of the primary goals of target-centric analysis, the model becomes a key part of the process.

There are a few steps that can help you get started with target-centric analysis:

1. Get buy-in from the other stakeholders for changing the way that things are done. If you have typically operated in a different fashion with little direct collaboration between roles, then this will be a significant change. Since effective target-centric intelligence involves input from decision makers, take the time to outline the business case for why you are starting a new approach and how it will benefit the organization. You can use the example of how more consistent collaboration between incident responders and threat intelligence analysts has supported an effective incident-response process and how this new approach to intelligence will help to extend that even further.

2. Begin developing the conceptual model of your "target." Many, though not all, targets are adversary networks, and the goal of understanding them is to determine how to best prevent, detect, and respond to any malicious activity you may experience from them. Depending on the adversary, you may have specific information about who and where they are; however, that is not necessary for a good model. Without any identifying information, you can still capture and describe a threat actor's recurrent patterns of actions, understand the key components of their operations against you, and detail the behavioral, physical, and functional nodes that they rely on when attempting to compromise your organization. Building this shared understanding of the threat should lean heavily on information that has been exploited throughout the process thus far. It is one of the many reasons that the Exploit phase, as tedious as it may feel at some times, is so important. Developing the initial model for target-centric intelligence analysis can also leverage several SATs, including things like brainstorming and Key Assumptions Checks.

3. Once the model has been developed, you need to outline the operating processes you will follow to ensure that you are truly conducting target-centric intelligence analysis that is collaborative, iterative, and, at times, predictive. Although the process needs to involve other stakeholders such as your intelligence customers, collectors, and other analysts, take ownership of driving the process and find a way to engage other teams without putting too much of a burden on them. This is one way to ensure that you can maintain a collaborative approach. Regularly outline logistics, such as during weekly syncs, to go over findings and identify new questions. Include an internal chat channel for asking time-sensitive questions and identifying secondary points-of-contact for when a primary stakeholder is out of the office or unable to participate due to other obligations.

These may not seem like exciting tasks, but they are critical to the success of this approach.

4. Now we get to work. Once the conceptual model has been developed and standard operating procedures outlined, we begin the process of understanding the questions customers have around the model, the answers we already have, and the answers we still need. The answers we have are considered *actionable intelligence*—intelligence that can be acted on or can answer questions. Actionable intelligence is shared with the customer, and if more or different information is needed, the model is updated and we move back through the collection and analysis process again. Target-centric analysis follows an iterative process, where information is gathered, analyzed to see whether it helps answer the questions presented, and occasionally ends up generating new requirements. If more or different information is needed, the collection and processing phases are reengaged, and all the necessary information must be made available to the collective group. This method also allows analysts to check in frequently with customers to see if the situation and needs have changed. Although every analyst wants to think that they can come to analytic judgments and conclusions while they are still needed, it is important to be honest about time constraints and how quickly things may change, which can alter intelligence requirements.

5. Repeat as needed and be open to change. The benefit of using the target-centric method of analysis is that it involves multiple check-ins between the various stakeholders involved in the process. Although you may have a few customers who are regular parts of the target-centric approach, it is beneficial to check in with all the recipients of the analysis, whether that is a CISO or a SOC analyst, to make sure that what is being provided meets their needs and to identify whether their needs have changed. This is a good way to not only ensure that the shared understanding that comes from the analysis continues to grow but identify when a customer may become a key stakeholder who should participate in the process more frequently.

Once you've identified the method that you will use for the analysis, take a step back and look at the context for the question you are answering and the situation you are analyzing. As we discussed at the beginning of the chapter, this pause is a key step in switching from system 1 thinking to system 2 thinking. It can be instinctual for an analyst to begin to formulate a hypothesis and start moving on to later steps—like how to communicate their findings—without ever conducting any formal analysis. This is your "fast" system 1 brain working (bless its heart). Stopping to think about additional context can activate the slow, deliberate thinking required in this phase of intelligence-drive incident response.

Conducting the Analysis

We spent the first part of this chapter building the analytic toolkit that can be used to conduct analysis in a way that counters biases, is repeatable, and allows you to explain how you came to a particular judgment. Now the work can begin—if you know what it is you are analyzing.

What to Analyze

Conducting analysis is incredibly difficult if you do not know what you are trying to analyze. Often, the thought of analysis conjures up images of someone standing in front of a wall with pictures and newspaper clippings haphazardly taped to it, waiting for that "aha" moment when everything suddenly makes sense. Or, maybe you think of Newton sitting under a tree as an apple falls on his head, a simple (and oversimplified) tale of an event that brings about sudden clarity, as everything you have been wondering about makes sense. If your approach is to stare at all the data you have collected with the vague idea that you want to understand what it means, you will have a far more difficult time analyzing it than if you asked specific questions of the data, such as, "Why were we targeted?" or "How could this attack have been prevented?" You can certainly ask multiple questions of the information, and the questions can build on each other to increase your understanding of an attack and its implications, but without a starting point, many analysts find it difficult to complete this phase of the process. As we discussed at the beginning of this chapter, analysis often seems to mimic a mini-intelligence cycle, and therefore identifying or revisiting requirements—the questions you are trying to answer—is the first step.

If you do not have specific requirements that are being analyzed for leadership or other internal teams, you can ask a standard set of questions that are helpful for analyzing each incident. However, some questions will always be unique to your organization or incident, so do not think of the following examples as the *only* things you should be analyzing. Here are some of the questions you can start with:

Why were we targeted?
> This question will provide a wealth of information on how to identify additional intrusions as well as how to protect your organization from future attacks. The nature of the attack—whether the attacker targeted integrity, confidentiality, or availability of your data, whether they used the attack to get access to third-party connected networks, and the actions they took after finding what they were looking for—can all provide insight into what you need to be looking for moving forward. Tactics and techniques may change, but an attacker's goals change far less frequently.

Who attacked us?

This is often the first question that executives ask, but it is not the first question that we mention for a specific reason. Whatever it is that makes you a valid target for a specific criminal group may not be unique to that group; the same information may be targeted by another group with similar goals. Focusing exclusively on the group may cause you to lose sight of the overarching threats. Once you do understand their goals, however, it can be useful to understand more about the particular attackers. Analyzing information about attackers can include things such as the tactics they employ, what they target, how careful and cautious they are, what hours they operate, what infrastructure they use, whether it appears to be an individual or a group, and any other patterns that can be identified by analyzing the data.

How could this have been prevented?

A significant goal of analysis is to understand what happened and why it happened so that it can be prevented in the future. When answering this question, you will focus on the things that went wrong within your own network. Were there unpatched vulnerabilities that the attacker exploited? Were there IDS alerts that were triggered but that no one looked into? Did a user reuse a password that had previously been leaked as part of an unrelated intrusion? This is not usually a fun analysis to conduct, because no one likes to hear or see what they did wrong, but if your organization simply wipes a piece of malware from a system without understanding or addressing how it got there, then you will likely have to go through the whole incident-response process again, as the root cause will not be identified or addressed.

How can this be detected?

This is where all of the delightful indicators you collected come into play. After the sometimes-painful process of analyzing how you could have prevented the attack, it is nice to know that you can put things into place to prevent or detect future attacks. What you are able to do will depend greatly on the security systems that you have in place. While answering this question, it is important to focus on aspects that are unique to this particular attack, such as malware hashes and command-and-control IP addresses, as well as the aspects of the intrusion that are not as ephemeral, such as the systems that were targeted or the tactics used as the attackers moved through the network.

Are there any patterns or trends that can be identified?

This type of analysis is especially relevant when comparing internal incidents to incidents that have been reported either through information-sharing groups or through open source channels. When answering this question, you can attempt to identify patterns at various levels—from patterns related to targeting of organizations that may indicate a campaign to patterns that identify reused or shared attack infrastructure or patterns in social engineering avenues used by an attacker. The output of the analysis that you conduct in this phase should enable action, whether that action is updating a threat profile, patching systems, or creating rules for detection. Focusing on the preceding questions and any other questions or requirements specific to your organization will help ensure that the work that you do in this phase will be able to cycle back into the operational phases of F3EAD.

Enriching Your Data

Once you have identified the questions you are trying to answer through analysis, you may need to move on to the next step of the mini-intelligence cycle—identifying any additional collection that is needed. Fortunately, we have spent a great deal of time on collection throughout the intelligence-drive incident-response process, and we even exploited the data (aka organized, sorted, and made sure we could fully leverage it in analysis). At this point, however, you may realize that to answer a specific question you need additional information about some of the data that has already been collected. This process is called *enrichment* and is useful whether you are trying to answer tactically focused questions around a particular malware family or more strategic questions around why you were targeted.

Enrichment data contains additional details about an indicator or a pattern of activity that usually aren't used for detection but for understanding more about a particular indicator and what it might mean if it is seen. This category of data can include things such as WHOIS information, autonomous system number (ASN), website content, recent and historical domain resolutions, and associated malware. The point of enriching your data is to gather more context around an indicator so that you can better interpret its meaning. When looking at enrichment data in the Analysis phase, you should focus on the patterns that emerge from the data rather than getting too caught up on one specific piece of information. One of the main reasons that many people end up with false positives and hundreds of thousands of indicators in block lists is that they take enrichment information and treat it as an indicator.

Enrichment sources

The types of enrichment data that will be used depend on the indicator you are investigating and your goals for the analysis. Most enrichment sources provide information that is beneficial for multiple use cases, but some are specific, so make sure that you know what you are looking for before spending a significant amount of time digging into a particular enrichment source. With all enrichment sources, it is key to record the date that the data was identified, as it is likely to change in the future. There is nothing more frustrating than finding a piece of information that is key to your analysis and not being able to identify when or how you found it after it changes again!

Now, we'll examine the types and sources of enrichment information in detail.

WHOIS information.   One of the most basic ways to get additional context and information about a domain or an IP address used in an attack is to get information about who registered or owns it. The WHOIS protocol, defined in RFC 3912 (*https://oreil.ly/toyDa*), was originally intended to pass additional information about the users of the original internet, ARPANET. In the past, you could get WHOIS information through a command-line query, and that functionality still works today, though additional resources are available now, including websites and tools to capture current and historical data. WHOIS has gone through several updates, as the user base grew and the scope of the internet expanded greatly. Currently, WHOIS contains information on the registrant's name, email address, and additional contact information. WHOIS information can enrich analysis in several ways:

Tracking attacker infrastructure
> Some (not all!) attackers reuse information when registering domains. By identifying a name or pseudonym used by a malicious actor, it may be possible to identify additional malicious domains related to the same attacker group.

Identifying compromised domains
> In many cases, a legitimate domain may have been compromised and is being used by an attacker. Knowing the WHOIS information can help identify whether a domain is being run by an attacker or has just been compromised.

Identifying researcher-run infrastructure and sinkholes
> Many researchers carry out activity on the internet that looks similar to attackers but is used for research or identifying vulnerabilities before actual attackers do. In most cases, the IP addresses used for this research will be identified through the WHOIS record, which can prevent an analyst from spending too much time digging into a non-malicious IP address.

Passive DNS information.   Hosts on the internet were originally able to identify and communicate with each other by using a single test file containing the names and IP addresses of all hosts. This file was aptly named *HOSTS.TXT* and was FTPed to all of the machines on the internet. This solution was sustainable when a limited number of hosts were on the internet, as shown in Figure 8-4. However, it was difficult to maintain, and as the file grew, it took more and more bandwidth to transfer.

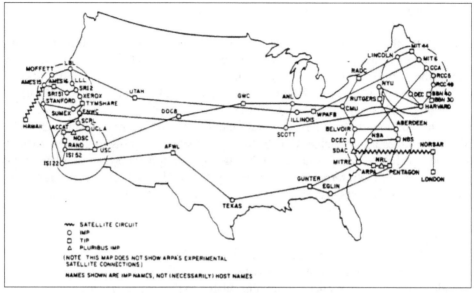

Figure 8-4. ARPANET access points in the 1970s

A more sustainable solution was developed, called the Domain Name System (DNS). It is essentially still a list of domains and hosts, but rather than a single file that is shared with everyone, the list exists on domain name servers that are queried when a host needs to look something up. The DNS is defined in RFC 1034 (*https://oreil.ly/zSLvD*) and 1035 (*https://oreil.ly/bOFcJ*), and RFC 7719 (*https://oreil.ly/0TwXN*) (released in 2015) defines modern DNS terminology. *Passive DNS*, originally called *Passive DNS Replication*, is a technique invented by Florian Weimer as a way to gather and reconstruct information from the global DNS. The original use case, outlined in Weimer's paper "Passive DNS Replication" (*https://oreil.ly/rDGXj*) and presented at the FIRST Conference in 2005, was the identification of domain names associated with botnet command-and-control IPs.[4] Weimer noted that botnet C2 often uses multiple domain names rather than hard-coded IP addresses and that these domains can resolve to multiple IP addresses, making filtering difficult. Identifying what IP address a domain resolved to at any given time, or vice versa, would require collecting the information ahead of time and storing it in a database so that it could be queried when needed.

Passive DNS provides an analyst with information on IP addresses and domains that were identified during an investigation. It can also provide information on the nature of the activity. Passive DNS information is especially useful when paired with WHOIS information to get a more complete picture of an IOC. Just remember that Passive

---

4 Florian Weimer, "Passive DNS Replication" (*https://oreil.ly/dWztl*), 17th Annual FIRST Conference, 2005.

DNS information, like WHOIS information, is not static, so make sure that you pay attention to the timeframe.

Certificates. Both modern encryption and code-signing certificates are another rich source of information. Because certificates come from signing authorities that require more information than registering a domain or IP address, they have multiple facets to pivot off of. Different kinds of certificates (code signing versus network TLS) and different providers will collect different information. Given many providers set a high bar, both in information, validation, and cost, for getting certificates, adversaries may be forced to reuse certificates, and this makes a great pivot point.

Malware information. Information on malware can be extremely useful in analysis, and similar to Passive DNS information, many of the details around a piece of malware tend to change as time goes on and more information is discovered. Resources such as VirusTotal are living resources—the information changes as new entries are made, new detections are recorded, or users identify additional details around a sample. Following are examples of enrichment information on malware:

Detection ratio
> This number will change over time and can be a useful indicator of the uniqueness of a sample that has been identified. When a sample first appears and is analyzed, the detection ratio, or the number of antivirus vendors that flag the sample as malicious, will be low. As time goes on, this number will increase.

File details
> This includes information that has been identified about a file, which is updated as more individuals or organizations analyze the sample. Even if you have conducted your own analysis of a particular malware sample, seeing what other analysis has been conducted can help to fill in any gaps you have and can also indicate how widespread the deployment is. It is helpful to know whether something has been used only against your network or is being seen across many networks in several industries.

Malware behavior
> In addition to static information such as the hash of a malware sample, it is also possible to identify additional aspects of the malware's behavior, including where it installs, other files it calls or relies upon to execute, and any automated or scripted actions it takes upon execution. These details can help you understand other malicious activities you may find on your network and provide a glimpse into the sophistication of the attacker and whether the malware is unique or is a variant of a common malware family.

Internal enrichment information

Not all enrichment information comes from external sources. Internal enrichment information provides additional details on things such as compromised hosts, users, or accounts. Internal information to be aware of includes the following:

Business operations
> Knowing what is going on in your network and in your organization at the time of an incident can help answer questions about why you were targeted and why the attack was successful. Did you recently announce new partnerships? Were you involved in a new merger or acquisition? These are important details that can help you understand the nature of an attack and often can be obtained only by talking to people within your organization.

User information
> Identifying which users were targeted or compromised can help you understand what information the attackers may have been after, if you have not already identified what was stolen. It can also provide information on the attacker's tactics, for example, if they initially target HR employees and then attempt to move to a user with more access, such as a systems administrator.

Leverage Information Sharing

Understanding when or if an indicator was previously identified can help put your particular incident into perspective. You should have identified some of this information during the Find phase, but it is useful to see what has changed or if any new information has been identified about the indicators you are using in your analysis.

A good source of timely, nonpublic information of this nature is sharing relationships with other organizations. Public information is useful as well and should be used in analysis, but information-sharing groups can provide details that often do not make it into the public domain, including specifics about when an indicator was seen, how it was identified, and what industry it was seen in. These are the types of details that many organizations do not want published but are often willing to share with partner organizations, especially when other organizations are sharing this sensitive information as well. There are formalized sharing groups, such as Information Sharing and Analysis Centers (ISACs), Information Sharing and Analysis Organizations (ISAOs), public/private partnerships, and informal groups. Many of the formal groups are arranged around industry or other shared interests. In some cases, information obtained from sharing groups can be used to detect malicious activity, but for the purpose of analyzing incidents, it can also be used as an enrichment source to help build your understanding of the intrusion you are analyzing. Once all information has been evaluated and enriched, it is time to move on to the next step: developing a hypothesis.

As you go through the process of collecting information, you most likely subconsciously start to form a hypothesis about whatever question you are trying to answer. Analysis involves taking all of the information you have and synthesizing and interpreting to determine its meaning and, ideally, what should be done about it. For analytic judgments to be complete, accurate, and reproducible, it is best to follow a structured process to conduct your analysis.

Developing Your Hypothesis

At this stage, we begin to get into the actual analysis, which begins with clearly stating your hypothesis. As mentioned previously, you usually begin to come up with some working answers to your question during the collection/enrichment process. At the hypothesis-development phase, you should start to document those working answers, no matter how speculative or far-fetched they are; the rest of the analytic process will weed out the ideas that are obviously incorrect. Make sure that when you document your ideas, you write them as fully as possible, and if specific information was found during collection that led to the formation of a particular hypothesis, make sure to note what it was. This will help with evaluating the hypothesis further down the road. If you cannot clearly articulate an idea or you discover that it is too vague or doesn't answer the question that you are asking, then it is not a good working idea, and you can move on to the next possible hypothesis.

In the case of our Road Runner intrusion, the first thing we want to understand is whether we were specifically targeted. Everything we have seen from this adversary indicates that they are a sophisticated threat group that is deliberate in their targeting, but we want to analyze the data we have to confirm that we were targeted. Our hypothesis, based on the information we gathered during the investigation and the internal enrichment data about who at our organization was targeted, is that this was in fact a targeted attack aimed at obtaining sensitive information related to our campaign. This hypothesis is specific and is based on our research, but it still needs to be verified by going through the rest of the structured analytic process.

Over the course of your career, developing a hypothesis will become easier for a couple reasons. First, many incidents have similarities, and it will become easier to identify indications of a particular behavior. While this can cut down on the time it takes to carry out the analytic process, it is important to *not* assume that this answer is correct; it is still just a hypothesis. Make sure that you go through the rest of the process even when the answer seems obvious, and make sure that you account for assumptions and biases, which we will discuss next.

The second reason that hypothesis development becomes easier is that after stepping through many investigations and iterations of this process, the mind often becomes more creative and less concerned when generating possible answers. After working through the analytic process and becoming comfortable with the fact that bad ideas *will* be identified and weeded out, an analyst can explore all possible ideas, often coming up with new ideas that they would not have identified before.

Regardless of how easy or difficult it is to generate, when you have a working hypothesis, the next step is to evaluate the assumptions upon which that hypothesis is based so that you can move into the judgment and conclusion stage aware of and accounting for your biases.

Evaluating Key Assumptions

As we discussed earlier, a *key assumption* is any part of a hypothesis that relies on a preexisting judgment or belief. Before continuing with the analysis, teams or individuals should take a few minutes or a few hours to identify these key assumptions and determine whether they are valid and should contribute to the analysis. For example, if an analyst has developed a hypothesis about how a particular attack could have been prevented, it is based on an assumption of how the attack was carried out, which would have been identified during the Find, Fix, and Finish phases. It should be relatively easy to evaluate whether that assumption is correct, but it should still be documented and discussed to make sure that all analysts have the same understanding of the information that contributed to the hypothesis.

We outlined the process for conducting a Key Assumptions Check earlier in the chapter; however, there are other methods for evaluating assumptions as a part of the analytic process, rather than as a standalone SAT. The CIA's Tradecraft Primer (*https://oreil.ly/m9qQI*) outlines how to evaluate key assumptions after hypothesis generation and highlights the many benefits of going through this process. These benefits include developing an understanding of the key issues that contribute to a hypothesis, identifying faulty logic, and stimulating discussions among analysts.

The process for evaluating key assumptions after hypothesis generation is as follows:

1. Identify all key assumptions about a situation or hypothesis.
2. Identify why the assumption was made.
3. Assess the confidence in the assumption.
4. Identify how the confidence rating was determined.
5. Challenge each assumption and determine whether it is true and remains true for the current situation.
6. Remove any assumptions that are not true or that have a low confidence; these should not be used in the analysis. It is important to note that you do not have to remove a hypothesis that has been generated because it was associated with an assumption that was removed; however, it is important that there is still

other evidence or other higher confidence assumptions for the hypothesis to remain plausible.

Our hypothesis that the Road Runner intrusion targeted us specifically is based on several assumptions. First, we are assuming that the actor who targeted us is Grey Spike and that the activity we are calling Road Runner was this actor's attempt to access multiple campaigns similar to ours. This is a key assumption, and it is made based on the fact that the information we obtained on the actor matched what we found in our network, including tactics, techniques, technical indicators, and targeting. We are confident in the accuracy of this assumption, based on the technical details and the timing. We are aware that additional information, especially information regarding deception activities on the part of the attacker, may change this assumption, and we will be prepared to change our analysis if any new information of that nature is identified.

Assumptions are not always easy to evaluate and include things such as cognitive biases, which are logical fallacies or flaws in thinking that can easily cloud an analyst's judgment. It is not possible to completely remove biases from analysis. However, when we are mindful of their presence in our analysis, we can ensure that they are not clouding our judgment in ways that may compromise the conclusions. In fact, understanding bias is so important that it warrants an entire section in this chapter.

Things That Will Screw You Up (aka Analytic Bias)

We have covered several different ways that you can use structured processes and step-by-step approaches to analysis, all with the goal of engaging system 2 thinking and intentionally avoiding mental shortcuts that may lead to faulty analysis. System 1 thinking and our mental shortcuts are deeply ingrained, however, and even using SATs and structured methods are not guaranteed to remove things like cognitive bias that can interfere with analysis. Understanding more about the mechanics behind these biases and some of the specific ways they show up in analysis can help you identify them.

Richards J. Heuer, Jr., one of the fathers of intelligence and the author of *Psychology of Intelligence Analysis*,[5] describes *cognitive biases* as "various simplifying strategies and rules of thumb to ease the burden of mentally processing information to make judgments and decisions." Cognitive biases are essentially shortcuts that our minds develop so that we do not have to go through the entire analytic process for every minute decision we make in our lives. A basic example is a child who complains of being cold and whose parents immediately tell them to put on a sweater. Years later, whenever that (now grown) child feels cold, they have the thought to put on

---

5 Richards J. Heuer, Jr., *Psychology of Intelligence Analysis* (Eastford: Martino Fine Books, 2019).

a sweater. They probably also tell their children to put on a sweater. Their mind does not have to run through the entire process of developing a hypothesis. (Maybe a hat would be best? Perhaps an extra pair of socks?) They can simply shortcut to something that their mind tells them is an appropriate response to the situation.

Accounting for Biases

Cognitive biases aren't always bad, and they do save a lot of time, but in intelligence analysis they can have a negative influence by causing an analyst to make assumptions and jump to faulty judgments. Another example of a cognitive bias at work is the use of previously identified malware, such as Poison Ivy. An analyst who has heard of or experienced several instances where sophisticated attackers used complicated, previously unseen malware may automatically generate the assumption that this actor is *not* sophisticated. In this instance, they would be using a cognitive bias called *anchoring* that lets one piece of evidence override any other piece of evidence without a sound analytic judgment.

Many types of biases exist. What follows is an overview of some that are commonly seen in intelligence analysis and incident response, along with ways that you can leverage the skills we have covered in this chapter to help counter them.

Confirmation bias

With confirmation biases, we tend to seek out or focus on evidence that supports our preexisting judgment or conclusion. If, in the back of our minds, we think that we are going to find evidence of a specific type of activity, any evidence that seems to support that conclusion will be given more weight than something that disproves or questions that judgment. In the Road Runner scenario, we may have run into the issue of an analyst who assumes that the actors were attempting to steal credentials, since we have seen the tactic in the past. If a phishing email appears similar to a credential-lure, the analyst may assume that as long as no password was provided that there is no lingering threat, without investigating the actual email any further. That same analyst may also identify the use of password-guessing techniques, also used by less-sophisticated actors, to prove this assumption. This judgment would require the analyst to ignore the historical cases where sophisticated actors also used password guessing, or give them less weight. Confirmation bias is one of the primary reasons that it is important to go through the exercise of evaluating key assumptions prior to coming to a final judgment.

Anchoring bias

In anchoring bias, analysts tend to become over-reliant on, or give more weight to, the first piece of information that they hear. Any subsequent information or evidence is compared to that initial piece of evidence, and the analyst often unconsciously debates whether the new evidence supports or refutes the first piece, making that first piece of information central to the investigation. If analysts were told, going into the process of analyzing an intrusion, that "we think it was Russia," then each piece of evidence will influence their interpretation of whether it was Russia, when that really is not the question that the analysts were meant to answer.

Anchoring bias is one of the reasons that some experts such as Robert M. Lee (*https://oreil.ly/KiB5D*) say that true attribution (attribution to a particular government or nation-state) makes it more difficult for analysts to do their job because that attribution becomes the anchor that they base their judgments off of rather than a useful piece of evidence to include in analysis.[6] Again, going through the process of focusing on the requirements and what question is actually being asked, developing a hypothesis, and evaluating key assumptions should help an analyst account for and counteract anchoring bias.

Availability bias

In availability bias, there is an overemphasis on the information that is available, whether that information has itself been analyzed. Richard Heuer calls this bias the Vividness Criterion, which means that information that you personally experience or are most familiar with will become more important than information you are not as familiar with. It has also been referred to as the "I know a guy" bias, as in, "I know a guy who smoked a pack of cigarettes a day and lived to be 100; therefore, smoking can't be that bad for you." A newer version of the "I know a guy" bias is the "I saw it on the internet" bias.

Incident responders and intelligence analysts need to be aware of this bias because this is what allows their previous experience to hurt rather than help them. If they focus on pieces of evidence that they are most familiar with because they have seen it before, then they may give that one thing too much weight or discount other pieces of evidence that they are not as familiar with.

Bandwagon effect

Bandwagoning occurs when an assumption seems more likely to be true as more people agree with it. Although there is something to be said for group consensus after a piece of evidence has been analyzed, the bias comes into play when this judgment occurs *prior* to analysis or when the fact that others support the assumption becomes a basis for believing that assumption is true. There is some interesting psychological reasoning with bandwagoning, and it can therefore be hard to overcome, but it is important to note that "because everyone says so" is not a valid justification for an assumption to be labeled as accurate. If there is evidence to back up a group

---

6 Robert M. Lee, 2018. "Attribution is Not Transitive" (*https://oreil.ly/KiB5D*), (blog post) December 31, 2018.

consensus, it is important to look at the evidence rather than the fact that everyone is in agreement.

Heuer also refers to an "oversensitivity to consistency" and writes that:

> Information may be consistent only because it is highly correlated or redundant, in which case many related reports may be no more informative than a single report.

To overcome this, Heuer recommends that analysts ensure that they are familiar with the body of evidence that previous analysis is based on—including the sample size and the information available—and question whether the same, consistent conclusion would likely continue with a larger sample size or the availability of more information. This is especially helpful with media reporting of an attacker. Multiple media reports may all be based on a single incident, so just because there are multiple reports does not mean that there were multiple incidents.

Mirroring

Mirroring, or mirror-image bias, occurs when an analyst makes an assumption that a target being studied thinks like the analyst and therefore would make the same decisions as the analyst would. This leads to an analyst making assumptions about what an adversary would or wouldn't do based on the analyst's own personal experiences, which are often completely different from those of the target. Instead of using the evidence to guide judgments, an analyst suffering from this bias uses their own opinions of what would have been a logical step, or "what I would have done" to determine whether an assumption is correct. Mirroring is often used during the generation of working ideas, but during the Evaluation phase, it is important to identify when mirroring, rather than evidence, is the basis of an assumption and remove that bias from the analysis.

Judgment and Conclusions

After the assumptions around evidence that supports a hypothesis have been evaluated and biases accounted for, the analyst can move toward making their judgment and conclusion about the hypothesis. Analysts can use several methods to interpret the evidence and identify whether a hypothesis is likely to be true or not or whether they need to generate a new hypothesis either in part or in its entirety. *Judgment* is the step where analysts have to use their knowledge, experience, and logic to fill in any gaps in known information to answer the questions that are facing them. SATs and target-centric analysis can help you clarify the limits of your evidence and what it is telling you, understand your assumptions and conjectures and how confident you are in your validity, and identify what new or changing information would impact those assumptions. At this point, analysts need to package this information as an analytic judgment.

One common misconception is that a judgment is when you determine the correct hypothesis and answer the question being addressed as part of an intelligence requirement. While that may be the judgment that you present to the majority of your audiences during the Dissemination phase, a judgment is actually required every time you determine that a hypothesis is incorrect as well. If you use a method such as ACH, then this step naturally flows from the process, as the later steps on ACH involve developing initial conclusions, which are often further evaluated using contrarian techniques. Even if you did not use ACH to conduct the analysis, a version of the final steps, outlined as follows, can still be useful in any type of analysis:

- Assess the likelihood of the hypothesis based on the evidence available. Focus on disproving the hypotheses rather than proving them to be correct. Identify if any information disproves a hypothesis.

- Review the information that led to your judgment of the hypothesis, whether it was accepted or rejected as a hypothesis. Was there a single piece of evidence that weighed most heavily? If so, how confident are you in that piece of evidence? This will help determine the overall confidence in a judgment.

- Record your conclusion on each hypothesis, citing the evidence that led to the conclusion and confidence in the assessment. This should be directly tied to the evidence that supported or refuted it and should be clearly articulated so that another analyst would be able to review the evidence and clearly follow the logic. The rule of thumb here is that an analyst shouldn't have to "be you" in order to understand the findings.

- Articulate under what circumstances the analysis would need to be reevaluated. What would have to change for you to determine reevaluation is needed? These criteria should become part of your indicator generation.

A good formula for capturing a judgment is as follows:

> I/we assess with [*low, moderate, high*] confidence that [*state your judgment*] based on [*state the evidence reviewed*]. I/we will be monitoring [state your indicators] to further support or refute this judgment.

If you follow this method, even if you end up changing the statement during the Dissemination phase, you will know that you have all of the pieces needed to make and support analytic judgment and conclusion.

Conclusion

If there is one phrase that can sum up the most effective way to approach analysis, it is: *slow down*. Not only will this help engage your system 2 thinking that emphasizes deliberate, well-articulated reasoning, but will also help you counter biases, help you know when and how to engage additional experts or get second opinions, and actually result in a smoother and more effective process overall. By slowing down, you will make it easier for others to follow your reasoning in support of the judgment that was reached and end up saving time in the long run.

When answering specific questions about an incident or investigation, analysts do best when following a process that is both predefined but flexible enough to account for the complexity of the problems they often face. The process is not exactly the same in every instance—sometimes enrichment information is needed and ACH is conducted, and other times all the information is available and the analyst uses red teaming to evaluate a judgment—but there *is* a process. Be flexible with your analysis, but be sure not to completely skip any of the steps; they are there to ensure that a sound analytic judgment is made based on the right information. After the analysis has been completed and a judgment made, it is time to decide how best to convey the findings to the appropriate audience, whether that is an executive or the security engineering team. We now get to ensure that all of the time you spent on analysis results in decision makers taking action.

## CHAPTER 9

Disseminate

People tend to do one of two things with data: they hoard it, or they dump it on people.
—General Stanley McChrystal
Tell me what you know. Tell me what you don't know. And then...tell me what you think...I will hold you accountable.
—Secretary of State Colin Powell, September 13, 2004, Intelligence Reform Hearing

At some point, the investigation needs to end, or at least pause long enough to create outputs useful to other teams, leadership, organizations, and/or customers. *Dissemination* is the process of organizing, publishing, and sharing developed intelligence. This is a skill set unto itself, and just like any other skill, effectively disseminating intelligence takes time to learn, and it means following processes. Good intelligence can be ruined by poor dissemination. Although writing up something after hours of analysis may seem unimportant, it's worth the time for any intelligence team to focus and build their skills in disseminating information.

Dissemination is such an important skill that in larger intelligence teams, resources may be dedicated just to the Dissemination phase. These dissemination-focused analysts need the following:

- A strong understanding of the overall dissemination process and importance of the information they're sharing.

- A firm grasp of the types and needs of stakeholders to whom the intelligence will be sent.

- A disciplined and clear writing style. (Intelligence writing is a little different from typical narrative writing; we'll get into that later in this chapter.)

- An eye toward operational security to protect the valuable intelligence products and materials.

No matter how your team is set up, from a dual-hat CERT analyst and intelligence analyst up to large, dedicated teams, it's important to develop processes for writing and editing and practice them regularly. Dissemination, and the written output (known as intelligence products) that results from it, can only be as good as the analysis it's based on. In addition, bad intelligence product development can render good analysis useless.

This chapter covers building intelligence products for distribution within your organization. We'll discuss how to make your written output audience-focused and actionable, as well as how to build effective writing structures and processes.

Intelligence Customer Goals

Understanding intelligence customer needs is all about understanding their goals. Usually, this is accomplished by contemplating the audience (we'll get to that next) and their needs. These two aspects define almost everything else about the product, from tone to structure to timeframe. *Understanding the goals for an intelligence product means understanding the stakeholder's expectations for the product.* For example, here's a common goal: Inform SOC on New Actor TTP. This indicates the need for a shorter-form tactical product aimed at a highly technical audience (aka a target package).

The intelligence team needs to figure out what kind of product will help the customer achieve their goal. That's why it can be helpful to start your planning by explicitly stating the customer's goal, or expectations, for the product. This is especially useful when building a product with a team. A stated goal, or mission statement, can provide a common vision.

Audience

Also known as *consumers* or *customers*, the *audience* is tied directly to the goal of any intelligence product. The execution of the goal is intrinsically tied to the stakeholders you're writing a product for. Every intelligence writer and team must develop an understanding of the audiences they're writing for—this understanding leads directly to creating useful and actionable products. This is never a one-time exercise; the customers you're writing for will change their needs, evolve their understanding, and learn to read and leverage intelligence more effectively over time. For instance, an organization may have a highly technical CEO who can digest highly technical reports and revels in disassembly. That can drastically change the approach an intelligence team takes to developing an intelligence product. Understanding your audience allows you to anticipate questions and needs more effectively. Executive teams will hear a topic and have a completely different set of questions than SOC analysts.

Although every situation, and every customer, is a bit different, a few common threads exist. Common customer types include executives or leadership, internal technical customers, and external technical customers. We will explore them in more detail next.

Executive Leadership Customer

For many analysts, the most intimidating audience to present to or provide an intelligence product for is executive leadership—whether it's your team leader, the C-suite, or even your organization's board of directors. In large part, this is due to the authority such leadership has and the fact that major leadership briefings often happen as a result of severe circumstances such as a major breach or threat (they don't usually make requests of the intelligence team when everything is going well!). The stakes are almost always high, both for the analyst and for the organization, and that tension leads to stress but also the opportunity to deliver much-needed context.

As customers, executive leadership can be a challenge. For one thing, every leadership team has a considerable range of skills and technical acumen. The same group can have former engineers and technicians turned leadership with deep technical skills alongside specialists from totally unrelated disciplines such as Finance or Human Resources that, while deeply skilled in their own areas, are not always well-versed in computers and networks. It's often challenging to effectively target these sorts of mixed audiences.

The following are common characteristics of C-suite executives:

- Deep knowledge in a specific area with above-average awareness of others (sometimes known as *T-shaped people* (*https://oreil.ly/29GfO*)).[1] Although most C-level executives have one area of expertise, they have usually spent enough time around other fields (HR or finance, for example) to have more than a passing familiarity.

- They tend to be strategically focused above all else. If the executives are running a business, all decisions will focus on how to make or save money. If the organization is a nonprofit, the focus above all else will be the mission.

Although it's easy to write off a leadership team as nontechnical, many have done this at their peril. It's easy to forget that members of leadership may have gotten to their position as skilled engineers. It isn't unusual to stumble across a CEO or senior director who still knows their way around C code and understands key pieces of malware disassembly code, or maybe just earned a master's degree in electrical

---

1 Katharine Brooks, "Career Success Starts with a 'T'" (*https://oreil.ly/29GfO*), *Psychology Today* website, April 19, 2012.

engineering for fun (true story!). While assuming too much technical competency and drowning executives in jargon is bad, so too is assuming no understanding.

The focus on your customers goes deeper than just technical comprehension. Executive leadership, especially the C-suite, have specific focus areas. A chief financial officer (CFO) is interested in threats to underlying finances of the company, expenses related to incidents (real or potential), and threats targeting the Finance staff such as W-2 social engineering. Conversely, the chief technical officer (CTO) is probably not as concerned about W-2 theft attempts; after all, their staff probably doesn't have access to W-2s but is likely to be concerned about DDoS attacks, which would impact the technology department's function.

It is important to consider how a single intelligence product can speak to multiple aspects of the business. Above all, listen to your customers. We are now in the feedback loop of the intelligence cycle, discussed in Chapter 2, when the final product is reviewed by the customer and they share their insight. These insights can be about the intelligence itself, but it's important to also pay close attention to the customer's response to formatting, process, and even wording. Taking these factors into account allows a team to evolve their products and improve them with each new release.

When writing intelligence products for leadership, a few major characteristics make them most effective:

Focus on intelligence necessary to make business decisions.
> Few executives, even the deeply technical ones, are highly interested in tactical intelligence. Their primary focus is on anything that will help them make better business-level decisions.

Use operational intelligence to tell the story of the threat.
> There can be great value, if done correctly, in sharing relevant operational intelligence with leadership. The benefit of sharing operational intelligence, especially at the campaign level, comes in leveraging most humans' love of stories. Using operational intelligence makes it easier to share a narrative: good guys, bad guys, tools, and actions (think of the four corners of the Diamond Model, which we discussed in Chapter 3). The focus should still be on the strategic aspects, but the operational side can help support it with a powerful and relatable story.

Keep it brief and to the point.
> In many cases, security is only one concern for this audience, and their time to focus on security is limited. Long reports may seem like they'll be impressive and thorough, but in most cases they'll end up sitting on a desk unread. This can be avoided with two interrelated techniques:

- When in doubt, be brief. A well-written one-page product is far more likely to be read in its entirety than 10% of a 50-page report.

- The more senior level you're presenting to, the less you can assume they'll read. A director may read your whole three-page product, but it helps to assume the CISO will barely read the full front page. As a result, every product should start with an executive summary covering the most important points. It may be the only piece that gets fully read, so make it count.

Techniques like this are valuable to most customers, not just leadership. Economy of language means the customer can move more quickly to using the data instead of consuming it. Getting to a certain page count with extraneous details may feel impressive, but using three words when two will do is never a good idea in intelligence writing.

 It's easy to assume that your intel team is the single source of truth for your customers. This is a dangerous assumption, especially with your board or executive team. In many organizations, these groups will engage outside resources and advisors. In fact, you may not be the only intelligence team within your organization. Be sure to keep this in mind when creating intelligence products. You should be prepared for a more in-depth critique and cross examination than you might expect.

Internal Technical Customers

For most analysts, the easiest customers to write for are other analysts. This is largely because this is a persona we understand wholeheartedly: It's writing for ourselves! It's easy to make assumptions based on our personal ideas, preferences, and needs, but it's still important to treat analysts, even if you are one, as an important intelligence product customer with their own needs. It's valuable to study them, solicit feedback, and work to improve products to meet your customers' needs rather than rest on assumptions.

Generally speaking, internal technical customers—such as SOC analysts, incident responders, and cyber threat intelligence analysts—want tactical- and operational-level products to help them do their jobs, which in most cases is intrusion detection and incident response. In some cases, these products will be aimed at developers or architecture-focused analysts or engineers trying to build more defensible products or networks. As a result, these internal technical customers ultimately have the most varied needs and uses of any group you're likely to build products for. Here are a few examples of the types of products you may need to create for internal technical customers:

- An operational-level campaign analysis aimed at keeping SOC analysts familiar with a major ongoing spear-phishing campaign.

- A strategic discussion of major compromises of the last year for the systems architecture and vulnerability management teams, trying to identify improvements in system and network architecture.

- A tactical IOC list of domain names, after filtering out likely false positives, to be blocked at the web proxy.

All of these product examples are focused on improving detection and minimizing false positives. Analysts want to understand what bad looks like (generally) and how to verify that it's actually bad (specifically). These are two sides of the same coin, and striking a balance is key when building products for other analysts.

As far as how to approach writing for analysts, the key is to keep the focus on the data. Some tips:

- In most cases, you'll develop these products from analyst notes. This approach keeps the product close to the *ground truth* that analysts crave.

- These products can and should be highly technical and descriptive, rich with references, including external research and internal telemetry. Analysts often want to trace individual pieces of data to their original sources, and the best way to help them is by providing easy-to-follow references.

- The highest-quality products should be backed up by machine-consumable products, such as IOCs in STIX format or YARA signatures, to make it easier for other analysts in your organization to review the technical details.

- Always make sure you have a method for internal customers to provide feedback and ask questions. This could be as simple as providing your email address, setting up a topic-specific chat room, or another method for readers to interact with the authors.

External Technical Customers

Sharing intelligence can be wildly powerful, but creating products for external technical customers presents its own unique challenges. Writing for external technical customers is similar to writing for internal technical customers, in terms of tone. The core differences are in the rules of engagement, which detail how to interact with external technical customers.

There are four main rules of engagement:

Get permission.
    Sharing intelligence internally with your own organization may have some sensitivities, but sharing intelligence outside your organization is often riskier.

In many cases, threat and incident data are considered highly sensitive and shouldn't be sent to third parties without sign-off.

Understand who you're sharing with.

Authorization may allow sharing with a certain type of organization (e.g., partners, law enforcement, ISACs), specific individuals, or even the internet as a whole. Sharing outside these authorized individuals may risk exposure to unexpected third parties, including partner organizations or even the media.

Create external intelligence products that focus on translatable intelligence.

Translatable intelligence is information that can be useful for both organizations. This is largely focused on indicators (for example, Snort signatures are useful to other organizations with intrusion-detection systems, but IP addresses are useful to almost all organizations) but should also be applied to timeline and narrative information. Taking the time to understand partner organizations will help with writing such intelligence products.

Have a method for feedback.

Although sharing intelligence internally generally means a customer will have a wide variety of feedback mechanisms, external customers will have far fewer available channels. It's important when sharing intelligence to explicitly lay out methods of feedback including channels, formats, and expectations.

Risks of Exposure

Even though organizations verify and trust those they share intelligence with (and do everything possible to protect information they receive), exposure happens. Intelligence customers' mail accounts get hacked, and insider threats leak intelligence. As an intelligence producer, it's important to consider that the intelligence you share may leak. This shouldn't discourage organizations from sharing but does mean you need to consider the repercussions of exposure, even if using strong cryptography.

Teams should avoid offensive or insensitive code names, use professional language, and avoid unfounded speculation. Consider the embarrassment or negative ramifications that would result if your intelligence product were shared on Twitter. For an example of how this could happen, look at the exposure of Google's "Peering Into the Aquarium" report (*https://oreil.ly/N45uL*). Want to take this protection against exposure to the next level? Consider working with your organization's public relations team and get their feedback.

Ultimately following these rules will mean working with your leadership, security, legal, and even (and I'd recommend it) your public relations teams. Taking the time to work with these stakeholders means lowering the level of ambiguity when something worth sharing becomes available, allowing you to publish the most actionable intelligence to your customers quickly, whether that means sharing privately to a peer organization or sharing a blog post to help the community overall.

Sometimes you will have more than one target audience for your intelligence; your SOC may be an internal technical customer of incident-related data, but the C-suite wants a brief as well. At times like this, it is important to keep track of what information you need to give to each customer, so we recommend that (regardless of your audience) you develop customer personas.

Developing Customer Personas

A highly useful exercise for understanding the audience of an intelligence product is developing customer personas, a technique pulled from common marketing practices. A *persona* describes a hypothetical, prototypical customer and defines their characteristics, challenges, and needs in order to find the best way to address these needs. Keep the personas in a place where they can be accessed by members of the team during the Dissemination phase.

The exercise starts with developing a template for the persona. Figure 9-1 provides an example template for a customer persona.

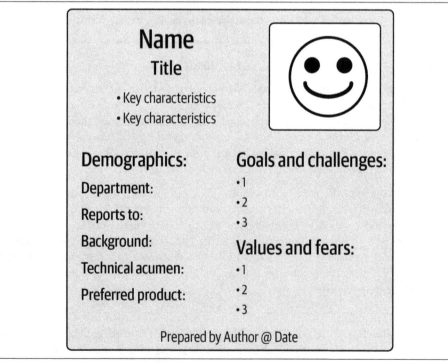

Figure 9-1. A simple customer persona template

Old Navy is famous for a whole family of customer personas, but their main persona is Jenny (*https://oreil.ly/YEdzQ*), a 25- to 35-year-old mother.[2] For intelligence products, the size of the audience is important. Intelligence teams with lots of customers may have a few generalized personas. Other teams may have a more limited number of customers and may be able to make specific, detailed personas for each customer. A hybrid approach is likely best for most teams, building a few detailed personas for high-priority customers and generalized personas for other groups.

The persona should help explicitly define many of the unknowns or generalizations about the customers. Is the CEO highly technical and thus likes reading full-on reverse-engineering reports? That should be noted in their persona. Does your SOC lead prefer short, one-page products? That should be called out in their persona. Ultimately, the persona should be a recipe for providing a customer with the most useful and stakeholder-relevant products. Take time to carefully consider (or even investigate and confirm) the persona's goals and challenges, values, and fears. This will help ensure that you hit your target and provide the most useful products.

Figure 9-2 shows a real intelligence customer profile. Shawn is a VP of Security, which naturally leads to certain expectations about him in terms of interest and technicality (a form of bias). This is where the profile is important because many of the assumptions we'd make about a vice president are wrong in this case. Shawn is highly technical and has high expectations about the accuracy and depth of any products sent to him. Whereas some VPs might be uncomfortable or intimidated at high levels of detail about packets and persistence mechanisms, Shawn expects this specificity. At the same time, many of his interests are typical strategic needs. By combining the understanding of both interest and acumen, we can design custom products specifically aimed at Shawn.

Although it's not crucial to build a detailed profile for every possible customer of your threat intelligence product, creating personas can be a valuable exercise for key stakeholders. On the other hand, it can be valuable to build generic personas based on common stakeholder roles, such as an SOC analyst. Such generalized profiles still provide key guidance when building intelligence products and function as an important yardstick for determining whether products are meeting stakeholder needs.

Many teams go through the persona process and treat those personas as gold. Personas should be only as static as the people or roles they're attached to. Is there a new CFO? Take the time to create a new persona for that person; they may be dramatically different from the previous CFO.

---

2 Ryan Flinn, "Old Navy's Target Customers: Working Moms, 25 to 35" (*https://oreil.ly/YEdzQ*), *The Seattle Times* website, July 12, 2011.

Shawn
VP of Security

- Former engineer, highly technical
- Security program management focus

Demographics:

Department: Security

Reports to: CEO

Background: Unix admin and security engineer

Technical acumen: High

Preferred product: 1 pager

Goals and challenges:

- Identify strategic threats to organization
- Tying together security for varied business needs
- Sec risk management

Values and fears:

- Strong situational awareness
- Intel leading to strategic improvements

Prepared by Scott @ January 3, 2017

Figure 9-2. A real customer profile

Authors

Whereas the audience dictates what the customers want, the authors dictate what your product can talk about effectively. Any great product combines both the capabilities of the authors and the needs of the audience.

Authorship is about establishing and maintaining credibility. Your customers (the audience) will get value only out of products they believe in, and much of this belief is based on the authors. In the same way that biases in analysis can discredit a team, so can trying to write about information outside your scope of knowledge. It's better to write strongly and authoritatively on topics that are well understood than to overrepresent.

Authors should be knowledgeable enough about the topic to write with authority and be familiar enough with the audience to convey information in the way the audience needs to receive it. Without the former, the product will be riddled with errors (which will damage credibility), and without the latter, good information will be wasted without any understanding.

As a report writer, you need to decide whether you're writing an intelligence product based on the analysts you have or the topic you want. If you're starting with a particular set of topics that you want to address in the product, you need to assemble a team capable of addressing the various details that topic needs to cover. On the other hand, if you have a set team, the product topics should be limited based on the capabilities of that team.

Automated Report Information in Intelligence Products

One common technique used by intelligence product writers is to include information that comes from automated tools, such as exporting directly from your threat-intelligence platform or having a script pull data from your security information and event-management platform. This approach is especially common in malware analysis, and many authors include output from sandboxes and online malware analysis services in their reports. This can be valuable, especially when the analysts and authors have limited experience, but in many cases, this is just data without context and may muddy the water. Automated malware analysis may be useless because of anti-reverse-engineering techniques that cause the analysis to fail.

Any time you include automatically generated information in a report, make sure of the following:

You completely understand the information.
Understanding the information is important not only for writing the report, but also so you can speak about it after delivery of the products. Many analysts, even companies, have made mistakes by misunderstanding automated output and including bad data. 8.8.8.8 and windowsupdate.microsoft.com are great examples and are commonly cited as malicious even by vendors. They show up in dynamic analysis since malicious code will often reach out to them to verify it has internet access as an anti-forensic technique.

Put the automatically generated information in context.
The automated report needs to be part of telling the story of the product. Without context, these automated reports are just data.

Provide links to the automated analysis for reference and updates.
For example, some samples may have a low-detection rate on VirusTotal early on, but as vendors start adding signatures, these detection rates will change. That context is important, so make it easy for customers to check that information.

By taking these three actions, you can ensure that your use of automated analysis improves intelligence products instead of muddying the water and confusing your customers.

Actionability

Intelligence products need to be actionable. A product is *actionable* when it provides the right information, in the right format, for the customer to take action or make a better decision than they would have without the product. An otherwise excellent intelligence product becomes useless if the customer can't use the information it contains to improve their network defense posture (Dragos CEO Robert Lee is famous for referring to this as the "self-licking ice cream cone"). In the F3EAD nomenclature, if a product doesn't improve a team's ability to Find, Fix, or Finish an adversary, the report is missing a key component. In the end, the goal of every intelligence product should be to lead to a meaningful decision or action.

Here are some do's for actionability:

- Provide information on adversary TTPs that makes it easier for the customer to detect or respond to an adversary they're likely to face.

- Ensure products that contain easy-to-use IOCs and signatures make it easier for a customer to add detection or hunt for malicious activity. Open formats used by vendors such as Snort and Yara are especially helpful.

- Answer specific questions from the customer that are relevant to their needs (we'll discuss this in the later section "Requests for Intelligence").

Here are some don'ts for actionability:

- Avoid overly broad descriptions of activity without meaningful details—this prohibits a network defense team from putting those details to use. For example, don't reference an attacker's phishing campaign without including information about the sender's email addresses, subject lines, attachments, or malicious links.

- Don't use tools or methods to hinder copying information out of intelligence products. For example, many vendors flatten their reports from text into images so that customers can't copy and paste information from them. This is especially frustrating for lists of hashes, domains, and IPs.

- Skip distribution of contextual information via vendor-specific formats that are useful only in that vendor's products. Also avoid sharing information that can be used only for host detection with a customer that only has network tools.

- Don't overclassify information so much that it can't be used. This can occur in both government-classified and TLP environments (see the following "Avoid TLP: Black" on page 225 sidebar).

Avoid TLP: Black

We've discussed the Traffic Light Protocol for protecting sensitive intelligence. In addition to the official Red, Amber, Green, and White designations, some analysts reference information as TLP: Black. This unofficial designation is meant to convey the highest sensitivity, so high it should not be acted on in any way and is shared only to contextualize activity. TLP: Black has a clandestine, spy sort of feel to it, but because TLP: Black intelligence is by definition unactionable, it's seldom useful. As an intelligence creator, avoid using TLP: Black if at all possible. As an intelligence receiver, if you receive data that's marked TLP: Black, consider pushing back or clarifying with the sender what they're trying to convey. In most cases they probably meant TLP: Red. If they really do insist on TLP: Black, you may want to consider if it's worth taking the intelligence at all given its inapplicability.

Actionability is a nuanced thing that varies greatly based on the customer and the maturity of their intelligence program. This can largely be tied to a customer's focus, whether tactical, operational, or strategic. In some cases, a product can be well-crafted, but if the customer is already highly aware of the threat, that product may not be highly actionable. Conversely, that same product could be highly actionable when shared with another team that's just discovered the threat. Information on TTPs that will help an analyst detect a threat would be useless to a strategically oriented CISO. At the same time, high-level, business-oriented strategic intelligence, which the CISO wants, likely won't be very applicable to the SOC analyst.

Ultimately, improving actionability requires listening to stakeholders and understanding the following customer characteristics:

Needs
> What problems do they have, and what questions are they trying to answer?

Technology
> What tools do they have available?

Maturity
> What is the skill level of their team and their ability to act effectively?

Methodologies
> How do they approach team tasks?

After we understand all of these characteristics, we can tailor products to help customers effectively take action.

The Writing Process

Many people think good writing is the result of being a good writer. Although one aspect of being a great writer may be innate ability, for most of us writing is a slowly learned and patiently practiced skill. Writing for digital forensics and incident response (DFIR) intelligence, or any rigor-backed analytic needs, requires not only a sense of style but also a particular process. This section covers a generalized process for developing intelligence products.[3] Intelligence writing consists of three major phases: plan, draft, and edit. Let's dive into these now.

Plan

Intelligence writing always starts with a plan. Though it's easy to just start putting pen to paper (or fingers to keys), this path doesn't result in the best output. Intelligence products are thoughtful, well-reasoned, and structured deliberately to provide the most value possible to stakeholders. To that end, remember to focus on the key aspects of intelligence products during the planning phase:

Audience
> Who are you writing for? What are their goals and needs? Intelligence needs to be understood to be used effectively.

Authors
> Who is doing the writing, and what are their skill sets? Intelligence requires deep understanding to contextualize, which means informed authors.

Actionability
> What actions should the intelligence receivers be able to take after reading the product? Intelligence should always drive decision making (and usually change).

All three of these aspects help plan what needs to be in the product and what format it should take. Keep these in mind throughout the various phases of creating intelligence products, from the draft to delivery to the customer.

Draft

While creating intelligence products, the drafting process is different for everyone. Nearly everyone has their own approach and process. Regardless of the approach, however, most people find that the most difficult part is getting the first few words on paper. For example, it took your humble authors about 45 minutes to type the first sentence of this section, and it wasn't even that great of a sentence. Most authors

---

3 Expert intelligence-generating organizations should create their own detailed guides, such as *The Analyst's Style Manual* developed by the Mercyhurst College Institute for Intelligence Studies (Bill Welch, editor) (*https://oreil.ly/uKaYY*).

agree that the best way to start a first draft is just getting something written down and then moving on from there. If you do not already have your own approach to drafting, here are several strategies for starting the process. You can use just one of these approaches or several—whatever works for you.

Start with the thesis statement

A *thesis statement* is a one-sentence summary of the entire product and makes an ideal place to start. By starting with the direction, it's easy to make sure that the resulting product answers the original stakeholder request. Put the thesis statement at the top of the document and then begin building out evidence that speaks to the direction, calling out facts and assessments. In some cases, it may make sense to leave the thesis statement as a distinct element of the product, but don't feel obligated. This is just a starting point.

Using Narrative in Intelligence Writing

Human beings are storytellers, and we like hearing stories. It's a format we're used to and find comfortable. We like characters, finding out what they're like, and hearing descriptions about what they do, how they do it, why they do the things they do, and how they relate to other characters. This narrative format is natural for both intelligence producers and customers. Rather than fight this instinct, embrace it. Stories are simple to remember and have a greater impact than dull statements. People relate to stories, so use narrative.

Start with facts

Another method for beginning a draft is to start with a list of facts that have been identified in the investigation (this is the *What* of the *What/So What* format). This technique is especially useful when the product creators have comprehensive notes. Focus less on format and prose, and instead try to get all facts, times, indicators, and any concrete pieces of information on the page. When the facts are all available, they become easier to rearrange, adjust, and contextualize with prose.

Start with an outline or bullet points

Creating an outline is a good way to start getting your thoughts on paper with some structure. At this point, it is not important to fill out the content for each section of the outline; just list the main subjects that will be covered in the report. If it is too soon in the process to understand the structure or order of your findings, start with bullet points instead. This can cover a wide variety of topics, including facts (more on that next) but also analysis, considerations, and anecdotes. Once the information is written down, the best way to arrange it often emerges organically. When in doubt, follow the *rule of threes*—the idea that people aesthetically like groups of three.

It's an easy rule to follow, but starting with three bullet points, and perhaps three sub-bullets, is a great way to start almost any product.

Edit

No draft should be the final product. Creating a truly great product, even from a great draft, requires great editing. For shorter products, editing may take nearly as long as drafting. For longer products editing can take days or weeks.

Editing is rarely a single-person job. Editing is hard, and the human mind has multiple glitches that can cause problems while editing. The worst by far is the human mind's ability to edit while reading, adding missing words, or ignoring misplaced words—in short, mentally replacing what's on the page with what you meant to say instead. The more familiarity you have with the content, the more inclined you may be to make these mistakes. You can use various techniques, including the following, to avoid these kinds of mistakes:

Don't trust yourself.
> The most obvious technique is having another analyst (in bigger shops, even a dedicated editor) read your product. A second set of eyes can often see things that the original writer cannot. Having a formal process for working with an editor is highly useful.

Walk away.
> One way to make the text fresh, even text you've written yourself, is to take some time away from it. Walk away from your desk, get a cup of coffee (or your beverage of choice), and take 15 minutes to clear your mind. When you come back and reread the text, you'll have fresh eyes and ideally a fresh perspective.

Read it out loud.
> When you read things silently, your mind lets you skip small and less significant words. This is useful for reading quickly, but bad for proofreading. One solution is reading out loud. It may feel a bit crazy, but you'll be amazed how often you identify mistakes in the small words you skip over otherwise.

Automate.
> Many tools are meant to help writers. Spellcheckers and grammar checkers are common and built into most word-processing systems. In other cases, you can go far beyond that. Tools such as write-good (*https://oreil.ly/CEslt*) identify grammatically correct but inefficient or counterproductive constructs including weasel words (words that don't describe much, like *really* or *very*) or using phrases like *So* or *There is/are* at the beginning of sentences. Any tools that automate editing of products will scale for an entire team's intelligence producers.

Editing should go beyond identifying misspelled words or a sentence that ends in a comma instead of a period. Good editing should improve organization, ensure accuracy, make the topic easier to understand, identify inconsistencies, and help the original writer focus on end-customer needs.

Here are common pitfalls, specific to intelligence writing, that an editor may help you avoid:

Passive voice (https://oreil.ly/XkdlQ)
Using the format *direct object-verb-subject* is known as passive voice (as is this sentence). Passive voice makes sentences sound complex but can often be confusing and may soften the action. Intelligence products should use the more straightforward *subject-verb-direct object* pattern, which conveys action and is easier for readers to understand. For example, "The child liked the ball," instead of "The ball was liked by the child."

Uncommon terms and acronyms
Consider the audience's technical proficiency. Using unknown terms causes the customer to lose interest. Not sure how technical to go? Look at the customer's persona. When in doubt, add a definition or explanation for a term. For short documents, this may be done in-line. For longer documents, consider adding an appendix.

Leading or unobjective language
Be careful not to mislead customers. It's critical to identify bias in any subjective language and ensure it's in line with any assessments. Customers can otherwise conflate facts and assessments, leading them to make bad decisions.

Imprecision about known versus suspected
One of the most dangerous mistakes you can make when creating an intelligence product is confusing what is known with what is suspected. Although customers want an analyst's suspicions (essentially leveraging their experience and bias), any confusion around what's suspected versus what is fact can have devastating consequences and cause bad decisions to be made by stakeholders.

Editing is also the phase where content is checked both for accuracy and completeness. This is especially important for IOCs or other data that may be used by the customer directly. In many cases, a dangling participle is less problematic to a security operations team than a mistyped IP address. A good editor won't just identify the mistakes but will call out gaps in information, confusing descriptions, or places where the content would benefit from a different approach.

Instead of using a text-only approach, consider visualizing data or adding graphics. "A picture is worth a thousand words" is good advice. Wherever possible, replacing information with graphs or images makes the data more engaging, easier to digest, and often more memorable. Creating custom graphics can be a challenge without access to a graphic designer, but in many cases even stock images or clip art can provide useful insight.

The last benefit that great editors bring to a product isn't what they add, but what they cut. Intelligence products benefit from brevity, which means a good editor pays as much attention to redundant information and opportunities to streamline the product as they do to what stays in it.

Intelligence Product Formats

After planning is complete, the characteristics we discussed—goals, authors, audience, and actionability—will help define the structure of your document. Structure is the actual format and layout of the intelligence product, including headings, length, even formats of data. The audience and actionability aspects, in particular, will naturally match up with specific products.

Making up products on the fly is a dubious proposition. You run the risk of neglecting audience needs or missing out on critical actionable information. Mature intelligence programs have a library of intelligence-product templates for analysts to choose from, as well as guidance on how to choose them.

Developing product templates is an organization-specific task that relies on an understanding of anticipated audiences, needs, and organizational tone. Customization of templates is ongoing, based on feedback from customers and analysts. In most cases, products (whether a single-page tipper document or a multipage report) can adopt the following simple intelligence writing structure (shout-out to Utah State University's Center for Anticipatory Intelligence (*https://www.usu.edu/cai*)):

- What? Describing the issues, laying out the facts.
- So What? Describing why these issues and facts are important to your stakeholders.

In some cases, you can extend this into a more policy-style, prescriptive structure:

- What? Describing the issues, laying out the facts.
- So What? Describing why these issues and facts are important to your stakeholders.
- Now What? Describing actions customers can or should take.

The best structure will depend on your customers' expectations. The intelligence style simply lays out the facts and presumes the customer will use that data to formulate a plan, avoiding the analyst's bias. In the policy-style writing, we presume the customer isn't an expert and wants feedback on not just what is happening and why it's important but what to do about it.

The best way to understand what these products should look like is to walk through our example report templates. These templates illustrate the kinds of products that teams can produce for a variety of stakeholders. We're sharing them so you can use them to start building products for your own stakeholders. Templates for all sample products described in this chapter can be found on GitHub (*https://oreil.ly/igP5Z*).

Short-Form Products

Short-form products are generally one to two pages in length and are meant to address specific tactical or operational intelligence needs. In general, these products are created quickly and consumed almost immediately. Often short-form products are directly linked to requests for information (RFIs) or generated to alert others in the organization to adversary actions. They are focused products that should emphasize being timely and quickly actionable. Short-form products have distinct goals and are usually not comprehensive, but meant to provide details on specific aspects of an investigation or to meet specific needs around a given event or actor.

Incident and Actor Names

When writing short- and long-form products, analysts often need a quick way to reference current or past incidents or the actors behind them. This is far easier than just referring to things as "that email thing from last year" or "those bad guys who use that tool." Having actor names or memorable incident names fits the concept that human beings like stories and thus names for characters and specific events.

Although these names are important, be careful when choosing them. Code names may make it out into the public, so they should be public-friendly. It's also important to use code names that are nonattributable; otherwise, they're marketing terms.

A great example of a good naming convention is the Microsoft Threat Intelligence Center (MSTIC) convention, which uses elements of the periodic table to group malicious activity. These names are distinctive and memorable, and a wide range of options is available.

Let's review a variety of short-form products, starting with the event summary.

Event summary

An event summary (Example 9-1) is a common product that bridges the gap between incident response and threat intelligence. This short-form product is useful for bringing incident responders, SOC analysts, and management up to speed on evolving situations. This product should be highly time-bound and tied to a specific action.

Example 9-1. Example event summary format

```
# Event Name

## Summary

> Most products start with a comprehensive summary. This is
> important so customers can determine relevance quickly and
> because in many cases the summary is the only part of the
> product that many customers will read.

## Timeline

- 2000-01-01 Event One Description
- 2000-01-02 Event Two Description
- 2000-01-03 Event Three Description

## Impact

> Describe what resources were impacted and what that means for
> operations.

## Recommendations

- Suggested Mitigation Action 1
- Suggested Mitigation Action 2
- Suggested Remediation Action 1
- Suggested Remediation Action 2

## Ongoing Actions

- What's Being Done Now Action 1
- What's Being Done Now Action 2

## References

- [www.example.com/1](http://www.example.com/1)
- [www.example.com/2](http://www.example.com/2)
- www.example.com/3 (http://www.example.com/3)
```

Target package

Whereas an event summary is focused on something that recently took place, often unattributed, a *target package* is a description of an actor, regardless of whether an event from that actor has been observed. Target packages (Example 9-2) are often useful for summarizing information pulled from vendor reports. They are one of the most useful products because they are often of interest to a wide variety of customers. A good target package won't dive too deep into attribution. This is a fact-based project that shouldn't get too far into estimative analysis.

Example 9-2. Example target package format

```
# Target Name

## Summary

> Most products start with a comprehensive summary. This is
> important so customers can determine relevance quickly and
> because in many cases the summary is the only part of the
> product that many customers will read.

| Alternative Name | Source    |
|:-----------------|:----------|
| Alternate Name 1 | Company 1 |
| Alternate Name 2 | Company 2 |
| Alternate Name 3 | Company 3 |

## Tactics, Techniques, & Procedures

- TTP1
- TTP2
- TTP3

## Tools

| Name   | Description | Notes |
|:-------|:------------|:------|
| Tool 1 |             |       |
| Tool 2 |             |       |
| Tool 3 |             |       |

## Victim Profile

- Victim Type 1
- Victim Type 2
- Victim Type 3

Example information on reasoning.

## Related Actors

| Name         | Type       | Notes |
|:-------------|:-----------|:------|
| Actor Name 1 | Group      |       |
| Actor Name 2 | Individual |       |

## References

- www.example.com/1 (http://www.example.com/1)
- www.example.com/2 (http://www.example.com/2)
- www.example.com/ (http://www.example.com/)
```

IOC report

IOC reports are highly tactical products, typically aimed at SOCs and responders, meant to share the context of indicators. An IOC report (Example 9-3) can be especially useful when used in conjunction with new detection or alerts (such as newly blacklisted indicators). Given that indicators require context in order to be intelligence, IOC reports can often provide the necessary context.

Keep in mind that references included in IOC reports may be external but are often more valuable if they point to internal sources. For example, it would make sense to reference the related target package for an associate actor, or even an event report from a time those IOCs were observed. Tracing back through multiple products often provides the context that analysts need to understand complex events.

Example 9-3. IOC report format

```
# IOC Report

## Summary

> Most products start with a comprehensive summary. This is
> important so customers can determine relevance quickly and
> because in many cases the summary is the only part of the
> product that many customers will read.

## Indicators

| Indicator | Context | Notes |
|:----------|:--------|:------|
| IOC1      |         |       |
| IOC2      |         |       |
| IOC3      |         |       |

## Related TTPs

- TTP1
- TTP2

## References

- [www.example.com/1](http://www.example.com/1)
- [www.example.com/2](http://www.example.com/2)
- [www.example.com/3](http://www.example.com/3)
```

Long-Form Products

Long-form products are multipage, often multi-analyst, intelligence products that cover a wide range of needs. Short-form products tend to have hard deadlines, and timeliness is key. Long-form products, while they may have a deadline, tend to be much less time-constrained. Whereas a short-form product may be put out in less than 24 hours, long-form products may take weeks or months to deliver. This is due partially to their length, often more than five pages with no solid upper bound, but also the level of effort and content expected. Short-form products are often the output of a small team or even a single analyst, whereas long-form products are usually developed by large teams covering a wide variety of skills and capabilities, from reverse engineers to graphic designers.

Long-form products are expected to provide a complete view of a given topic. One of the first major long-form products was the Mandiant APT1 report (*https://oreil.ly/DPYVa*). This was a campaign analysis report that dove into multiple years of investigation and analysis of the Chinese APT group People's Liberation Army Unit 61398. The APT1 report involved multiple perspectives from a variety of victims, discussed the actor and the actor's common TTPs, explored their infrastructure, and analyzed motivations.

Given the deeper technical, writing, editorial, and overall effort requirements, long-form products are used primarily by more mature intelligence teams, and even then only sparingly. Because these tend to be long, customized products that have a strategic focus, it's important to remember that strategic customers, often leadership, may read only bits and pieces that are relevant to them. So, it's important to start with a wide-ranging executive summary covering major points and a comprehensive table of contents to let a stakeholder jump straight to aspects that are most useful to them.

What follows are three templates for common long-form products (one tactical, one operational, and one strategic).

Malware report

The tactical long-form example product is the malware report (Example 9-4). Generally an output from a reverse-engineered analysis, malware reports provide a wide range of benefits to multiple teams, from SOC analysts and incident responders who will use this information to identify new or ongoing attacks to systems architecture folks who will use this information to build future defenses.

Make sure to include outputs from automated tools such as sandboxes in these tactical, long-form reports. Although longer-form narrative tells a useful story, hunting through these reports for usable IOCs slows response actions.

Example 9-4. Malware report format

```
# Malware Report: Sample

| Key                     | Value         |
|:------------------------|:--------------|
| Reverse Engineer        | Analyst Name  |
```

```
| Date                  | 2017          |
| Requester             |               |
| Associated Intrusion Set |            |
```

Summary:

> Most products start with a comprehensive summary. This is
> important so customers can determine relevance quickly and
> because in many cases the summary is the only part of the
> product that many customers will read.

Basic Static Analysis:

- File Name:
- File Type: Portable Executable
- File Size: 0

Hashes:

> Static file hashes useful for pivoting

Hash Algorithm	Value
MD5	ddce269a1e3d054cae349621c198dd52
SHA1	7893883873a705aec69e2942901f20d7b1e28dec
SHA256	13550350a8681c84c861aac2e5b440161c2b33a3\
	e4f302ac680ca5b686de48de
SHA512	952de772210118f043a4e2225da5f5943609c653\
	a6736940e0fad4e9c7cd3cfd...f41
Ssdeep	<FOO>

Current antivirus detection capabilities:

> Gathered from VirusTotal, these are useful for understanding
organization wide detection

Vendor	Sample
Vendor 1	Signature.xyz (http://signature.xyz/)

Interesting Strings:

> Unique static file strings helpful for building detection such
as Yara signatures

- foo
- bar
- baz

Other Relevant Files or Data:

- c:/example.dll

- sysfile.exe

Basic Dynamic Analysis:

> Input from an automated sandbox

Behavioral Characteristics:

> Descriptions of how the malware accomplishes its major goals, based on kill chain methods

Delivery Mechanisms:

> How the malware got to the victim system

Persistence Mechanisms:

> How the malware runs at startup and continues running

Spreading Mechanisms:

> How the malware migrates between systems

Exfiltration Mechanisms:

> What the malware uses to move data outside the victim network

Command-and-Control Mechanisms:

> How the malware is given tasking by the attacker

Dependencies:

> System-level requirements for the malware to execute

Supported Operating Systems:
- Operating System 1

Required Files:
- c:/example.dll

Second-Stage Downloads:
- c:/example.dll

Registry Keys:
- /HKEY/Example

Detection:

> Unenriched information from the sample useful for identifying infections.

```
### Network Indicators of Compromise:

> Network strings, domains, URLs, tls certificates, IPv4, IPv6
Addresses, etc.

- 10.10.10.10
- [example.com](http://example.com/)

### Filesystem Indicators of Compromise:

> File strings, file paths, signing certificates, registry keys,
mutexes, etc.

- foobar

## Response Recommendations:

> Incident-response-centric steps for pausing and removing the
malware.

### Mitigation Steps:

- Block initial installation by remediating exploit vector.
- Update antimalware definitions to block installation actions.

### Eradication Steps:

- Update antivirus software to remove implant.

## Related Files:

> Important for establishing relationships between exploits,
droppers, RATs, etc

- C:/example.dll
```

Campaign report

The most common operational long-form report is the campaign report (Example 9-5), an end-to-end breakdown of an entire intrusion campaign. These are useful for identifying analysis gaps (places where your team doesn't fully grasp the adversary action), which may lead to RFIs. These reports are also useful for identifying missing response actions, as well as for bringing new responders, intelligence analysts, or other stakeholders up to speed on long-running investigations. For most teams, campaign reports are the longest products that analysis teams create on a regular basis.

Example 9-5. Campaign report template

```
# Campaign Report: Sample

| Key                     | Value                                     |
|:------------------------|:------------------------------------------|
| Lead Analyst            | Analyst Name                              |
| Analysis Team           | Analyst Name 1, Analyst Name 2, Analyst Name 3 |
| Date                    | 2017                                      |
| Requester               |                                           |
| Associated Intrusion Set |                                          |

## Summary

> A one-paragraph summary of the campaign and the impact.

## Description

> A comprehensive, multiparagraph summary of the entire incident,
> including the malicious activity, the actor, and the response
> actions taken by the incident-response team.

## Kill Chain

> The campaign maps against the kill chain and breaks out the
diamond model characteristics for each.

### Reconnaissance

> How the attacker gathered pre-attack information.

#### Diamond Model

- __Adversary:__ The attacker or attacker persona
- *Capability:*
 - Capability/TTP 1
 - Capability/TTP 2
- *Infrastructure:*
 - Infrastructure Resource 1
 - Infrastructure Resource 2
- __Victim:__ Target person/system of this stage

### Weaponization

> A description about the setup and configuration of the attack.

#### Diamond Model

- __Adversary:__ The attacker or attacker persona
- *Capability:*
 - Capability/TTP 1
 - Capability/TTP 2
```

- *Infrastructure:*
 - Infrastructure Resource 1
 - Infrastructure Resource 2
- __Victim:__ Target person/system of this stage

Delivery

> A description of the methods used to introduce the exploit
> into the target/victim environment.

Diamond Model

- __Adversary:__ The attacker or attacker persona
- *Capability:*
 - Capability/TTP 1
 - Capability/TTP 2
- *Infrastructure:*
 - Infrastructure Resource 1
 - Infrastructure Resource 2
- __Victim:__ Target person/system of this stage

Exploitation

> This introduces the method of exploitation, how the adversary
> took control of their target system.

Diamond Model

- __Adversary:__ The attacker or attacker persona
- *Capability:*
 - Capability/TTP 1
 - Capability/TTP 2
- *Infrastructure:*
 - Infrastructure Resource 1
 - Infrastructure Resource 2
- __Victim:__ Target person/system of this stage

Installation

> A description of how the attackers achieved persistence on
> host after exploitation.

Diamond Model

- __Adversary:__ The attacker or attacker persona
- *Capability:*
 - Capability/TTP 1
 - Capability/TTP 2
- *Infrastructure:*
 - Infrastructure Resource 1
 - Infrastructure Resource 2
- __Victim:__ Target person/system of this stage

Command & Control

> How the attacker communicates with their compromised resources.

Diamond Model

- __Adversary:__ The attacker or attacker persona
- *Capability:*
 - Capability/TTP 1
 - Capability/TTP 2
- *Infrastructure:*
 - Infrastructure Resource 1
 - Infrastructure Resource 2
- __Victim:__ Target person/system of this stage

Actions On Objectives

> The attacker's ultimate goal and what tools and techniques
> they use to achieve those objectives.

Diamond Model

- __Adversary:__ The attacker or attacker persona
- *Capability:*
 - Capability/TTP 1
 - Capability/TTP 2
- *Infrastructure:*
 - Infrastructure Resource 1
 - Infrastructure Resource 2
- __Victim:__ Target person/system of this stage

Timeline

Index	DateTime	Actor	Action	Notes
1	20170101 12 (tel:2017010112):00+00	Actor1	Action1	
2	20170102 12 (tel:2017010212):00+00	Actor2	Action2	
3	20170103 12 (tel:2017010312):00+00	Actor3	Action3	

Indicators of Compromise

> A collection of all IOCs identified, including enrichment and
pivoting, and useful signatures

Network Indicators

> Individual Network IOCs

- 10.10.10.10
- example.com (http://example.com/)
- www.example.com/path (http://www.example.com/path)

Host Indicators

> Individual Host IOCs

- /HKEY/foobar
- example.exe
- foobar

Network signatures

> Individual Network Detection Signatures (Snort, etc)

Signature for 10.10.10:

alert ip any any → 10.10.10.10 any (msg: "Bad IP detected";)

Host Signatures

> Individual Host Detection Signatures (Yara, etc)

Example Rule for foobar

```
rule example: example
{
 meta:
 description = "This is just an example"
 threat_level = 3
 in_the_wild = true

 strings:
 $a = "foobar"

 condition:
 $a
}
```

Observations

> It's useful to keep track of even casual observations
and analyst notes.

Datetime	Analyst	Observation
20170101 12:00+00	Analyst 1	Observation One
20170102 12:00+00	Analyst 2	Observation Two
20170103 12:00+00	Analyst 3	Observation Three

Related Products

> Other related intelligence, short- or long-form products

```
### Internal Products

> Internally generate related intelligence products

- product1
- product2
- product3

### External Products

> In many cases external vendor products are useful to hold on to

- www.example.com/product.pdf
```

Intelligence estimate

Intelligence *estimates* are long-form products that comprehensively explore a major strategic issue. This product originated in one of the precursors to the CIA, an agency in the State Department called the Office of National Estimates (ONE). This agency created the National Intelligence Estimate, a yearly State of the Union-esque intelligence product meant to identify and explore major strategic threats to the US.

A typical intelligence estimate–style product is a wide-ranging, largely strategic product aimed at the highest level of stakeholders, providing context necessary for making strategic decisions throughout the year. Although it is not perfect in every case (it is supplemented throughout the year), an intelligence estimate sets a baseline and provides stakeholders a starting point for understanding a wide variety of issues.

Instead of a sample intelligence estimate, a highly tailored document, we recommend looking at some declassified examples from the CIA (*https://oreil.ly/MWc63*).

The RFI Process

As we discussed earlier in this chapter (as well as in Chapter 4), a *request for information* (RFI) is a specialized product meant to answer a specific question, often in response to a situational awareness need. A requester submits a very short-form question to the intelligence team. At that point, the intelligence team either answers it directly based on information already collected (if possible) or treats this as a request for collection, kicking off a new intelligence cycle. To keep the process orderly and consistent, it helps to have a template, not only for the response product but also for the initial request. The RFI process, illustrated in Figure 9-3, needs to stay focused. An RFI can be used for tactical, operational, and strategic requests.

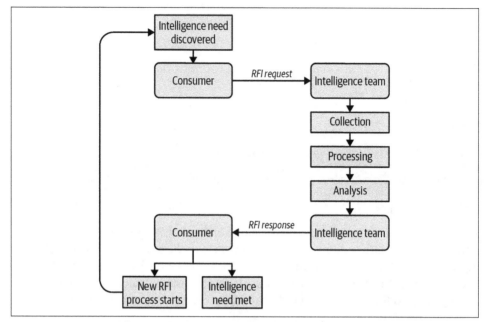

Figure 9-3. RFI workflow (including the intelligence process)

An easy way to implement an RFI workflow is by using email-based requests. Customers send a request, using the team template, to a common mailbox such as *rfi@company.com*, where the intelligence team can pick up requests. Because RFIs come in two parts, the request and the response, your workflow will include two templates.

RFI request

The request from a customer follows a strict and limited structure, as shown in Example 9-6.

Example 9-6. RFI request template

```
# RFI-1

- _FROM:_ Requester
- _TO:_ Intelligence Team
- _Response By:_ 2016-11-12

## Request:

> The RFI request needs to be a straightforward question with a
> distinct description of what a good answer would look like.

## _Request References:_
```

```
- www.example.com/request_source_1 (http://www.example.com/request_source_1)
- www.example.com/request_source_2 (http://www.example.com/request_source_2)
```

The *To* and *From* fields should direct the request from the customer to the intelligence team. The Response By field specifies how quickly the customer needs the intelligence (an alternative is using severity levels such as high, medium, or low). Next is the Request. This should be a directed question with a description of a concrete answer. Finally, a requester may provide Request References or other background to the question as a starting point for the intelligence team.

RFI response

The RFI response also follows a strict and limited structure, as shown in Example 9-7.

Example 9-7. RFI response template

```
# RFI Response - 1
- _FROM:_ Intelligence Team
- _TO:_ Requester
- _TLP:_ red/yellow/green/white
- _Response At:_ 2016-11-13

## Response:

> The response should be crafted to be complete but succinct,
> directly answering the question in the request.

## Response References:

- www.example.com/response_source_1 (http://www.example.com/response_source_1)
- www.example.com/response_source_2 (http://www.example.com/response_source_2)
```

The *From* and *To* fields direct the response back to the original requester. The TLP field specifies the sharing rules that the response recipients should follow. It's also key to call out the date the response was sent back to the customer (Response At) for reference and metrics. Success for the RFI process hinges on whether the Requester receives a meaningful Response to their request. The response should address the specific question asked and not stray into secondary issues. Finally, it's useful to include sources of information that the intelligence team used for the RFI as Response References.

RFI flow example

What follows is an example of a typical RFI workflow. We'll start with the request from the customer.

RFI request. A useful RFI request could look like this:

- *From: Security Operations Center*
- *To: Intelligence Team*
- *Response By: 2017-02-20*

Request:

What are the useful network IOCs for detecting X-Agent malware?

Request References:

- *https://attack.mitre.org/software/S0161/*

RFI response. The response (after going through an intelligence cycle) might look something like this:

- *From: Intelligence Team*
- *To: Security Operations Center*
- *Response By: 2017-02-22*

Based on public sources, we recommend the following network indicators for detection of the APT28 X-Agent malware:

- Snort alert tcp $HOME_NET any -> $EXTERNAL_NET $HTTP_PORTS (msg:"Downrage_HTTP_C2"; flow:established,to_server; content:"POST"; http_method; content:"="; content:"=|20|HTTP/1.1"; fast_pattern; distance:19; within:10; pcre:"/^\/(?:[a-zA-Z0-9]{2,6}\/){2,5}[a-zA-Z0-9]{1,7}\.[A-Za-z0- 9\+\-\_\.]+\/\?[a-zA-Z0-9]{1,3}=[a-zA-Z0-9+\/]{19}=$/I";)
- *hxxp://23.227.196[.]215/*
- *hxxp://apple-iclods[.]org/*
- *hxxp://apple-checker[.]org/*
- *hxxp://apple-uptoday[.]org/*
- *hxxp://apple-search[.]info*

Further intelligence could be developed with a follow-up request.

Response References:

- *https://oreil.ly/tWK6m*
- *https://oreil.ly/tKDvC*

Date and Time Formats

Few things can cause as much consternation and confusion for a security operations team as inconsistent datetime representations. In the US, it's common to use the MM/DD/YYYY format that, while familiar, is often hard to use globally. European custom is typically DD/MM/YYYY, which is more straightforward. Unfortunately, both of these formats may cause problems in intelligence products since they're difficult to sort and can often be jarring to read in-line. Instead, consider the YYYYMMDD format, which is easy to read, especially in timelines, and easy to sort. Time is also better when it's sortable, so consider using the 24-hour system and use a consistent time zone, preferably UTC; for example, 20170219 22:02+00. This is also easier for scripts and tools to ingest.

Automated Consumption Products

Automated consumption products are grouped IOCs meant to be used by tools such as detection, alerting, or analysis systems. These differ from IOC reports, which are meant to be read by human analysts. Used in conjunction with written products, which provide useful context, automated consumption products make it much faster to start using threat data effectively and improve accuracy. Automated consumption products fall into four categories:

- Unstructured/semi-structured IOCs
- Network signatures with Snort
- Filesystem signatures with Yara
- Automated IOC formats

In the following sections, we'll explore all types of automated consumption products.

Unstructured/semi-structured IOCs

Generalized IOCs are groups of indicators (a piece of data plus context), typically in basic text-based lists, which make them easy to integrate into other tools or formats. When sharing information for automated consumption by scripts and tools, the most important consideration is what tools or scripts will be ingesting the product. A variety of complex standards such as OpenIOC (*https://oreil.ly/pC_fN*) and STIX (*https://oreil.ly/7T6wv*) are incredibly expressive but limited to the tools that implement those standards. If your customers can't use these formats, they are often more trouble than they're worth. We'll discuss them at the end of this section.

Even after the advent of these security-centric standards, most IOC sharing is still done using lists in text files or semi-structured CSV files. While lacking in context, these formats are easy to consume, easy to read by people (as well as computers), and easy to write scripts against.

Road Runner unstructured IOCs. Generalized IOCs can be incredibly simple. Here's an example of hashes from Road Runner.

```
Family, sha256
ZoxFamily,0375b4216334c85a4b29441a3d37e61d7797c2e1cb94b14cf6292449fb25c7b2
ZoxFamily,48f0bbc3b679aac6b1a71c06f19bb182123e74df8bb0b6b04ebe99100c57a41e
...
Plugx,fb38fd028b82525033dec578477d8d5d2fd05ad2880e4a83c6b376fa2471085c
Plugx,ff8dbdb962595ba179a7664e70e30e9b607f8d460be73583af59f39b4bb8a36e
...
Gh0st,ff19d0e8de66c63bcf695269c12abd99426cc7688c88ec3c8450a39360a98caa
PoisonIvy,ffc3aa870bca2da9f9946cf162cb6b1f77ba9db1b46092580bd151d5ed72075f
...
ZxshellModule,6dc352693e9d4c51fccd499ede49b55d0a9d01719a15b27502ed757347121747
...
```

This format is incredibly simplistic, but easily scriptable for use with other tools. These lists of IOCs are most often shared as plain text, Markdown, or Excel/CSVs.

Network signatures with Snort

In general, when we reference *network signatures*, we mean Snort signatures. Snort, as we've discussed earlier in the book, was one of the earliest intrusion-detection systems and uses a text-based, open signature format. Snort has a verbose and effective signature language that has been adopted by many other vendors, implemented in a wide variety of tools, and thus is the standard for describing network traffic.

Snort signatures are shared as simple text files, making them easy to ingest with a variety of tools and easy to manage using scripts (see Example 9-8).

Example 9-8. Sample Snort signature

```
alert tcp any any → 10.10.10.10 any (msg:"Sample Snort Rule"; sid:1000001;\
rev:1;)
```

Road Runner network signatures. There are signatures for Road Runner. Specifically, here is a Snort Community signature (*https://oreil.ly/68Jtv*) for Road Runner's Hikit malware:

```
alert tcp $HOME_NET any → $EXTERNAL_NET any (msg:"MALWARE-BACKDOOR
Win.Backdoor.Hikit outbound banner response";
flow:to_client,established;
content:"|5D 00 20 00|h|00|i|00|k|00|i|00|t|00|>|00|";
fast_pattern:only; metadata:impact_flag red, policy balanced-ips
drop, policy security-ips drop, ruleset community, service http,
service ssl; reference:url,www.virustotal.com/en/file/aa4b2b448a5e24\
```

```
(http://www.virustotal.com/en/file/aa4b2b448a5e24/)
6888304be51ef9a65a11a53bab7899bc1b56e4fc20e1b1fd9f/analysis/;
classtype:trojan-activity; sid:30948; rev:2;)
```

If you need a reminder of how Snort signatures work, refer to Chapter 5. Here are some key pieces:

```
alert tcp $HOME_NET any → $EXTERNAL_NET any
```

The Hikit malware used by Road Runner sits on a server in the victim's network demilitarized zone (DMZ), where the attacker then connects to it from the outside. (This is an unusual architecture, because most remote-access Trojans *phone home* from inside the victim's network to a command-and-control node outside.) To model this, the Hikit Snort signature uses $variables, which make it easy to set network ranges for different network locations. ($HOME_NET is typically an organization's range, and $EXTERNAL_NET is basically everything else.) As a result, the Hikit signature should trigger only when the server (the system inside $HOME_NET, usually the victim's DMZ) is sending a message back to the client (the attacker's system outside somewhere in $EXTERNAL_NET).

As important as what this clause specifies is what it doesn't: ports. If ports were hard-coded in, changing the server port could be trivial for the attacker, depending on the malware. Because client ports are almost always random ephemeral ports (picked at random from higher port numbers (*https://oreil.ly/cpkYI*)), specifying universally correct ports would be difficult. If the attacker guessed the port, the attacker could easily avoid detection. Given the specificity of the content bit string and directionality, this wildcard for the port will not likely cause too many false positives. Specifying ports can be important for signatures impacting specific services, such as attacks on SMB (445/TCP for those of you playing along at home).

```
flow:to_client,established;
```

These flow clause characteristics help model a similar directionality as the To/From in the alert clause. The key is this clause adds established, meaning this signature shouldn't trigger on the first few packets of a connection. This improves accuracy and prevents someone from generating packets with the Hikit bit string shown here:

```
content:"|5D 00 20 00|h|00|i|00|k|00|i|00|t|00|>|00|";
```

The second key piece of this signature is the byte signature of the communication (this byte signature is where the malware got its colloquial name). This combination of bytes is always observed in the command-and-control communication of the Hikit malware (at least the sample it was based on, which is specified with the reference to VirusTotal).

Combined, these three characteristics (directionality, flow specification, and the content) create a comprehensive signature for the Hikit malware.

Filesystem signatures with Yara

When describing file content, information analysts rely on Yara. Staying true to its tagline—*"The pattern matching swiss knife for malware researchers (and everyone else)"*—Yara makes it easy to describe a variety of patterns useful for identifying malware; not just individual files (as with hashes), but entire families. Yara signatures are an ideal way to share this data because they're usable with any tools that implement the open source Yara detection libraries. This means customers can use Yara with a variety of command-line tools, automation tools, host and network detection tools, and even while hunting for samples on VirusTotal.

Yara signatures (see Example 9-9) are also shared as simple text files, like Snort signatures, making them similarly easy to ingest with a variety of tools and easy to manage using scripts.

Example 9-9. Sample Yara signature

```
rule sample_signature: banker
{
 meta:
 description = "This is just an example"


 strings:
 $a = "foo"
 $b = "bar"
 $c = {62 61 7a}

 condition:
 $a or $b or $c
}
```

Automated IOC formats

Fully automated and comprehensive formats such as STIX 2 (*https://oreil.ly/TtOVr*) are useful only for teams that use tools built for them (or that are capable of building tools to use these standards). These can be used as general intelligence consumption but may require translation to more accessible formats. In the past, one thing that has limited the adoption of these formats outside of vendors is that both Mandiant's (now deprecated) OpenIOC and MITRE's (also now deprecated) STIX version 1 were based on Extensible Markup Language (XML). XML was a data format for many years, but as REST interfaces have overtaken SOAP, so has JavaScript Object Notation (JSON) overtaken XML.

In keeping with the times, the STIX 2 format is being updated to JSON. Example 9-10 shows a C2 indicator based on Oasis's GitHub (*https://oreil.ly/vAE2L*).

Example 9-10. STIX 2 Command-and-Control IOC[4]

```
{
  "type": "bundle",
  "id": "bundle-93f38795-4dc7-46ea-8ce1-f30cc78d0a6b",
  "spec_version": "2.0",
  "objects": [
    {
        "type": "indicator",
        "id": "indicator-36b94be3-659f-4b8a-9a4d-90c2b69d9c4d",
        "created": "2017-01-28T00:00:00.000000Z",
        "modified": "2017-01-28T00:00:00.000000Z",
        "name": "IP Address for known Grizzley Step c2",
        "labels": [
            "malicious-activity"
        ],
        "pattern": "[ipv4-addr:value = '146.185.161.126']",
        "valid_from": "2013-09-05T00:00:00.000000Z"
    }
  ]
}
```

STIX 2 is especially valuable when authors want to share indicators with a variety of customers but they don't know what tools or formats the customers use. This can be especially useful in public reporting, such as the US-CERT's GRIZZLY STEPPE report (*https://oreil.ly/b17hL*). In this case, US-CERT released both a written report (a similar format to our campaign reports) along with indicators in multiple formats including in STIX 1. The use of STIX was appropriate because, as a TLP:White general public report, it was impossible for the authors to know what formats the customers would want. STIX provides a middle ground that any threat intelligence team should be able to use, and some teams could make use of quickly.

Establishing a Rhythm

Intelligence teams must establish their own rhythm for releasing intelligence products. Some products benefit from regular release, such as situational awareness reports and intelligence estimates, while others make more sense released in an ad hoc nature based on ongoing events, such as RFIs or tipper products.

Regularly released products are useful for keeping stakeholder interest, establishing and maintaining situational awareness, and solidifying lines of communication. That said, it's important to work with stakeholders to calibrate frequency, length, and content of regularly distributed intelligence products. Too often, and the analysis team runs the risk of having nothing of consequence to put in the products, giving little value to the customers, wasting their time, and eventually causing them to lose

---

4 Based on CISA's "Enhanced Analysis of GRIZZLY STEPPE Activity" report (*https://oreil.ly/tu9rr*).

interest. Conversely, if intelligence products get released too infrequently, no forward momentum is established, and too much time must be spent reorienting the customer each time a new product is released (this is especially important because, like writing, reading intelligence effectively is a skill unto itself and practice helps).

Distribution

Once a product is written and edited, it's ready for distribution to customers. Like all other aspects of the Dissemination process, the method of distribution must make sense for the target audience and at the same time must effectively display the product content.

Ease of distribution must be balanced with intelligence product protection, as well. Government classification systems are one example of intelligence product protection. While establishing an elaborate protection system may seem useful, in many cases it's far more trouble than it's worth. Within analysis teams, portals are effective for distributing intelligence products. Wikis or CRMs, such as Microsoft SharePoint, provide a centralized point for creating, updating, and sharing information. They're commonly searchable, which is useful for gaining context around indicators. Intelligence teams can set up CRMs off the internet, such as in an isolated noncompany SOC or intel team network.

Depending on sensitivity, products for leadership can be distributed in multiple ways. Common channels, such as email, are useful for less-sensitive products, especially regularly distributed products. Most executives won't go to extensive lengths to view intelligence products, so email and printed hard copies are most effective. To that end, consider the fact that many executives work extensively on mobile devices. This means two things: small screens and a likelihood they won't be on VPNs. Tailor your products and distribution to take that into account, since an intelligence product on a one-off intelligence distribution platform behind your company's VPN will likely go unread.

Feedback

Let's return to the intelligence-writing process. Often overlooked, the feedback stage is a core piece of establishing a rhythm. During feedback, the intelligence customer shares what would make future products more useful. This largely breaks down into two categories:

Technical feedback
> The first and most important piece of feedback from a customer is whether the original direction was met and whether the stakeholders got the information they needed. In many cases, there aren't simple *yes* or *no* answers to these questions; the intelligence team may instead need to conduct another round of

the intelligence cycle. Generating more specific requirements and providing a new direction is its own form of success.

Format feedback

Another form of feedback is whether the products were useful for the stakeholders. In many cases, the intelligence itself is useful, but the product type could be better, either for the original customer or for a new customer. For example, a campaign report is useful for the SOC team, but the SOC team lead could ask for a new, shorter-form version aimed at executives.

Intelligence teams greatly benefit from establishing open lines of communication and getting regular feedback from their customers. Regular feedback guides change to processes, formats, conventions, and even how to staff the intelligence team.

Getting feedback can be a difficult problem, though. The simplest solution? Reach out to intelligence customers and solicit feedback. Want to go the extra mile? Combine gathering feedback on intelligence products with improving customer personas. These interviews can improve a variety of intelligence products, and once the floodgate of feedback is open, it's easy to gather information about a variety of topics, including improving intelligence products.

Regular Products

One of the keys to establishing a rhythm for creating intelligence products is having regular intelligence product output. Many successful intelligence programs use regular products to great effect. Here are the reasons regular products make an impact:

- Regular intelligence products inform customers on important topics such as imminent threats, situational awareness items including security news, and activity of the intelligence and incident-response teams.

- Regular intelligence products keep the intelligence team at the front of customers' minds, reminding them of the option to make requests (whether RFIs or formal) and to be on the lookout for future products.

- By producing regular products, the intelligence team keeps security priorities on the radar of the customers, even when not necessarily related to the incident response.

Establishing a cadence for developing intelligence products depends greatly on the incident-response team's operational tempo, the intelligence team's bandwidth to create regular intelligence products, and customer needs.

One way to get started is with a weekly threat report. This basic one-page product should focus on ongoing investigations and incidents, as well as situational awareness in the form of security news. This type of product is valuable to a variety of customers, from SOC analysts to C-level stakeholders. It keeps them informed, keeps everyone aware of the status of urgent matters (either internal or external), and acts as a conversation starter for intelligence and incident response.

Conclusion

Analysts need to create great products to share their intelligence successfully. Effective dissemination requires taking the time to create products that are accurate, audience-focused, and actionable by focusing on the presumed customer, understanding how they plan to use the information, and planning accordingly.

In addition, analysts should ask themselves the following five questions during the writing process to ensure that the intelligence products they develop will be well-received and will meet the needs of their intelligence customers:

- What is the goal?
- Who is the audience?
- What is the proper length of product?
- What level of intelligence? (tactical, operational, strategic?)
- What tone and type of language should you use? (technical or nontechnical?)

Your answers to these questions inform the final product. Learning to pair the product's goals and its audience is a skill, not a formula. It takes time and feedback to develop an understanding of how to approach this. Building processes on how to plan, draft, and edit content will dramatically speed up the entire process.

Ultimately, the entire Dissemination process relies on developing a continuous feedback loop between analysts, writers, editors, and customers. Only through this cycle can the process develop, the products improve, and the intelligence program mature.

## PART III

The Way Forward

Intelligence-driven incident response doesn't end when the final incident report has been delivered; it will become a part of your overall security process. Part III covers big-picture aspects of IDIR that are outside individual incident-response investigations. These features include strategic intelligence to continually learn and improve processes, as well as implementation of an intelligence team to support security operations as a whole.

## CHAPTER 10

Strategic Intelligence

Our products have become so specific, so tactical even, that our thinking has become tactical.
We're losing our strategic edge because we're so focused on today's issues.

—John G. Heidenrich

Once you've worked through the F3EAD process—from day one of Find all the way through Disseminate—you may be wondering what comes next. Well, in most situations, there is barely enough time to work all the way through the entire intelligence-driven incident response process before you need to jump right back to the beginning with another intrusion or some other pressing task. While it may seem urgent to move onto something else, you are not quite done yet. Taking a little bit of time to understand if and how the recent incident fits into the strategic threat landscape is a task that will pay dividends down the road. It is one of the best ways to make sure that your organization actually learns from the incident and moves forward in a more resilient, informed manner.

All too often, incident responders must deal with the same situation manifesting itself in the same way, with the same vulnerabilities, the same lateral movement, maybe even the exact same stolen or reused passwords, and very often the same adversaries. At that point, many find themselves shaking their fists at the sky, asking how this could have happened. Didn't we learn from the last time? Didn't we fix the problems? Unfortunately, the answer is often "no." When the last incident was resolved, there were other things to worry about, other problems requiring the attention of everyone—from the security team to the IT manager to the CIO—and since the problem had been "resolved" there was no more time to spend thinking about it. Lessons were not learned, and although some small changes may have been made, there was no lasting impact on the security of the organization because new, urgent problems took priority. Investing time in strategic intelligence, both understanding the "big picture" and assessing how individual incidents validate or change that understanding, will help prevent incident déjà vu and not only help protect your organization but also help your security teams stay focused on emerging threats rather than the same threats time after time. In this chapter, we will cover what strategic intelligence is, how it fits into the intelligence-drive incident response process, and how you can utilize it—whether you have a team or 1 or 100.

What Is Strategic Intelligence?

Nothing happens in a vacuum, especially not network intrusions. Everything happens within a specific context—the strategic environment—and that context is important across the entire F3EAD process and beyond. The strategic environment extends far beyond your own networks, data, and the tactical and operational impacts of an intrusion. It includes geopolitical, economic, social, and technological issues, along with many other variables. *Strategic intelligence* provides the necessary information for planning future actions and policies and helps decision makers tackle long-term projects and initiatives.

Strategic intelligence gets its name not only from the subjects that it covers, typically a high-level analysis of information with long-term implications, but also from its most common audience. Strategic intelligence is geared toward decision makers (most often business/agency senior leadership) who have the ability and authority to act, because this type of intelligence should shape policies and strategies. This doesn't mean, however, that leadership is the only group that can benefit from these insights. Strategic intelligence is extremely useful to all levels of personnel because it can help them understand the surrounding context of the issues that they deal with at their levels. Helping individuals understand why certain policies were created, or why an emphasis is being placed on a particular area, will help them to fulfill their role more effectively.

In his paper "The State of Strategic Intelligence" (*https://oreil.ly/Ccggp*), strategic intelligence expert John G. Heidenrich wrote that "a strategy is not really a plan but the logic driving a plan."[1] When that logic is present and clearly communicated, analysts can approach problems in a way that supports the overarching goals behind a strategic effort rather than treating each individual situation as its own entity. When that logic is NOT there, following any plan can become incredibly difficult and knowing when the plan should be modified is even harder.

Strategic intelligence supports intelligence-driven incident response processes by helping analysts prioritize responses, identify when an intrusion is particularly significant to their organization, and ensure that the lessons learned from each incident are

---

1 John G. Heidenrich, "The State of Strategic Intelligence" (*https://oreil.ly/Ccggp*), Studies in Intelligence 51(2), 2007.

analyzed and acted upon. Without strategic intelligence, intelligence-driven incident response can still provide insight, but strategic intelligence can drastically improve an organization's ability to understand and posture itself to prevent, identify, and respond to subsequent intrusions. But how does one *get* strategic intelligence? How can you identify the logic that will help dictate the plan that you will follow, especially when there are so many other time-sensitive needs competing for your attention?

Sherman Kent: Father of American Intelligence Analysis

Sherman Kent is known as the father of American intelligence analysis and quite literally wrote the book on intelligence analysis with *Strategic Intelligence for American World Policy* (still a great read almost 60 years later).[2] He was so instrumental to the intelligence discipline that the CIA's school to train new intelligence analysts is called the Sherman Kent Center for Intelligence Analysis.

Kent received a doctorate in History from Yale University and taught on the faculty until World War II, when he joined a new division of the newly formed foreign intelligence service (and CIA precursor) Office of Strategic Services (OSS) called the Research and Analysis Branch (R&A). There, Kent used his experience as a historian, combined with an ability to lead, to bring together economists, scientists, philosophers, poets, and military members to conduct some of the most influential analysis of the war. Kent and the R&A analysts were not planning operations or tactical skirmishes; they were analyzing the underpinnings of the enemy and operating environment. They analyzed the cultures and the resources available (food, finances, and transportation) to help the US determine what actions would have the most significant impact to the national strategy. They generated strategic intelligence that helped not just a single mission, but the entire war effort.

In many cases, one of the most significant differences between strategic and tactical intelligence is the modeling process. In tactical intelligence, analysts use pre-existing models, whether that model is an actor dossier or an internal network map, to solve the problem at hand. In strategic analysis, those models are often being updated or developed for the first time. In fact, when strategic analysts start leveraging only pre-existing models, whether mental or tangible, they run the risk of missing significant changes in the way the world functions, making their analysis less effective and in some cases flat out wrong.

While it is beneficial to have a corpus of work to look back on when applying these principles to modern intelligence-driven incident response, it is also important to

---

2 Sherman Kent, *Strategic Intelligence for American World Policy* (*https://oreil.ly/7GjYj*) (New Jersey: Princeton University Press, 1966).

understand how the world has changed since World War II and how that may change some of the doctrine intelligence analysts rely on.

The Role of Strategic Intelligence in Intelligence-Driven Incident Response

The strategic intelligence of Sherman Kent's day was designed to inform policy makers at the strategic level of what they needed to know in order to make the right decisions. Analysts often had access to information that no one else did and were able to provide insight that would otherwise have been lost to policy makers. Things have changed quite a bit since that time, and leaders are often dealing with *too much* information rather than too little.

As we mentioned, strategic intelligence can be thought of as the logic behind a plan and so it plays a primary role in intelligence-driven incident response before or after an incident, rather than during, with a few exceptions. When leveraged before an incident, strategic intelligence can shape the response process, helping to identify how critical the response process is to an organization and whether there are any particular requirements to keep in mind—for example, legal requirements about when and how to report the incident, and what type of data exposure warrants reporting. It can also help position defenses based on an understanding of the strategic threat landscape and any significant world events that may have an impact on security. After an incident is the time when new information that was learned through the intelligence-driven incident response process is integrated into the organization's understanding of the strategic threat landscape. At this time, the key questions that are often asked by leaders and executives include:

- Who is targeting our organization?
- What are they after?
- How effective are we at preventing attacks?
- What is the impact of a successful intrusion?

Answers to these questions should be based on information from your own incidents, but also from intrusions that have occurred elsewhere that you learned about via threat information sharing or media reporting. If you are basing updates to strategic intelligence on media reporting, however, it is important to make sure that you have enough insight into what happened and trust the validity of the reporting before making significant changes to the way your organization views threats. There are, as always, exceptions. While most often applied before and after, there are times when strategic intelligence can be directly leveraged *during* the incident-response process. In these cases, analysts are often not generating strategic intelligence—after all, the direct focus of incident response is often tactical in nature, which requires a different way of thinking—but are instead turning to strategic intelligence to help understand a potential contradiction that is stalling or even halting analytic progress. As Father Richard Rohr wrote, "Dictionaries define a *contradiction* as two things that cannot be true at the same time. I would say it this way: a contradiction is two things that cannot be true at the same time *by your present frame of logic.*"

As analysts, we always view the information that we are analyzing through a specific frame, and when something does not make sense or does not seem like it should be possible, that often means the analyst needs a new frame. The process of reframing a mindset can be very difficult when remaining "in the weeds" (where many incident responders like to stay). Reframing, or changing your present state of logic, often requires taking a step back and looking to the bigger picture, which is what strategic intelligence provides. When using a structured analytic technique like a Key Assumptions Check, it can also be beneficial to turn to strategic intelligence to help counter biases and identify information that may make the assumptions untrue.

Intelligence Beyond Incident Response

This is as good a time as any to bring up a key concept that the threat intelligence world is still coming to terms with: Intelligence can go far beyond just supporting detection engineering, intrusion detection, and incident-response activities. Throughout this chapter, we're discussing strategic intelligence and how threat intelligence can support an organization's leadership in making better decisions, but many other security decisions benefit from this support.

Red Teaming

One way to use intelligence beyond tactical/operational defense is to inform adversarial operations. In *red teaming*, an internal team acts as an adversary to challenge the intrusion-detection and incident-response teams (or blue teams, in this scenario). In many organizations, the red team develops their own persona, often based on the capabilities of the red team's engineers. If the red team engineers know how to build zero days, then the red team adversary will leverage zero days. If the red team engineers typically use the Metasploit framework, then the simulated adversary will use Metasploit. Even more complex is if the red team engineers know a programming language like Python, then the adversaries' tools will end up being written in Python.

You might be noticing that the only adversary we've talked about at this point is the artificial one. That's the problem. Giving your blue team an adversary to track and respond to teaches them how to track and respond to that simulated adversary. But if the simulated adversary isn't similar enough to the real adversaries an organization faces, then the blue team won't learn useful lessons. For example, if the red team uses HTTP beacons over 80/tcp (because it's easier to build or download sample remote-access Trojans that just use well-understood protocols like HTTP) but the organization's main adversary uses C2 encoded in DNS, then the TTPs developed by the blue team (yep, defense has TTPs, too) may not be very effective. So, what way would be better? Well, the most obvious approach is for red teams to act more like real adversaries. Unfortunately, most red teams don't know what real adversaries act like. This is somewhat expected. Most red teamers migrate out of one of three other roles, which explain their...lack of perspective (sorry, red teamers!):

Application security analysts

> They are focused on hunting through code for vulnerabilities. Some write fixes, some write exploits. Either way, their approach is always going to be more focused on the vulnerability/exploit itself than how it's used in the real world.

Vulnerability analysts

> Most of these folks focus on using tools like scanners to understand where there are network vulnerabilities. They know how to interpret the outputs of these tools but don't understand the kinds of objectives adversaries are after or the stages after initial exploitation.

Former offensive engineers

> While rare, there are a small number of folks who were "real" offensive engineers. These folks, usually former government staff, have actually conducted intrusions. They do know what adversary tradecraft looked like, at least at one point in the past, but often can't disclose it. Subconsciously they may emulate it, but not all nation-state adversaries operate the same way, and chances are your new red teamers' former employer is not your company's current adversary (and, if they are, you may be in bigger trouble).

The fact is most red teamers will welcome being more relevant and useful. Their goal is to help defense be as effective as possible. By taking the time to share and review adversary profiles that your organization faces, the red team can adjust their TTPs to better emulate the threats your defenses will actually face, such as testing more effectively, using more realistic tools, and even setting up a similar infrastructure. All of these things help your defense better prepare for their actual adversaries.

Vulnerability Management

Closely related to red teaming is vulnerability management. *Vulnerability management* seeks to reduce attack surface by identifying, mitigating, and remediating vulnerabilities before an adversary can exploit them, usually by working with, or being, a member of the organization's patching team.

Most of security operations is built on metrics, but vulnerability management more than most—whether it's a Common Vulnerability Scoring System (CVSS), the time since the patch was released, the criticality of the system, whether it's a full moon, or some combination of all of the above! While the CVSS score does take into account things like whether there's a public exploit, the idea that a known adversary is using it, how it's being deployed, and what malware is being deployed using the vulnerability can all make a difference in how remediation of a particular vulnerability is prioritized.

For example, think about the Log4Shell attacks aimed at CVE-2021-44228, CVE-2021-45046, and CVE-2021-44832 (*https://oreil.ly/lyDIz*). Initial reporting, largely from GreyNoise and CISA, identified the primary vector for Log4J exploitation as aimed at Java web services such as Tomcat and games like Minecraft. While these reports were 100% valid, intelligence teams quickly started hearing about other ways it could be exploited, such as putting the Log4Shell exploit strings in documents going through content proxies like web security gateways. That new knowledge caused a fundamental shift in which systems the vulnerability management team needed to focus on. Suddenly, it was less about externally facing systems and more about a wider variety of internal systems. It was not until after this analysis was conducted that the CVSS score was updated to take this into account.

Architecture and Engineering

Those last two concepts were pretty straightforward, but there are lots of ways threat intelligence can better inform more complex things like network and even application engineering and architecture. In a lot of ways, this is an extension of our vulnerability analysis discussion: By understanding how adversaries are attacking systems, we can better improve the resilience of those systems by whatever means make the most sense. Ultimately, systems engineering and architecture is a series of decisions about trade-offs, and better information means better decisions, and intelligence supports better decisions.

A (Exceedingly) Brief Introduction to Resilience

While a topic of growing interest, *resilience* is the ability for a system to resist external threats while returning to its ability to function effectively. According to Utah State University's Center for Anticipatory Intelligence, a system's resilience is dependent on four Rs:

Resistance
> How well do you keep the threat out?

Retention
> How can you keep the system's core functions going during disruption?

Recovery
> How quickly can you get the system's core functions to bounce back?

Resurgence
How do you make a system stronger and smarter after the disruption?

Only one of these, resistance, is *left of boom*, before exploitation. The rest come *after* the adversary has started to gain control. Through intelligence, we can use knowledge of past incidents to anticipate what steps an adversary will take and prepare to respond to them.

Privacy, Safety, and Physical Security

Networks aren't the only things that need protection from threats in cyberspace. Human systems, including individuals and communities, face vulnerabilities and threats and need resilience as well. Many of these vulnerabilities and threats are amplified by technology, and while technology can't solve these problems, it is incumbent on us to build systems that don't exacerbate them. Building resilient human systems ends up being a task that's wildly specific to the system, and outside the scope of this book, but is certainly worth keeping in mind. It's a different sort of system, but it can still benefit from the same kind of decision support that strategic intelligence brings.

Now that we understand more about the role of strategic intelligence in intelligence-driven incident response and beyond, we can move onto the hard part: conducting and leveraging strategic analysis.

Building a Frame with Strategic Intelligence

Daniel Kahneman and Amos Tversky, whose groundbreaking research (*https://oreil.ly/aFNum*) on framing and decision making has had a far-reaching impact on fields such as psychology and economics, advocate for building what they call a *broad frame* for making decisions.[3] In a talk given at the CFA Institute's conference, Kahneman urged listeners to "see a decision as a member of a class of decisions that you'll probably have to make" rather than a single, stand-alone decision.

A traditional "frame" in intelligence analysis is viewed like a picture frame on the wall. Everything you are looking at is contained within the frame, and the viewer is outside, looking in. Framing is a way of defining what it is you are looking at and breaking a problem or issue down into its component parts to be more closely studied. In this sense, we can think of many of the models we covered in Chapters 4 and 8 as analytic frames. With strategic intelligence, however, it is even more crucial that our frames be based on both analysis and synthesis.

---

3 Amos Tversky and Daniel Kahneman, "The Framing of Decisions and the Psychology of Choice" (*https://oreil.ly/aFNum*), *Science 211* (1981): 453–457.

In addition to strategic analysis—or breaking down large-scale concepts into their individual parts so that they can be understood—we also need to think critically about *strategic synthesis,* or understanding how different pieces work together in a complex system. As Josh Kerbel explains in his paper "The US Intelligence Community's Creativity Challenge" (*https://oreil.ly/MMGKg*), complex environments are defined not just by their parts but how those parts interact in often unpredictable and unanticipated ways.[4] In complex situations, analysis alone will not help us understand what's going on in a complex system. For a truly complex system, in addition to breaking down an issue into parts, framing must also include information on how the different parts interact and under what circumstance the parts impact other parts. This process is called *strategic synthesis* and is a crucial part of framing for strategic intelligence in an increasingly complex world. In fact, synthesis is one of the primary reasons it is so important to translate intelligence-driven incident response findings into strategic intelligence—this synthesis helps identify relationships between parts of the system and highlight the changing nature of the landscape in which an organization or business is operating.

Frames can be either mental frameworks for approaching problems (a descriptive way to present the problem to others) or, as mentioned, a visual representation of a system or situation. Considering strategic intelligence is used by many people in many different roles, ranging from analyst to CEO, a documented (often visual) frame is one of the best ways to keep all necessary parties aligned. In the next sections we will cover a few of the models that can help with framing in strategic intelligence.

Models for Strategic Intelligence

In *Psychology of Intelligence Analysis,* Richards J. Heuer Jr. points to models as a key method to overcome several shortcomings analysts face, including the limitations of working memory and the challenge of clearly recalling multiple details, their connections, and the often-complex context surrounding them at any given point in time. We have used models in several different ways throughout this book precisely because they are such good tools to support analysis. With strategic intelligence, we will use models primarily to create a detailed visual representation of a problem to assist with framing, analysis, and synthesis.

Target models

In some ways target models are the ultimate model for framing. If we carry forward our art analogy, a target model is a landscape painted in a realistic fashion by an artist with an eye for detail. As a whole, the painting tells the story of a moment in time,

---

4 Josh Kerbel, "The US Intelligence Community's Creativity Challenge" (*https://oreil.ly/MMGKg*), *The National Interest* website, October 13, 2014.

with enough interesting details and components to help the viewer understand more about the situation the more they look. Stepping back from the art analogy, *target models* are representations of an area of focus. They can describe things such as a broad problem area (food insecurity), a specific entity (a corporation or a nation), or even a process (the ransomware-distribution lifecycle). When using target models in strategic analysis, the goal should be to show the component parts as well as the relationships between different parts.

Developing these models can be time-consuming, and the larger or more complex a target is, the more complex the model will be. Don't let that stop you from beginning—once developed, target models can be some of the most useful tools for understanding a particular issue and can easily be updated when new information is identified (such as information gained from the intelligence-driven incident-response process). The first step in developing a target model is to determine what it is you are hoping to explain or understand by creating it. If you are hoping to understand where in your organization's network you see the most successful or attempted intrusions, you can start with a network infrastructure map, which can then be overlayed with information from recent intrusions. If you are looking at something broader, such as how cybersecurity issues are likely to impact emerging multinational markets, then your target map will likely be focused more broadly on the components of multinational markets and then overlaid with examples of cybersecurity impacts for each of the components.

In both cases, it is perfectly acceptable to start with a hand-drawn map of what you are envisioning. In many cases getting started is the hardest part of the process. Once you have developed a working target model, the hardest part is done. However, models are rarely static; they must be updated periodically to remain applicable and effective. In the case of an organization's network infrastructure map, for example, it must be updated frequently to remain current. With organizational structure maps, it can be necessary to update them whenever there is a reorganization or when key leaders change or leave, which can occur almost as frequently as network changes. Developing models is an investment but will provide a solid frame for future analysis, whether it is used in the next intrusion you are supporting or used to propose a plan to increase the security budget or staffing of your incident-response or threat-intelligence teams. In addition to target models, which can represent nearly any topic, there are some forms of specialized target models that can be useful is specific situations.

Hierarchical models. Some sets of information, such as organizational structure, fit best as *hierarchical models*. These models use a parent-child relationship style to illustrate the chain of command, or leadership structure, of a target. This can help an analyst identify all the components of a target that need to be further analyzed. It can also help identify any choke points or bottlenecks that could be significant. This information can be gathered from many sources and needs to be updated periodically as personnel or organizational structures change. A hierarchical model (Figure 10-1) is best used to display a closed system that is not likely to change based on outside variables.

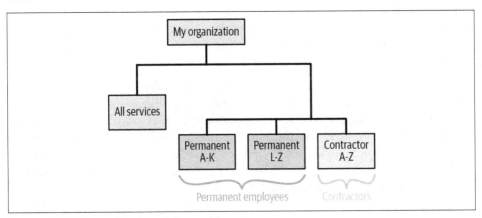

Figure 10-1. Hierarchical model example

Hierarchical models are traditionally used to show personnel or roles, but one unique application of this model is to identify the data that is important to an organization and which departments are responsible for it. A hierarchical model for data includes the broad categories of data, such as financial information, customer information, and sensitive company information. Any information that is valuable to the organization, and that an attacker may try to access or impact in some way, should be identified. When taking this approach, it is useful to be as specific as possible with the types of data. Financial information may break down further into credit card information, payroll information for employees, and future projections for the company. All of this data likely sits in different places within the organization, with different teams responsible for maintaining and securing it. Owner information for each data type should also be built into the model. This type of model will help organizations understand the data they are protecting and where it resides and can be used to identify which data types are most targeted over time. As with all of the models we discuss in this chapter, it can take some time to build an accurate model, and this should not be done during an active incident.

Network models. *Network models* are useful when representing the relationships or interactions between individuals or groups that are interconnected in a nonhierarchical way. Network models are commonly used to develop computer network diagrams, both of an organization's own network and often of an attacker's infrastructure. In his keynote talk at the 2023 SANS Cyber Threat Intelligence Summit (*https://oreil.ly/KcphK*), Dr. Chris Sanders spoke about the importance of "friendly intelligence" and "threat intelligence." Friendly intelligence includes intelligence about things that we are trying to protect, and in intelligence-driven incident response we are often trying to protect our networks. Having a well-defined, up-to-date, and accurate model of the network is invaluable for defenders and should be part of strategic intelligence work. In addition to building a model of the physical and logical connections of the network, it is also helpful to include details that are relevant to your organization's operations, including regulatory compliance requirements for any portions of the network and international requirements if your organization operates globally.

Strategic-level threat intelligence network models have also been used to show the relationships between attacker groups and the relationships between victims of an intrusion. As more and more advanced opportunistic attacks take place, understanding the relationship between victims can help better understand the nature of the threat itself. Network models must be updated more frequently than any of the other model types discussed, because they have many moving parts that change quickly and often. Figure 10-2 shows a sample network model.

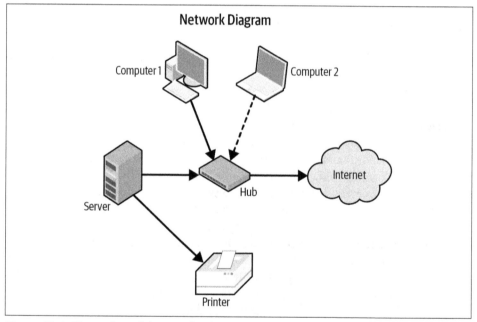

Figure 10-2. Network model example

Process models. *Process models* illustrate the various actions and decision points that make up a structured process. Process models are especially important when conducting analysis as part of a team, as it helps keep people on the same page as they move through the analytic process. The cyber intrusion kill chain is a kind of process model. In earlier chapters, it was used to capture indicators of a specific incident, but the kill chain can also be used to document the steps an attacker takes at a more strategic level to assist in the development of the target model.

There are two approaches to take when designing process models that support strategic analysis. You can either look at the often-undocumented processes or standard operating procedures (SOPs) that you are already doing and build them into a process, or you can look through examples of process models used in different types of analyses and pick one that best fits your way of operating. Either option is fine—process models are meant to be useful, not to dictate how you work, so do not feel that you need to change a good process just to fit a model someone recommends. We have found, however, that looking through models that others have developed does provide a good opportunity for reflection and optimization of existing methods.

In addition to the kill chain, there are several other models that can be used as guides for developing a strategic intelligence process model. In 2020, after reviewing several process models in fields ranging from criminal psychology to meteorology, Nicole Hoffman introduced her model: Cognitive Stairways of Analysis. Hoffman described her motivation for publishing her model in her blog post (*https://oreil.ly/qHteR*), "Everyone talks about analysis, but no one goes into detail about how to perform analysis." The Cognitive Stairways model (Figure 10-3) includes "steps" that are taken by an analyst that follow a set pattern; however, the pattern can be tweaked to fit whatever particular task you are undertaking. In her example for brainstorming, a key component of any type of analysis, she includes the following steps:

Brainstorm/Generate hypothesis/Think steps
1. This step will help you determine what your analysis will focus on, similar to your intelligence requirements (though not always that specific).

Determine the scope
2. Identify the frame that your analysis will focus on, the context through which you will conduct your analysis.

Key assumptions check
3. What assumptions will you take with you into the analysis? Make sure that the assumptions are valid before beginning, or they will need to be tossed out.

Compile data/Quality of information (QoI) Check
4. Gather data relevant to the topic you are focusing on, while evaluating the source and completeness of the data.

Clean data/Omit useless data
5. To properly use the data in analysis, it needs to be in a format and used with a taxonomy that will make it possible for you to both leverage and reference it within your analysis.

Exploratory data analysis (EDA)/Visualization and regression

6. What does that data you have gathered tell you about a topic? Try not to focus too much on the general hypothesis or think steps you developed in step 1. The goal of that step was to get you on the right path, but now you must look at the data, using visualizations and regressions if helpful, to understand what the data indicates. Findings in this step may require you to hop back down to step 4 again to gather more data, and that is perfectly fine.

Confirmatory

7. *THIS* is the step where you check your analysis and findings against your original think steps or hypothesis to come to an analytic judgment.

Disseminate

8. This is where you conclude your analysis and share your findings, ideally updating any pre-existing target models that may be changed based on the new findings.

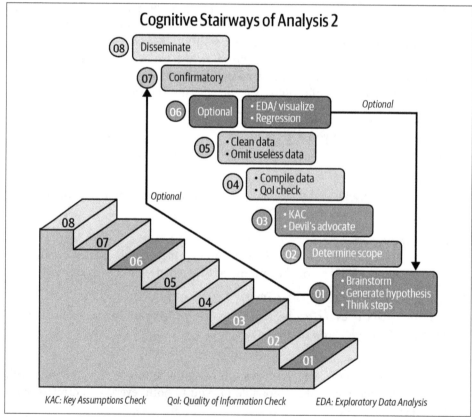

Figure 10-3. Cognitive Stairways of Analysis model (Source: Nicole Hoffman)

Process models can take many forms. The most important thing is that you have a process model that works for you, that is documented, and that can be leveraged by others.

Timelines. Timelines are linear models that show the time-based relationships between activities. Incident responders are most familiar with attack timelines that show when specific actions were taken during an incident, but many other timelines can be helpful in an incident-response situation. Understanding the timeline from vulnerability discovery to remediation is useful to help a network defender know how long they will remain vulnerable to a particular attack and can help decision makers determine when they will need to act. A timeline indicating when different actor groups were seen using a particular exploit or tool can help an analyst determine the threat from that malware, as well as understand how quickly or slowly tool-reuse propagates after a tool is identified. Visualizing the temporal aspects of various activities provides analysts with a framework for understanding how those aspects will impact their organization's goals and objectives.

Building and Maintaining Models

If developing models is so time-consuming, why bother developing them at all? Models are critical to developing a common understanding of a situation, and this common understanding is what enables people to learn to respond to situations in a consistent, informed way and work toward a common goal. In a business, that common goal is usually increased revenue, and network defense supports that goal by preventing breaches that result in loss of intellectual property, brand damage, and incident-response expenses. In the government or the military, the goal is to support the national strategy and ensure national security. Without understanding what those things mean, however, it can be difficult to respond in a way that supports the primary objectives. Developing models is one key area of strategic intelligence that will influence decision making as well as operational and tactical analysis. Taking the time to develop and update models will almost always be time well spent.

The Strategic Intelligence Cycle

Chapter 2 covered the intelligence cycle extensively, but the primary focus was on tactical and operational-level intelligence—following the cycle in order to respond to a specific and often immediate threat. At the strategic level, the intelligence cycle follows the same process, but each step (from setting requirements to dissemination) looks different than it does when dealing with an immediate threat. Let's examine these differences.

Setting Strategic Requirements

The task of setting requirements at the strategic level may seem more vague than at the tactical level. With tactical intelligence, there is a specific threat to focus on, which helps direct requirements. That is not often the case with strategic intelligence; and when requirements are passed down, they are often something vague like, "Tell me what we need to know." Although the scope and the timeframe are much larger with strategic intelligence, the requirements should still be specific.

Strategic requirements often follow the military concept of commander's intent. *Commander's intent* is what allows large, dispersed units to make decisions about when and how to conduct operations. Using the models that were developed as part of the strategic process, the commander (or the CEO or CISO) can state their goal or objective (aka intent) and trust that all decision makers are on the same page and will take actions that will support that objective without the need to micromanage. For example, if the intent is to ensure that a company is first-to-market with a new product, then making sure that the manufacturing schematics, marketing plans, and other sensitive information are not leaked is a task that would fall under the commander's intent. Developing a model of the attackers who may target that sensitive information is a strategic intelligence requirement that is necessary to protect that information.

Strategic requirements, unlike tactical or operational ones, have the luxury of time on their side. Requirements can be planned far in advance, allowing them to be larger or broader in scope, depending on the needs of the organization, and they can also specify timing or periodicity. For example, a strategic requirement may be to update a company's threat model twice a year or to analyze what new threats may impact a business if they move into a new market or a new geographic region.

When setting strategic requirements, it is helpful to identify early on if the requirement is ongoing, when analysis needs to be completed, and how often the findings will need to be reviewed or updated. It is also important to periodically review standing strategic requirements to identify whether they are still relevant and necessary. Strategic requirements, just like tactical and operational ones, can become stale if they are no longer relevant. However, it can take much longer to realize that strategic requirements are stale.

Collection

The type of collection we have focused on so far in this book has been centered around logs and external sources such as threat feeds and information sharing. Although these types of collections still play a part in strategic intelligence, the scope of what you are collecting and from where will greatly increase, which is pretty exciting for those of us who are intelligence nerds at heart. Depending on your requirements—which have been specifically called out, *right*?—you may find yourself pulling information on economic, political, and cultural sources, or any number of other sources. This type of collection will also be more extensive than tactical collection, where any information older than a few days or even hours may be obsolete. With strategic intelligence, you may be searching for information that goes back years in order to capture trends or look for changes. The following sections describe useful types of strategic information to collect.

Geopolitical sources

Geopolitical sources provide information on what is going on in the world, including conflicts, alliances, tensions, and other factors related to international relations in a particular region. There was a time when many people, maybe even some of the people reading (or writing) this book, disregarded geopolitics when it came to incident response. It is possible to hack a network from anywhere, so why would it matter if conflicts existed in certain areas of the world? Well, it turns out that there are many reasons geopolitics are important for incident response. Although it is possible to access networks from anywhere in the world, regional conflicts and international tension can still impact intrusion targeting and planning. As we've seen numerous times over the past decades, understanding geopolitical intelligence is critical to understanding and responding to cyberattacks. Consider the following:

- The 2022 invasion of Ukraine by Russia coincided with a series of cyberattacks, including massive DDoS attacks, malware targeting government systems, an increase in phishing attempts, and even attacks against cyber-physical systems such as power and water systems.
- In 2021, the South Korean government was targeted by threat actors from North Korea, who used phishing emails to target members of the Ministry of Foreign Affairs and exfiltrate sensitive government information.
- In 2018, a threat actor was identified as they were targeting multiple organizations with trade ties to China. The targets included organizations involved in China's Belt and Road Initiative, a massive China-led effort focused on infrastructure projects that stretch across the globe.

What is going on in the world, whether it is in our own backyard or across the globe, matters to strategic cyber threat intelligence. Understanding political climates, conflicts, triggers, and tactics of adversaries can assist in strategic planning.

Although it is normal to focus outward on international threats, some aspects of geopolitics are local and should be considered as well. Good sources of geopolitical intelligence are peer-reviewed articles, white papers, and assessments. For this type of intelligence, is it often useful to look for historical information as well as current information about a situation. Understanding trends and patterns is particularly useful with geopolitical intelligence, where history often seems to repeat itself.

> ## Is News Intelligence?
>
> It is possible to get a lot of information related to current events from the news, and it can be easy to interpret those as geopolitical intelligence. However, the information provided by news outlets may not be a complete assessment of a situation and should be used with caution. Current events and the news should be used to understand what threats an analyst should look into more, but from there the analyst can begin to research the events and their implications by seeking peer-reviewed sources such as academic journals and white papers.

Economic sources

Economic sources are incredibly important to network defense. Economics, the study of the production, consumption, and transfer of wealth, is not just useful for situational awareness, but for understanding the motivations of many threat actors. The vast majority of intrusions are economically motivated, whether that involves stealing credit cards for direct monetization or stealing intellectual property for strategic economic gain, and economic intelligence sources can provide insight into an adversary's motivations.

Economic intelligence can include details about how stolen information is monetized, the types of information that criminals target, the types of information that is being targeted for industrial espionage, and economics associated with nation-states that are likely to target you or have targeted you in the past. Even with a broad understanding of economics, this type of information can help organizations understand the strategic threats they are facing. A specialized knowledge can provide an even greater level of insight, though it is harder to find someone specializing in economics on a network security team.

Historical sources

Historical sources, such as analysis of a nation's tactics or priorities from a previous conflict, is another often-overlooked aspect of intelligence analysis when it comes to responding to cyber threats. The internet is new, relatively speaking, so how could historical sources possibly support cyber threat intelligence? If we consider the cyber realm to be an extension of the physical world, any activities that take place in the physical world will likely end up manifesting in the cyber realm as well. Because of this, history becomes important. If we can understand how adversaries targeted organizations before the internet existed, we can begin to pick up on ways that they will attempt to achieve the same goals by using new tactics and new mediums.

This is one of the reasons that military doctrines like Sun Tzu's *The Art of War* and Carl von Clausewitz's *On War* are so often quoted in cybersecurity presentations. Just because they were written long before modern incident response doesn't mean they're not relevant to the prevention and detection of attacks in this new domain. Con men were operating long before email was invented, and many of the tactics they used are similar to modern phishing scams, which just use a new avenue for their schemes. One tactic to help integrate historical sources into strategic intelligence analysis is to look at the most common threats an organization sees, whether that is phishing emails targeting employees or targeted intrusions aimed at obtaining corporate information, and then to look for how those attacks have been carried out in the past. The goal of this type of analysis is to identify any lessons learned or patterns that can help the organization better understand the threats and better posture itself to defend against those threats.

Business sources

Strategic intelligence, when used to support business operations, relies heavily on an understanding of the defending organization's business. Many security professionals struggle with supporting strategic-level business decisions because they do not take the time to understand the problems that the business is facing or what information is critical to operations. Without understanding the business, it is nearly impossible for intelligence analysts or incident responders to produce strategic intelligence that will help leaders make the best decisions for their organization's security.

Like all things in security, business operations and priorities are not static, so it is important to continually update and gather new information as it becomes available. *Business sources* include information on the markets an organization operates in, competitors, challenges to the business, new regions or markets that the business is planning to expand into, key personnel changes, and other aspects of business operations that have been identified as significant.

 In addition to these sources of information (geopolitical, economic, historical, and business), which are more strategically focused than the collection sources discussed in earlier chapters, it is also important to incorporate information from previous incidents into strategic analysis. Doing so allows the analyst to present a holistic picture of what is being seen in the network combined with additional insight into historical, political, and economic trends that may influence the threats that an organization faces. All of this information will be pulled together in the strategic analysis phase.

Analysis

Analysis at the strategic level follows the same process described in Chapter 8. Requirements are clearly stated, collection and processing occur, and hypotheses are developed and tested by researching and reviewing evidence that supports or refutes them. Strategic intelligence teams, however, must analyze a larger and more diverse data set. Therefore, these teams should ideally be larger with members from diverse backgrounds and experiences. Keep the following points in mind when conducting strategic-level analysis:

- The evidence to be considered will come not just from network information, as is often the case with incident response, but from many sources that the analysts may or may not have expertise in or substantial knowledge of. In those cases, understanding the source is especially relevant because analysts often take information from these various sources at face value. Look for information that comes from peer-reviewed, reputable sources. If a particular piece of evidence is deemed to be a key during a process such as analysis of competing hypotheses, it is best to try to find more than one source that is reporting the same information.

- Biases can run rampant in strategic intelligence, where there is often a smaller amount of tactical evidence and more evidence that is open to interpretation.

Processes for analyzing strategic intelligence

Some specific processes are more conducive to analyzing strategic-level intelligence, and others are far less effective at this level. For example, the target-centric model, which is an asset to an analyst investigating an intrusion or working at the operational and campaign level, is not as useful at the strategic level because, as we discussed, many of the target models are developed during the analysis. Several models and processes stand out as particularly useful for analyzing strategic intelligence, including SWOT analysis, brainstorming, and scrub down.

SWOT analysis. *Strength, Weakness, Opportunity*, and *Threat* (SWOT) is a model that is commonly used in risk management. SWOT takes into consideration internal aspects (strengths and weaknesses) as well as external aspects (opportunities and threats). It also lends itself to strategic intelligence specifically around network security and defense, because in many cases it will identify big-picture problems and concerns that need to be addressed. Using the SWOT model requires that an organization have a solid understanding of its core competencies and where they excel, be honest and up front about the issues that they face, and understand the external threats that are facing them. The basic outline for SWOT analysis is pictured in Figure 10-4.

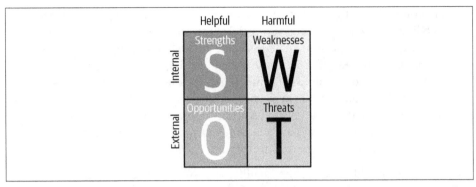

Figure 10-4. SWOT analysis

For example, if documentation indicates that 90% of successful intrusions into the network come from phishing emails, this demonstrates a weakness of the organization that needs to be addressed. Identifying strengths can help determine steps that can be taken to mitigate those weaknesses. SWOT analysis is useful not only for determining an organization's own strengths and weaknesses. It can also be used to analyze a foreign government, a criminal organization, or an attack group. To conduct this analysis, it is important to pull heavily from the research that was done in the Collect phase. An important tip when using SWOT analysis is to look for places where an adversary's strengths line up with your organization's weaknesses. Those are places that need to be addressed.

Brainstorming. Strategic intelligence analysis should not be the work of one individual. As we mentioned, it is helpful to have multiple analysts with different backgrounds identify the issues that will have a significant impact on an organization moving forward. An analysis on past intelligence failures (an analysis of analysis, one might say) has found that many times an intelligence failure is the result of groupthink, which discourages creativity and thinking outside of the box. General James Mattis said, during his Senate confirmation hearing, there is no place for groupthink, especially when it comes to national policy. He said, "In the national security decision-making process, as you know, you need different ideas to be strongly argued. You don't want the tyranny of consensus of groupthink."

Brainstorming, especially with a group that comes from different disciplines, is a good way to counter groupthink by encouraging new and creative approaches to problems. Brainstorming can be used on its own or with nearly any other analytic method. Although it sounds as if it is unstructured, the CIA's Tradecraft Primer notes that brainstorming should be structured in order to be most effective. One of the most critical components of successful brainstorming is to allot enough time at the beginning of the process to enable the group to explore a variety of possibilities. When a group is time-constrained or feels rushed, they are more likely to select a smaller group of hypotheses that sounds realistic rather than exploring a larger set of possibilities that may generate new insight into an issue. It is also a good idea to ensure that at least one person participating in the brainstorming has a different role or approach than the rest of the team. Although getting together a group of incident responders to brainstorm will likely bring more than one point of view, it is still likely to be constrained to the typical experiences of an incident responder. By bringing in an outsider, whether that is a systems administrator, security architect, or someone from human resources, having new and different perspectives in the group will also discourage group thinking and force the rest of the team to consider new angles.

Brainstorming should result in the identification of a new set of hypotheses and at that point the team can focus on identifying specific evidence from the collected information to support or refute the hypotheses, and then use an analytic method such as ACH to complete the analysis. It is fine if it is not possible for the entire group to see the analysis to completion. One of the most important aspects of brainstorming is having the group identify new hypotheses, call out our unfounded assumptions, and identify bias *at the beginning* of the analytic process. If one or more analysts take the lead on completing the analysis, it is still critical that they consult or check in with the group from time to time.

Scrub down. The term *scrub down* (also known as a murder board) was originally coined to describe a process used to help a candidate prepare for oral presentations. During a scrub down, an analyst presents their findings to a review board, which then questions not only the findings but the analytic processes used to generate those findings. The scrub down process helps identify any biases that are present in the analysis, any key assumptions that were not validated, and any analytic leaps that were not founded in evidence. Even if the analysis is sound and no obvious errors exist, a scrub down helps an analyst vocalize the process used and explain the methods and findings—something that many intelligence analysts struggle with.

When questioned about how a certain conclusion was reached, especially at the strategic level that has more variables and pieces to tie together, an analyst will often default to using vague terminology or anecdotes to explain how they conducted the analysis. That type of explanation often does not inspire confidence in decision makers. Being prepared to describe not just the conclusion, but the analytic process itself, is a skill that takes time and practice to develop.

Rob Dartnall, an analyst from Great Britain, reminded us of the importance of the scrub down, especially when it comes to strategic intelligence where the stakes are high, in his presentation "Conventional Intelligence Analysis in Cyber Threat Intelligence" (*https://oreil.ly/GpFho*), given at the CTI Summit in 2017.

When analysis that you have done is about to lead directly to important and potentially drastic actions, it is imperative that your analysis is sound and that you are prepared to defend it under scrutiny.

Check Your Egos at the Door

Strategic intelligence analysis is no place for egos. The goal of this type of analysis is to provide intelligence to decision makers so that they can act, which also means identifying the level of confidence an analyst has and any intelligence gaps and updating the assessment when new information is identified that changes the findings. When egos get involved, it becomes difficult to objectively assess things like confidence, and it is difficult to go back to stakeholders and acknowledge when mistakes were made or when information changes. Processes such as scrub downs help remove ego from the equation. It is important to note, however, that the presenter's ego isn't the only one that needs to be checked. Individuals participating in a scrub down and asking questions should also be careful not to let their egos get in the way and cloud their judgment. It can be tempting to try to "prove the presenter wrong" for the sake of ego, which can lead to the participant's own biases running rampant.

Dissemination

Dissemination of strategic intelligence is only slightly different than at the tactical or operational level, and those differences are due to the scope and nature of strategic intelligence. The recommendations that are being made have the potential to significantly impact a businesses' operations moving forward and therefore, unless there are specific time requirements, accuracy and thoroughness take precedence over speed.

Many of the same principles that we discussed in Chapter 9 are directly applicable to dissemination of strategic intelligence, but there are some unique aspects, too. Specifically:

The audience is especially key at this level.
It is important to identify who the audience will be before beginning the process of writing or creating the final deliverable. If multiple audiences would like to receive information in different ways, it is a good idea to make sure that the information is presented to each audience in the way that will be most useful to them. Make sure that the different versions of intelligence products or reports tell the same story, though. The last thing you want is for different leaders within an organization to have a different interpretation of the analysis and its meaning.

It is important to specifically call out any intelligence gaps or trigger events that would result in a change to the analysis.

It can be difficult to tell leadership that the analytic findings have room for doubt, but setting these expectations will make it easier to communicate changes as they occur.

Moving Toward Anticipatory Intelligence

As the saying goes, "All models are wrong, but some are useful." Strategic intelligence is ultimately a model, and while it's useful today, it is not (and never was) perfect. As a result, like so many models, it will evolve or get replaced. At its core, the US intelligence community's concept of strategic intelligence was based on a "two body problem" originating in the 1950s—the Cold War conflict between the US and the USSR. Nearly everything was looked at strategically as conflict between these two adversaries; even secondary and tertiary conflict was rolled up with the assumption that at a strategic level it was ultimately about the US versus the USSR. The actions of the Vietnamese Viet Cong were really just a proxy for the Soviet intelligence and military apparatus. The 1970s Mujahideen in Afghanistan were a proxy force for the US intelligence community. The modern era is not nearly so straightforward. There are multiple sets of adversaries leveraging asymmetric threats (of which cyber is just one) and emergent problems like cryptocurrency and climate change.

Strategic intelligence is designed to provide information to decision makers on long-term, broad topics with perceived implications to national security for years to come. It requires time to conduct solid analysis on strategic intelligence, and when a situation occurs before a complete analytic picture can be formed, decisions are often made without it. Urgency often remains the primary focus even in a business decision making context and often results in actions with unintended consequences. As the world changes and needs change, many believe that it is time for strategic intelligence to change as well.

An approach that may begin to make more sense for organizations and governments large and small is *anticipatory intelligence*—the practice of studying a situation and the surrounding context, environment, and related situations to anticipate future events and their implications. This is not the same as predicting a specific event—something that most analysts wish they could do regularly. While predictions are narrow and describe a specific event or outcome, anticipatory intelligence uncovers a broader spectrum of possible outcomes. Josh Kerbel, a strong proponent of moving toward anticipatory intelligence, proposed a new definition (*https://oreil.ly/9R4YP*) of anticipatory intelligence: "The intelligence process or practice whereby potentially emergent developments stemming from the increasingly complex security environment are foreseen via the cultivation of holistic perspectives." The good news is that moving toward anticipatory intelligence does not require an entirely new intelligence process—just the reapplication of existing processes and practices, along with new ways of thinking about situations. This is a growing and developing field but will be a critical component of intelligence-driven incident response in years to come.

Conclusion

We consider strategic intelligence to be the logic behind the plan, and it is no wonder that many incident responders struggle with finding the time to conduct this level of analysis. In many organizations, incident responders would be hard-pressed to identify a plan at all, much less understand the logic behind the plan. Strategic intelligence, when properly analyzed and adopted by leadership, not only can inform leadership of the long-term threats to an organization, but can also provide incident responders with policies and procedures that will support their ability to meet the needs of their organization.

Strategic intelligence for incident response not only enables you to make smart decisions about the visibility of your networks, but also feeds directly into the requirements for tactical and operational levels of analysis, and helps you move toward anticipatory intelligence. Strategic intelligence will help you answer the following:

- Which threats are most significant to the organization? Where should incident response prioritize and focus?
- Which types of information are important to capture? What findings warrant a brief to the CISO or other executives?
- What situations may emerge as the outside world changes?
- How do external situations such as financial crises, global conflict, or pandemics impact the security posture of the organization?

There is a misconception that there is simply no time to conduct strategic intelligence. There is so much happening on a daily—and in the world of incident response, sometimes an hourly—basis, that many people feel overwhelmed by trying to keep up just at the tactical level. Strategic intelligence, often viewed as a "nice to have" rather than a "need to have," gets relegated to the pile of things to do when time allows, and time rarely allows. However, strategic intelligence is critical to our ability to do our jobs, and although it does take time away from the daily emergencies, it can position us to better deal with those emergencies, and therefore it should not be overlooked.

All actions that take place during the strategic intelligence cycle can be tied back to strategic requirements. As you understand the logic and reasoning behind the requirements (and once you start adding to that logic yourself), you will be able to adapt and respond when situations change, without having to revisit the entire process. Strategic intelligence takes time, but when it is done correctly, it can set up entire programs for success long into the future. It is well worth the time and effort.

## CHAPTER 11

Building an Intelligence Program

Great things in business are never done by one person. They're done by a team of people.
   —Steve Jobs

Working with an intelligence team can be a game changer for many security opera-tions programs. However, there needs to be a system in place to get everyone on the same page, both within the intelligence team and with the customers that the team will be supporting. A structured intelligence program will provide the benefit of a robust intelligence support capability while avoiding many of the struggles teams go through when they are thrown together rather than purposely built. This chapter covers the various elements to consider when building an intelligence team or function at your organization.

Are You Ready?

One question that frequently gets asked is, "What are the prerequisites for forming an intelligence team?" Many things need to be done before a formalized intelligence function will be beneficial. We are not of the mindset that an intelligence program is the last thing that should be created at an organization, but we do view the intelligence function as the glue that holds many other security functions together. If you do not have those existing functions, you will just end up standing around, holding a bottle of glue.

Here are some fundamental questions to ask before beginning to develop an intelli-gence program, which will require funding, time, and effort:

Is there a security function at the organization?
   This seems like an easy question, but it is surprising how many organizations start thinking about developing a threat-intelligence capability with a one-person security team or even a one-person team responsible for *both* IT operations

and security. Although an intelligence-driven approach would probably benefit the poor individual responsible for keeping everything from catching on fire, the intelligence team would take budget away from additional security-focused personnel and tools, meaning that the intelligence team would likely *become* the security team rather than focusing on intelligence work.

Is there sufficient network, host, and service visibility?

Intelligence programs rely on access to information, both internal and external, with internal being some of the most critical information needed to conduct intelligence analysis and apply the outputs. When there is no visibility, whether that is because of technical limitations or privacy or legal concerns, the effectiveness of any intelligence team will be limited. If visibility is a technical issue, the best approach is to work with other stakeholders, such as the overall security team, network team, and IT teams, and focus on gaining that visibility prior to establishing an intelligence program. If there are legal or privacy concerns, it is probably best to discuss those concerns with legal counsel to determine what can be done and whether an intelligence program is a good fit at all. At times, intelligence can help overcome some of these types of hurdles for an organization, providing additional insight into external threats to compensate for the lack of visibility, but these types of situations are the exception rather than the rule. Remember to focus on the opportunity for improvement, what these new capabilities will allow, and how this positive protection will enable the business.

Are there multiple teams or functions to support?

As we mentioned, intelligence can be thought of as the glue that holds together multiple functions by enabling all of them to do more and make better decisions. Intelligence gained from incident response can help with prevention and detection, assist with vulnerability management and security architecture, and inform strategic planning. That is a lot of work for a single individual. When multiple facets of intelligence work need to be done in an organization, that is a good sign that it is time to set up an intelligence program with multiple team members. If the plan is for intelligence to support a single aspect, such as incident response, it is probably best to start with an intelligence-focused role on that individual team.

Is there room in the budget?

The answer to this question is usually "no," followed up with, "But if we need it, we will make it work." Either of these answers is a good sign that now is *not* the best time to start an intelligence program. Intelligence is almost always a cost center rather than a profit center (even though it can have a high return on investment), which means that it will not generate additional revenue to sustain its operations. The big exception to this are intelligence teams within security vendors. Getting the appropriate level of funding can be difficult. Intelligence programs do not need to be budget breakers, but the one thing that will almost always be a high-ticket item is personnel, usually with third-party collection sources and services as a close second. If you are just developing a program, it is important to find the right person, whether internally or hiring externally, to get the program started on the right foot. A much better answer to this question would be "Yes, we have some room because this has been identified as an important step in maturing our security program." OK, we know that an answer like that doesn't come around often, but if it does that is a good sign that you are ready for an intelligence program.

Avoiding Knee-Jerk Reactions

At the far end of the spectrum of determining budget is the answer, "We just had a horrible incident and now we have to show what we are doing differently ASAP so that it never happens again. Go buy things. All the things." Even though the knee-jerk reaction to a significant breach often comes with substantial budget, it is important to know that a breach is not the best reason to start an intelligence program, and if key prerequisites (network visibility, guidance and requirements, and budget) are not met, then what looks like a good opportunity now could turn into questions about ROI a few years down the road. Without sufficient ability to create, sustain, and use the intelligence output, a program will quickly be seen as a large group of expensive analysts with a pile of expensive tools and data sources. If your organization is in this situation, be sure to take a pragmatic approach to the program, follow the guidelines described in the next section to determine goals and audience, and ensure that you are capturing meaningful metrics to ensure that the intelligence program will not fall victim to the first round of budget cuts after your organization has recovered from the initial knee-jerk reaction to the breach.

After determining whether a formalized intelligence program is the best option, many other aspects of the program still need to be defined before hiring and product generation begins. Developing a new program requires a lot of work up front in order to make sure that it is successful in the long term. It is important to clearly define your program so that everyone is on the same page about what you are trying to create.

Planning the Program

Three types of planning go into the development of a solid program: conceptual planning, functional planning, and detailed planning:

Conceptual planning
> This sets the framework that the program should work within. Stakeholders contribute the most to conceptual planning, but it is important for them to understand what intelligence can offer them, especially if they are unfamiliar with intelligence work.

Functional planning
>   This involves input from both stakeholders and intelligence professionals to identify requirements to complete goals, logistics such as budget and staffing needs, constraints, dependencies, and any legal concerns. Functional planning provides structure and realism to the sometimes-abstract conceptual planning phase.

Detailed planning
>   This is conducted by the intelligence team and will determine how the goals identified by the stakeholders will be met within the functional limits.

All three phases of planning are important to ensure that all aspects have been considered, from budgeting to the metrics that will be reported to stakeholders.

Defining Stakeholders

It is crucial for the intelligence team to understand its stakeholders so that the analysis it conducts and the reports it provides are useful and understandable. Those stakeholders should be clearly defined. Defining stakeholders should take place during the early phases of conceptual planning, because the stakeholders will contribute to the rest of the process.

In this section, we'll look at a few common stakeholders.

Incident-response team

Incident response is an ideal stakeholder because this team will not only benefit from intelligence support of operations, but it also provides additional information back to the intelligence team that will feed into other functions.

Security operations center/team

Intelligence teams can provide SOCs with information on emerging threats, whether they are general threats, threats targeting an industry, or even threats specifically targeting the organization. Intelligence can also provide technical indicators for alerts, enrichment information to provide context on alerts, and information to help with prioritizing alerts. SOCs can also provide information to the intelligence team on attempted attacks that never reach the point of a full-blown incident. Even if the incident-response team is not involved, there is still a great deal of information that an intelligence analyst can gain from failed attempts.

Vulnerability management teams

Vulnerability management teams often deal with vulnerabilities numbering in the hundreds, if not thousands. Intelligence teams can help prioritize patching based on the most significant threat to the organization. Many vendors will provide information on the severity and the impact of the vulnerability, but an additional level of analysis still needs to be done to identify the threat that the vulnerability presents to a particular organization. An intelligence team is ideally situated to assist with this analysis. The intelligence team can also work with the vulnerability management team and the security operations team in tandem to ensure that the security team can monitor for exploits that are targeting unpatched vulnerabilities while an organization is in the process of remediation.

Red teams/offensive engineers

First things first, most red teamers are really blue teamers in disguise. Their goal is not to *pop shells* and *pwn noobs*; it's to help the organization better understand what would happen if an adversary attacked them, what would be detected, what wouldn't be detected, and ultimately how prepared the team is to respond to an incident.

What makes this most effective is if the red team can emulate an actual adversary that's in the threat model for the organization. Often red teams don't, instead creating an odd amalgamation of what they *think* adversaries do, mixed with the red team's organic capabilities and their own internal bias and understanding of the environment, which an adversary wouldn't have. Without any other concept of an adversary, the red team has to make it up as they go! If instead they based their actions on a threat-intelligence profile of an adversary, including a set of constraints around an adversary's TTPs, the red team could conduct a more effective exercise by demonstrating a more realistic experience of the challenges the blue team might face.

Trust and safety teams

Intelligence can be applied to more than traditional cyber threat actors attempting to phish or watering-hole attack a victim. By taking an adversarial mindset, threat-intelligence professionals can focus on the goals an adversary might have, especially in emerging scenarios. More and more often, intelligence teams are able to provide insight to functions such as Trust and Safety teams, which are working to identify inauthentic behavior, misinformation, harmful content, and other types of online harm not typically addressed by traditional security teams. While the subject area is different, there are still adversaries on the other end of Trust and Safety issues, and threat-intelligence processes and models such as kill chains and target models can be useful in supporting this function as well.

Chief information security officers

The CISO is responsible for understanding and managing the risk to an organization's information, and intelligence can provide insight to help them both understand and manage that risk. As a stakeholder, a CISO will likely have the broadest intelligence requirements, both tactical and strategic in nature. It is important to understand what a CISO expects from an intelligence program and how that information relates to other teams within security operations.

End users

End users are most often an indirect stakeholder for intelligence. Often, an intelligence program will support end-user security training by providing information on recent or evolving threats and helping users understand the impact of those threats and how they should respond. If end-user education or awareness is something that the intelligence program will support, it is important to identify what team will be responsible for this relationship, because it is impossible for the intelligence team to directly communicate with each end user in an organization.

After stakeholders have been identified, it is important to document them. The format shown in Figure 11-1 is an example of a way to document stakeholder identification. It includes basic information, including the name of the stakeholder, the point of contact (who should be informed that they are responsible for this relationship), and a brief description of what the intelligence program will provide to the stakeholder.

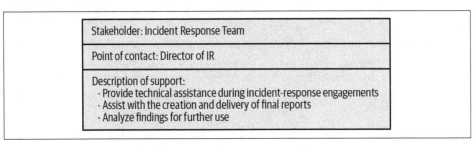

Figure 11-1. Sample stakeholder documentation

Defining Goals

After stakeholders have been defined, it is time to identify the goals of the program with respect to each stakeholder. This is a more in-depth process that involves discussing the needs of the stakeholders and the ways the intelligence program can meet these needs in a concrete way. This dialogue is necessary because the stakeholders know best the types of support they need, and the intelligence program representatives know best whether a particular goal is achievable.

During goal setting, you should not define how a goal will be met or what tools or personnel will be used to meet the goal. At this stage, the intelligence team may not be staffed or have acquired tools, and defining these details puts arbitrary boundaries on the team's processes.

Defining Success Criteria

Defining concrete goals gets the stakeholders and the intelligence team on the same page by using the same definition of *success*. In the stakeholder documentation template in Figure 11-1, different people likely will have different definitions of *support*. One of the definitions may be "to provide technical assistance during incident-response engagements." To one person, that may translate to providing technical IOCs, and to another person, that may mean that the intelligence team will conduct log analysis to identify anomalous behaviors. Those different definitions drastically change the nature of the support; one is external facing, and the other is internal facing. This is a good example of how setting concrete goals should clarify the support that is provided. In this case, although providing technical support is an overall requirement, the goals could clarify that this technical support could include (1) identifying external intelligence, including IOCs, to assist with the investigation, or (2) assisting incident-response teams with analyzing anomalous behaviors in logs—or both, depending on requirements.

Here are some key questions to discuss with stakeholders when defining success criteria:

- What current problems are the stakeholders dealing with?
- What are the ways that an intelligence program can help with those problems?
- What are the ideal outcomes of intelligence support to the stakeholder?
- If there are multiple outcomes, how should they be prioritized?
- How will the support be initiated? Is it continuous or on-demand?
- Are there any dependencies for support?

After success criteria has been determined, the process can move to identifying potential ways to achieve success. There is rarely just one way to achieve a goal, and the best choice is often determined by the resources required by each option.

Identifying Requirements and Constraints

Requirements and constraints fall into the functional portion of planning. Once success criteria have been outlined and ideal outcomes identified, it is important to also identify the things that are needed to accomplish the tasks that have been set out. These things usually fall into two buckets: requirements (things needed to accomplish the goals) and constraints (things that hinder the ability to accomplish goals).

One way to identify requirements and constraints is to conduct a walk-through or a tabletop exercise of the problem, stepping through the various ways that the problem can be addressed with a potential solution. The goal of this exercise is not to solve the problem but to identify the things needed to achieve the goal (requirements) as well as to identify potential issues or problems that need to be addressed (constraints). These should be documented for each potential solution, and the results can be used to identify the best course of action. This should be done at a high level still and should not focus on the particular details of a requirement. For example, a walk-through of a potential process may determine that an automated solution would be necessary to provide results at the scale required, but at this stage it is not important to determine *what* that solution is, just to identify it as a requirement.

Success criteria and requirements and constraints should be added to the stakeholder documentation to continue building a comprehensive picture of the intelligence program, as shown in Figure 11-2.

Stakeholder: Incident Response Team

Point of contact: Director of IR

Description of support:
- Provide technical assistance during incident-response engagements
- Assist with the creation and delivery of final reports
- Analyze findings for further use

Success criteria
- All incidents are reviewed by an intelligence analyst
- Incidents deemed significant are worked in tandem with an IR analyst and intelligence analyst
- Intelligence analysts contribute contextual information on threats to IR reports
- Finding from engagements are used to create alerts for the SOC and include contextual information

Requirements
- Criteria for determining "significant" incidents
- Staffing to support average number of significant incidents
- Analysis platform for IR and Intelligence to coordinate
- Communications channel with SOC

Figure 11-2. Advanced stakeholder documentation

Think Strategically

Some people in this industry, ourselves included, often bite off more than they can chew (almost chronically in our case, just ask our editor!). Whether it is because of pride, dedication to the mission, or a firm belief that a human can operate on less than four hours of sleep a night (false), we sometimes take on tasks we shouldn't. Even when we identify that there are constraints that have not been addressed, that doesn't always stop us.

Though it is tempting to take on exciting tasks even when there are obvious constraints, make sure to think through the long-term impacts of that decision and whether it is sustainable. Identify whether things can be done to ensure that the constraints are at least recognized and earmarked for future attention, even if they cannot be addressed immediately. Sometimes it is necessary and appropriate to say "yes" to a task that is not completely resourced, but it should be done in a way that will not allow it to have a negative impact on operations for years to come.

How do you make sure you're doing this effectively? In many cases, the best way is to work with another team member or peer who can tell you if you're taking on an unsustainable level of effort. An outside observer can look at your plans objectively and tell you if your ambition is outstripping your working hours. It is also critical to have a vision and mission clearly articulated for the intelligence program—when in doubt, check whether the task directly supports the mission and vision. If it doesn't, direct the task to a different group.

Defining Metrics

Good metrics tell a story, and they are best received when they tell a story about something that the stakeholders care about. Many intelligence programs start operating without thinking about how they will routinely communicate progress to stakeholders, especially in a quantitative rather than a qualitative manner. The planning stage of a program is the best time to determine the metrics that will be gathered and reported. This activity falls into the detailed planning phase, but it relies heavily on both the conceptual and functional planning phases.

Metrics should speak directly to the conceptual issues that stakeholders identified during planning. When you start defining your intelligence program, one of the first questions that should be asked is what the stakeholder gaps or requirements are that need intelligence support to fulfill. It may not be possible to determine the exact metrics that will be captured initially, but even identifying what success looks like and how it can be measured will help set up the program to report on progress. If stakeholders have specific results that they would like to be informed of, these can be built into the process at the beginning, and functional planning can ensure that the necessary resources are being captured and accounted for. If teams wait until they have been operating for a year or more before trying to identify whether the program is meeting its goals, they might not only lack the data to show success but also lose sight of what success looks like for the program.

Different stakeholders will have different goals and therefore different definitions of success, which will be demonstrated through different metrics. Capturing what success means and how it can be measured for each stakeholder will make it much easier to stay focused on the tasks at hand and identify success as the program moves forward.

Stakeholder Personas

Some people may think it is a little odd to have dossiers of fellow employees laying around, but we are intelligence professionals, and that is just what we do. Stakeholder personas are incredibly valuable to an intelligence program because they ensure that intelligence analysts are able to focus on the specific needs of the individual stakeholders throughout their work. Understanding your intelligence customers is key to providing them the right information at the right time in a way that they can best receive and act on the information.

Stakeholder personas can be developed for a group of stakeholders, such as a team of SOC analysts or threat hunters, but the best approach is to develop a persona for the individual point of contact within a stakeholder group. Maintaining a persona on an individual means that it will have to be updated when the role changes or when someone new assumes that role. It is important to develop a persona for the individual because that individual is responsible for the relationship between the intelligence team and the stakeholder team and will carry a great deal of weight as far as how the support relationship progresses. Different individuals likely will have different ways of interacting with the intelligence team and different preferences for receiving and sharing information. The better an intelligence team understands the personas that they support, the better value they will be able to provide them through their intelligence work.

When developing a persona for either a group or an individual, you need to take several important things into account. For an individual, it is important to capture information specific to the person, such as background, the things they are passionate about, the triggers they have related to their roles, and the way they typically operate.

Stakeholder personas are similar to the personas developed for intelligence dissemination, which we covered in Chapter 9. In fact, similar templates can be used with only a few minor adjustments to include things such as triggers and the specifics of the requirements between the stakeholder and the intelligence team. We also recommend documenting the individual's coffee or tea order—you never know when that will come in handy.

Tactical Use Cases

Use cases are a staple of program development, and intelligence programs are no different. If you are fortunate enough to work in an organization that already has intelligence use cases identified and documented, you are ahead of the game, as that is something many teams struggle with. Even if the use cases are intuitive and well-understood without much documentation, putting something in writing is good practice to ensure that everyone stays on the same page and to provide a concrete reference for new team members.

Tactical use cases involve intelligence that is useful on a day-to-day basis. This type of intelligence will change rapidly but can also be some of the most directly applicable intelligence in a security program. The following sections cover some of the most common tactical use cases for an intelligence team.

SOC Support

SOC support is one of the primary customers of an intelligence program. Within SOC support are three primary and unique use cases.

Detection and alerting engineering

Intelligence analysts provide intelligence, both internal and external, to generate detection system rules or signatures as well as alerting content for SIEMs and logging systems. Based on the program requirements, this may involve seeking out intelligence to generate signatures and sharing them with the SOC or creating alerts or rules based on that intelligence.

Triage

Intelligence provides context to SOC analysts to assist with the triage and prioritization of alerts that are generated. Intelligence can help the SOC understand the significance of an alert, which can then be triaged based on its severity and impact. Intelligence can also tell an analyst the steps that should be taken to identify whether the alert is a false positive by providing examples of true positive and false positives for comparison or by providing secondary indicators to look for. Triage intelligence often includes handling guidelines, as well, so that analysts have instructions on how to respond to a threat.

Situational awareness

Intelligence can provide situational awareness to SOC analysts to help them understand emerging and significant threats to their organization, both of which can help with generating rules for alerts and performing triage on those alerts. SOC analysts, while often more focused on the tactical, day-to-day application of threat intelligence, still benefit from a strategic understanding of threats faced by their organization. Providing situational awareness may involve a daily or weekly brief or may be on-demand when a significant threat warrants additional information. *Tactical* does not always have to mean *reactionary*, and intelligence can provide situational awareness to the SOC to help them understand and prevent threats from ever impacting their networks.

Indicator Management

Another tactical-level use case for intelligence is indicator management. We have touched on indicators in multiple places throughout this book, and the bottom line is that indicators can be useful intelligence tools when they are properly generated, actioned, and maintained. Indicators are used heavily in rule generation, threat detection, and information sharing. They can also be used in operational- and strategic-level analysis to help create a holistic picture of a threat. Managing indicators is not a trivial task. The more indicators that are being maintained, the more difficult it becomes. This section covers several aspects of indicator management, including managing a threat-intelligence platform, identifying and documenting context for tactical indicators, and integrating threat-intelligence feeds.

Threat-intelligence platform management

In many cases, the intelligence team is responsible for managing a threat-intelligence platform, sometimes known as a TIP, which usually consists of a database for storing indicators and adversary behavior, as well as a user interface for assigning context, pivoting/enrich, and creating relationships between the indicators and behaviors. TIPs should be query-able to assist in analysis and many also provide ways to export indicators to security appliances.

 A threat-intelligence platform makes managing indicators easier, but it is important to have a clear idea of why you are storing indicators in the first place. This understanding will ensure not only that you are managing them properly, but also that the team does not fall into the trap of gathering indicators for the sake of having more indicators. Collections are good; hoarding is not.

Third-party intelligence and feeds management

Threat feeds and third-party intelligence are another source of indicators that must be managed by an intelligence team in order to be useful to an organization. In many cases, these feeds are fed into a TIP. However, in some instances, they are directly tied into a security system such as a SIEM system. In most cases, a direct feed is not ideal, because it can be difficult to know what information is being shared across automated feeds. However, the practice is so widespread that many organizations believe that threat feeds are the cornerstone of threat intelligence. Threat feeds and intelligence from external sources must be carefully vetted and applied cautiously. A better method is to use third-party intelligence and feeds as an enrichment source. They can provide context around internally generated indicators and can be used to maintain and update existing indicators and rules.

It is important to understand the sources of these threat feeds so that you can properly use the information. For example, third-party feeds derived from honeypots will be useful in different situations than feeds of community-sourced incident-response data.

Updating indicators

Indicators are not static. They may, as with most network-based indicators, be malicious for a time and then disappear or become benign. Or they may, as with many host-based indicators, remain malicious even as the context around them changes or evolves. In many cases, malware that is originally linked to one attack or group is adopted by different actors or used in new campaigns. Tracking that information and linking new uses or tactics to existing indicators while weeding out or deactivating indicators that are no longer valid will ensure a steady stream of reliable, high-confidence indicators for tactical uses. Always remember that these indicators should be used; they should not just sit in a repository being carefully curated and maintained.

Additionally, some indicators may not be useful in their raw form, but with enrichment or pivoting they can be. Remember the Pyramid of Pain. For example, it may start with a singular IPv4 address, which an adversary can quickly move away from, but may have been used with a domain name that the adversary wants to keep using. Intelligence teams that practice proper indicator management can give detections and indicators more applicability and durability.

Operational Use Cases

Operational use cases for an intelligence program focus on understanding campaigns and trends in attacks, either against your own organization or against other organizations similar to yours. The sooner a campaign can be identified or a series of intrusions tied together, the less likely the attackers will successfully achieve their goals.

Campaign Tracking

A *campaign,* as we've discussed throughout the book, is a series of actions or attacks that support a common goal or objective. The island-hopping campaign in World War II is a good illustration of the concept. The US wanted to defeat Japan and therefore needed land from which to carry out attacks against the Japanese mainland. The island-hopping campaign was a series of attacks that targeted the less-defended Pacific Islands. After an island was taken, the military would build landing strips and fortify defenses and then use the newly established base to launch further attacks to gain the strategic advantage. Even though they may have employed different forces to carry out the attacks or used varying tactics based on terrain and fortification, the goal of the campaign was the same, and the various actions taken were all aimed at achieving that same goal.

This is the way that many adversaries operate: They have a goal or a target in mind, but achieving it is not always as easy as simply attacking the primary target. Often many steps are involved, and many organizations may be targeted by the same group in an island-hopping fashion, or an attacker may carry out a string of attacks against one or two organizations over a long period of time. It all depends on the goal of the campaign, so when it comes to campaign tracking, understanding the goal will provide far more insight than tracking only the various discrete indicators. Campaign tracking has various aspects, including identifying the campaign focus, identifying tools and tactics being used, and responding to the activity. We dive into those aspects here.

Identify the campaign focus

Many campaigns are focused on a particular industry, and identifying and under-standing campaigns that target other organizations in your industry can provide early warning that something may target you soon or may have already targeted you and threat hunting may be required. Identifying the industries that are targeted involves industry-based sharing communities such as ISACs, commercial intelligence, or open source intelligence.

Identifying tools and tactics

Once a campaign has been identified or is suspected to be part of a larger operation, the next step (after identifying the goal or intent of the operation) is to identify tools and tactics that are being employed in order to prevent and detect their use. Network-based indicators associated with an ongoing campaign are often useful for monitoring for threats. However, remember that they will not remain malicious forever, and their usefulness will eventually pass. Attacker tactics and behaviors are better places to focus, as long as you have the ability to monitor for them.

Response support

It is important to understand not only what campaigns are active but also what should be done after an intrusion, whether successful or failed, is identified in an organization. Campaign reports often provide information on the threat actor group behind the attacks, including tactics and tools, and sometimes even how the actors respond if they are detected or lose access to a network. All of these pieces of infor-mation can support SOC operations, as well as incident response if necessary, and can be used to provide updates and situational awareness to the CISO or other executives.

Strategic Use Cases

Strategic intelligence should always have a place in an intelligence program, regardless of how small that part is. As we discussed in Chapter 10, strategic intelligence enables an organization to truly learn from its previous incidents and begin to change long-term, large-scale behaviors and policies to combat those experiences. To be most effective, strategic use cases require support and buy-in from executive leadership, because many of the actions that need to be taken in response to strategic-level intelligence need to be made at the executive level. Strategic intelligence will always be useful for providing situational awareness, but it will not be as effective if the right stakeholders are not involved. The primary strategic use cases are architecture support and risk assessments.

Architecture Support

Strategic intelligence can provide information not only on the ways an organization should respond to intrusions or attacks but also on the ways it can posture itself to minimize attack surface and better detect these attacks. This intelligence is primarily based on two things: internal incident-response information and campaign analysis. Using these two primary sources, several things can be done to help focus on the right protections for a network.

Improve defensibility

Intelligence teams can work with IT and security operations to improve the defensibility of a network by understanding how adversaries have attacked or attempted to attack it in the past. Although attackers are clever, they will often repeat the same tactics as long as they work. If a network is designed or configured in a way that provides an easy attack vector, they will continue to use that vector until they are successful or until the opportunity is removed. Identifying these tactics can help identify an attacker's next logical move and can help structure network defenses to protect against these threats.

Focus defenses on threats

All systems, whether large networks or individual computers, will always have vulnerabilities. It is simply a part of operating systems, application, firmware, and protocols that are created by humans. Not all vulnerabilities are created equally, however, and some deserve more attention than others. A threat-based approach can help identify which vulnerabilities to focus on. Outside of patch management, intelligence can also support vulnerability management at a higher level by providing insight into the threats posed by potential network architecture changes. For example, if an organization was debating a bring-your-own-device policy or planning to introduce smart TVs into conference rooms across the organization, intelligence can help identify the threats to those devices and make recommendations before the policies are rolled out.

Risk Assessment/Strategic Situational Awareness

As we've discussed, one of the primary roles of a CISO is to understand and manage the risks to an organization's information. Understanding threats is a critical part of risk assessment, and intelligence can provide information on the threats facing an organization. For example, let's say an organization was reevaluating their IT travel policy to determine what processes employees should follow while traveling. With an intelligence team involved, they could provide context to the treats associated with specific locations and help the IT team policy better address the risks inherent with certain countries.

Here are some key steps an intelligence team can perform to support risk assessments and strategic situational awareness:

Identify when risk changes
> Risk does not stay the same, and external as well as internal factors may change the risk level to an organization. Intelligence teams, by working with multiple internal stakeholders, can provide information to the CISO when there is the potential that the risk to an organization has changed.

Identify mitigations
> Another aspect of risk management that can be supported by intelligence is identifying mitigations to reduce risk. Often security professionals assume that when there is a significant threat, the organization will not accept the risk, but at the end of the day, organizations must find ways to mitigate risks so that business can continue. Shutting down operations or halting the deployment of a new program that will increase efficiency is simply not an option. Mitigations become important to business continuity. These mitigations take many shapes, and an intelligence team can help a CISO identify what can be done to bring risk down to an acceptable level.

Organizations rarely focus all of their attention on one level of intelligence, whether it is strategic, operations, or tactical. Most organizations have a multilevel program. Moving between levels of intelligence itself requires planning and consideration as well, which we will discuss in the next section.

Strategic to Tactical or Tactical to Strategic?

You can organize a multilevel intelligence program in two ways. Intelligence can take either a *top-down approach* (strategic to tactical) or a *bottom-up approach* (tactical to strategic). With a top-down approach, strategic intelligence at higher levels guides policies and strategy and determines what tactical-level indicators the team should focus on and how they should be used in day-to-day operations. With a bottom-up approach, intelligence is primarily focused on tactical operations, and only significant information is pushed up to the strategic level. Both approaches have advantages and disadvantages based on the stakeholders involved and the needs of the organization.

Top-down planning is the standard approach of traditional military planning. In military operations, planning is a key responsibility of the commander. The commander is responsible for knowing the overarching goals, what is important to sustained operations, and the status and disposition of forces. In situations where the leadership has a clear understanding of what they want to accomplish and how intelligence can support those plans, you can expect to see more of a top-down approach. Strategic intelligence support is important with the top-down approach because it keeps the leadership up to date on the threat landscape, which they integrate into their overall understanding of how to protect their networks.

Many organizations do not have a robust strategic intelligence function to provide overarching guidance but still believe in the value of intelligence to support operations. In those situations, a bottom-up, or tactical-to-strategic, approach may work best. Operations focus on the tactical levels, such as supporting the SOC or incident-response teams, but the intelligence team will push significant information or trends up to executives when they deem it is important. With the bottom-up approach, there is no guarantee that leadership will respond to information as expected, and even if things run smoothly at the tactical level, there may always be a degree of uncertainty at higher levels. Bottom-up planning can be difficult to implement unless the strategic level of leadership has bought into the concept and has simply decided that, for the time being, operations are best left at the tactical level.

Critical Information Needs

Whether an organization is employing a top-down or a bottom-up approach, one concept can remain consistent: the critical information needs of executives. Critical information includes things that leadership has determined they need to know about ASAP. It often includes things such as successful intrusions that result in loss of protected information, intrusions into sensitive portions of the network, information on breaches, or compromises at partner networks. The need for this information may be compliance-based, or it may be driven by business needs, but whatever the case, it is important to understand the priorities and the timeframe in which executives expect to be informed of one of these situations.

The Intelligence Team

Now comes the fun part! Planning has been painstakingly carried out, the stakeholders for the intelligence program have been identified, goals have been set, and requirements identified. Now is the time to find the individuals who will do the work. Based on budget and the requirements, this may mean hiring a single individual or a team, but the important part is to find the right people based on all of the objectives that have been identified during the planning process.

Building a Diverse Team

It should go without saying that, while specifics of skill sets and experience levels will be determined based on the stakeholders and goals that have been outlined for the program, one key tenet in assembling an intelligence team is diversity. Having a variety of experiences and backgrounds is important to developing a well-rounded team capable of tackling complex issues. Diverse skill sets will strengthen the overall team, and diverse perspectives will strengthen your analysis. Exercises we have talked about throughout this book, including Key Assumptions Checks and red team analysis, are far more effective the more diverse the group conducting them is. While the team that is hired will often have core skills that they have been trained in, either at school or in a previous role, they are also bringing their background, experiences, gained knowledge, and the myriad biases all people have (which we talked about at length in Chapter 8). You do not want a team where everyone has the same or similar biases. This can result in groupthink, a snowball effect of confirmation bias, and a situation in which assumptions are far less likely to be checked. In addition to the many benefits of diversity and inclusion in the workplace—such as increased creativity and innovation, a higher sense of belonging, and higher job satisfaction—intelligence work itself is strengthened by differences.

Depending on the requirements the team is focusing on, an intelligence team may include professionals with cultural, geopolitical, and language knowledge. It can also include those with a background in business intelligence or knowledge of the organization's operations, incident handlers, penetration testers, programmers and tool developers, and management. With such a variety of potential team members, it is critical that hiring the team is an intentional, thoughtful step in the process of building an intelligence program.

While it's important to be mindful of gender, cultural, socioeconomic, and age diversity on your team, the *Harvard Business Review* (*https://oreil.ly/fQt_r*) has also highlighted the importance of cognitive diversity.[1] Cognitive diversity has shown to

---

1 Alison Reynolds and David Lewis, "Teams Solve Problems Faster When They're More Cognitively Diverse" (*https://oreil.ly/fQt_r*), *Harvard Business Review*, March 30, 2017.

increase a team's ability to solve complex problems. *Cognitive diversity* is defined as "differences in perspectives and information processing styles" and can also show up as different problem-solving processes and preferences for different types of models or approaches to solving problems. This is one of the reasons that there are so many different conceptual models in intelligence analysis—different people work better with different cognitive scaffolding supporting them.

HRB's study used the AEM-Cube™ (*https://oreil.ly/0uALm*), developed by Human Insight, which measures three variables (hence the "cube"): Attachment, Exploration, and Management of Complexity. The study showed that teams that were highly diverse across these three aspects were able to solve a challenge more quickly; in fact, two of the three teams with low AEM diversity were not able to complete the challenge at all. While you may not hire specifically for cognitive diversity, especially because it can be very difficult to truly understand someone's information processing style until you've actually worked together, understanding and encouraging cognitive diversity should be a key part of team and process development.

Team and Process Development

Intelligence teams are not static—you do not just assemble a team and assume that it will function well in perpetuity. Both teams and processes need care and feeding. While this will always look slightly different for each organization and team, there are a few things to keep in mind to support and grow healthy intelligence teams and processes.

Most everyone has thoughts about how they want their career to grow and evolve and where they want to be at some point in the future. Few people expect that what they do on day one at a new job will be all they ever do—they have expectations that they will grow their skills, grow their influence, and ideally grow their salary—though that last one is outside the scope of this chapter. In addition to individual growth, it is also important to think about team growth. How will the collective efforts of the team evolve over time? What does increased influence look like at an organizational level? At what stage of increased influence and responsibilities does the team need to physically grow in size? The way you approach these considerations will depend on your role in the team (e.g., individual contributor versus manager; team of one/two versus team of five), but there are some basics to keep in mind:

Have a plan for growth and development.
   Everything is better with a plan, and professional growth is no exception. It doesn't have to be a strict plan with "complete by" dates and Gantt charts, but there should be a written record of an individual's current skills and responsibilities, their current proficiency level versus where they would like to be in the future, and what additional skills and responsibilities they are interested in pursuing in the future. Ideally, areas of interest should be tied to the team's function,

either current or anticipated, though this is not necessarily a requirement, as many people move into different roles or teams throughout their career, bringing their previous skills to their new roles as they transition. There should also be a plan for the team's growth over time. With both of these, it is important to maintain cognitive flexibility, as there will always be forces outside of your control influencing changes that may need to take place.

Identify key skills outside of the basic intelligence-focused skill set.
Growth isn't only about progressing in your professional area of focus—it also includes expanding skills to include things that are distinct but complementary to the team's work, and things that will support the team's mission and make them more effective. Some examples of skills that are routinely used in intelligence work are presentation skills, interpersonal communication skills, and project management skills. In addition, members of an intelligence team will typically need to learn tool-specific skills (which will vary by team)—a critical part of functioning as a team that should not be overlooked. If there are additional skills that you identify as important to the team's functionality, you can look to hire someone with those additional skills, or you can provide training opportunities to existing team members. When growing new skills, remember that they do not just appear on their own. You cannot just say, "I am going to be better at project management." Skills need to be developed, either through a specific curriculum or program or over time through self-study or shadowing someone who has already mastered those skills. Regardless of which path you choose, make sure to have a plan for growing these skills.

Demonstrating Intelligence Program Value

Once the program has been implemented and the team begins operations, they will inevitably have to demonstrate the value of the program. If the program was properly planned and the necessary resources were allotted, you should already have an idea of what will show value to stakeholders. While it may be important to report daily or weekly statistics or metrics on the work that is being done, what will really show value is being able to convey the impact of the intelligence program. How has the program supported stakeholders? What is the organization able to do or focus on now that they could not have done without intelligence support? What risks was the organization able to take based on a better understanding of the threats facing them? Be sure to answer these questions as explicitly as possible when reporting on your program's activities.

It is also important to capture and discuss the lessons learned when things did not always go as expected. Identifying what worked and what didn't, and why, can provide information to help others avoid making the same mistakes. Intelligence teams will not always get everything right the first time, but learning from missteps is an important part of maturing a program.

Conclusion

The move from selective support of incident-response engagements to a full-fledged intelligence team is a big jump. This book focused on how to become proficient and add value as an individual supporting incident response, but once your organization sees how much value a single incident-response person can provide, key stakeholders will realize how valuable it would be to have an entire team of incident-response professionals. Intelligence is the glue that can bind together multiple diverse teams operating at different levels with different priorities. Although they may not often work together directly, there are many benefits of having those teams support each other, and an intelligence program can enable those interactions.

Moving toward a formalized intelligence program, especially one that is properly planned and resourced, can help organizations build upon the foundations and processes of intelligence-driven incident response and move even closer to intelligence-driven security.

Index

consumers (see audience, for intelligence product)

Containment phase of incident-response cycle
    defined, 41
    skipping, 41

Coordinated Malware Eradication (CME), 10

credential reuse, 107

CRITs (Collaborative Research into Threats), 174

CRUD (create, read, update, delete), 112

CTI (see cyber threat intelligence)

Cuckoo's Egg, The (Stoll), 4, 8

customer personas, 220-221

customers (see audience, for intelligence product)

cyber threat intelligence (CTI), 7
    defined, 7
    destructive attacks, 5
    first intrusion, 4
    history of, 4-7
    intelligence-driven incident response and, 10
    Moonlight Maze, 6

CybOX (Cyber Observable eXpression), 165

D

D3FEND, 67

damage assessment, 152

data, 200-204
    (see also information; threat data, extracting/storing)
    intelligence versus, 17

data exfiltration, 110

data standards/formats
    ATT&CK, 168
    CAPEC, 170
    for IOCs, 164-168
    MILE Working Group, 166-168
    OASIS suite, 165-166
    for strategic information, 168-170
    VERIS, 169

date/time formats, 247

DBIR (Verizon Data Breach Incident Report), 169

deception, 60, 69, 147

deconfliction of naming, 27

deductive reasoning, 180

defender-defender OODA loops, 25

degrading, 60, 69, 147

delivery
    alerting on, 106-107
    mitigation of, 137

Delivery phase of alerting, 106-107
    alerting on command and control, 107-109
    attachments, 106
    links, 106
    metadata, 106

Delivery stage of kill chain, 55-56

denial/deny action, 59, 68

denying access, 145

Department of Homeland Security (DHS), 12

deployment stage, of monitoring lifecycle, 154

destroy action, 59, 70, 148

detection systems, SOC and, 293

devil's advocate technique for SAT, 193

DFIR (digital forensics and incident response), 226

DHS (Department of Homeland Security), 12

Diamond Model of intrusion analysis, 22, 63-65
    basic model, 63
    extending the model, 64
    kill chain and, 64
    victim-centric targeting and, 89

digital forensics and incident response (DFIR), 226

direction phase of intelligence cycle, 26

disassembler, 130

disk analysis, 125-126
    applying intelligence to, 125
    gathering data from, 126

disproven hypothesis, unproven hypothesis versus, 188

disrupt stage, 146

disrupting, 60, 69

Disseminate phase, F3EAD, 73, 213-254
    actionability, 224-225
    audience, 214-221
    authors, 222-223
    establishing a rhythm for releasing intelligence products, 251-254
    intelligence product formats, 230-251
    understanding intelligence customer goals, 214
    writing process, 226

dissemination
    defined, 213
    of strategic intelligence, 279

dissemination phase, intelligence cycle, 30

automated consumption products and, 247-251
automated formats, 250
data standards/formats for, 164-168
indicator generation/validation/evaluation, 191-193
preparing an indicator list, 191
reports, 234
tactical intelligence and, 33
unstructured/semi-structured, 247
validating/evaluating, 192
inductive reasoning, 180
industrial control systems (ICS), 91
information
behavior, 83
indicators of compromise, 83
intelligence versus, 17, 82
internal enrichment information, 204
malware, 203
useful information during the find phase, 82-84
information gathering
during Exploit phase, 161-164
gathering external information (literature review), 163
goals for, 162
mining previous incidents, 163
information management, 172-175
information sharing, leveraging, 204
infrastructure
defined, 64
victim-adversary connection, 91
victim-capability connection, 90
victim-infrastructure connection, 90
infrastructure development, 53-55
certificates, 53
domains, 54
nontechnical needs, 54
servers, 54
Installation stage of kill chain, 56-57
network persistence, 57
system persistence, 57
installation, remediating, 141
intelligence
addressing biases in analysis, 33
basics, 15-36
collection method, 32
confidence levels, 35
context, 32

cyber threat sources of, 20
data versus, 17
date of collection, 32
defined, 9
incident response as part of, 9
information versus, 82
levels of, 33-34
military jargon and, 21
models, 21-32
operational, 34
as part of incident response, 4-8
qualities of good intelligence, 32
research and, 16
risks of exposure, 219
strategic, 34
tactical, 33
traditional sources of, 18-20
writing process (see writing process)
intelligence analysis, 15
intelligence cycle
analysis, 29
collection, 27
direction, 26
dissemination, 30
F3EAD and, 70
feedback, 30
naming deconfliction, 27
processing, 28-29
using to learn about new adversary, 30
intelligence estimates, 243
intelligence products
actionability, 224-225
audience for, 214-221
automated consumption products, 247-251
automated report information in, 223
characteristics for effective products, 216
distribution, 252
establishing a rhythm for releasing, 251-254
formats, 230-251
importance of regular product output, 253
incident and actor names, 231
long-form products, 234-243
RFI process, 243-247
short-form products, 231-234
intelligence programs, 283-303
architecture support, 297
defining goals, 288
defining metrics for, 291
defining requirements/constraints, 289

About the Authors

Rebekah Brown has spent more than two decades working in the intelligence analysis community. Her previous roles include NSA network warfare analyst, operations chief of a US Marine Corps cyber unit, and US Cyber Command training and exercise lead. She has helped develop threat intelligence and security awareness programs at the federal, state, and local levels, as well as at multiple Fortune 500 companies.

Scott J. Roberts is a security leader, analyst, software developer, and author. He is head of Threat Research for Interpres Security and has led security teams and projects in the defense industrial base and at GitHub, Apple, Splunk, and most recently, Argo AI. He is also a student and researcher at Utah State University, where he is focused on anticipatory intelligence, tackling emergent problems in national security and cybersecurity. Scott has served on an advisory committee for SANS CTI and DFIR Summits. Along with Rebekah Brown, he authored *Intelligence-Driven Incident Response* (O'Reilly) and has spoken at numerous industry events on incident response and cyber threat intelligence. He is passionate about improving security via automation, especially on macOS, and developing open- and closed-source tooling in Python, Go, and Swift.

Colophon

The animal on the cover of *Intelligence-Driven Incident Response* is a fan-tailed raven (*Corvus rhipidurus*). It is a member of the crow family and is the smallest of the raven species. These birds are native to countries of the Arabian Peninsula and those across the pond (the Red Sea) in Northeast Africa. These days, they can also be found further west and south in the Sahara, Kenya, and Niger with nests on rock ledges, cliffs, or trees.

The fan-tailed raven is completely black in plumage, beak, and feet, with overall shades of purple, gray, or brown in certain light. Both males and females average about 18 inches in length, with wingspans of 40 to 47 inches. With its rounded tail, broad wings, and long primary remiges, this bird resembles a vulture when in flight.

The diet of the fan-tailed raven is omnivorous and consists of insects and other invertebrates, berries, grain, and food scavenged near human populations. Like a parrot or other talking bird, the fan-tailed raven is capable of vocal mimicry of humans, but only seems to do so if in captivity.

Many of the animals on O'Reilly covers are endangered; all of them are important to the world.

The cover image is from *Riverside Natural History*. The cover fonts are Gilroy Semibold and Guardian Sans. The text font is Adobe Minion Pro; the heading font is Adobe Myriad Condensed; and the code font is Dalton Maag's Ubuntu Mono.

O'REILLY®

Learn from experts.
Become one yourself.

Books | Live online courses
Instant answers | Virtual events
Videos | Interactive learning

Get started at oreilly.com.

Printed in the USA
CPSIA information can be obtained
at www.ICGtesting.com
JSHW062020261223
54313JS00027B/86